D0122594

The Jericho Principle

How Companies Use Strategic Collaboration to Find New Sources of Value

Ralph Welborn
Vince Kasten

Foreword by
Steve Ballmer
Chief Executive Officer of Microsoft Corp.

WILEY

John Wiley & Sons, Inc.

Published by John Wiley & Sons, Inc., Hoboken, New Jersey.
Published simultaneously in Canada.

For general information on our other products and services please contact our
Customer Care Department within the United States at (800) 762-2974, outside the
United States at (317) 572-3993 or fax (317) 572-4002.

Wiley also publishes its books in a variety of electronic formats. Some content that
appears in print may not be available in electronic books. For more information about
Wiley products, visit our web site at www.wiley.com.

Library of Congress Cataloging-in-Publication Data:

Welborn, Ralph, 1961–
   The Jericho principle : how companies use strategic collaboration to find new
sources of value / Ralph Welborn, Vincent Kasten.
       p.   cm.
Includes bibliographical references and index.
   ISBN 0-471-32772-7 (CLOTH : alk. paper)
   1. Business strategy.   2. Strategic alliances (Business)   3. Business
enterprises—Computer networks.   I. Kasten, Vincent A.   II. Title.
   HD69.S8 W45   2003
   658.4′02—dc21

                                                            2002014325

Printed in the United States of America.

10   9   8   7   6   5   4   3   2

To Darlene and the boys
Vincent Kasten

To my parents, Howard and Florence
Ralph Welborn

Contents

FOREWORD

When I told my parents 22 years ago that I was dropping out of Stanford Business School to join a small company called Microsoft in the far northwest corner of the United States, my father asked the first question: "What's software?" My mother asked me an even more interesting question: "Why would a person ever need a computer?" The fact that no one asks such questions any more is a reminder of how much the world has changed. Back then, Microsoft's vision was "a computer on every desk and in every home." People thought we had stars in our eyes. Today, more than one billion PCs have been sold, and information technology is helping people and businesses everywhere to realize their potential.

Change—anticipating it, preparing for it, initiating it—is a crucial part of what leadership is all about. And leadership is not getting any easier, not with change coming faster all the time, accelerated by technology that instantly disseminates new information and ideas around the globe. To be successful in riding the wild, unpredictable waves of change, organizations today must be smoothly agile—able to adjust quickly to abrupt shifts in the marketplace, and able to move quickly to exploit suddenly emerging business opportunities. And because no single entity can possess all of the competencies it may need to respond to change, the ability to collaborate seamlessly must be a core competence of every agile organization.

That is why the book before you is incredibly timely and important. As Ralph and Vince aptly put it, collaborations are "innovation engines" that can curb costs, improve quality, reduce risk, and expedite the movement of new products and services to market. But as they also point out, the devil is in the executional details. There are many different forms of collaboration, all potentially relevant, all possibly effective. The key is knowing what kinds of collaboration meet your organizational needs, and how to design specific collaborative relationships to achieve the greatest synergy. This book is an invaluable guide to collaborating effectively and avoiding the pitfalls.

At Microsoft, respect for the vital importance of collaboration is bred in the bone. When Bill Gates and Paul Allen founded the company in 1975, they recognized that it alone could not put a PC on every desk and in every home. They adopted a strategy of enabling other firms to generate revenue for themselves using Microsoft's operating system as a platform for their computer hardware, applications, and services. By any measure, this strategy has been a success. Today Microsoft partners with more than 750,000 hardware manufacturers, software developers, and service providers in every region of the world, providing them with expertise, training, software tools, and other resources to expand their business and exploit new opportunities. IDC estimates that revenues from hardware, software, and services based on Microsoft products accounted for over $200 billion in 2001, meaning that every $1 of Microsoft revenue generates $8 in sales for other companies.

For the future, we are placing big bets on the value of collaboration with Microsoft .NET—software that connects information, people, systems, and devices. As *The Jericho Principle* notes, one of the key challenges in collaborating effectively is constructing and using a shared vocabulary to reconcile different understandings, expectations, and processes. Microsoft .NET meets this challenge in the technological domain with software built on the shared vocabulary of XML-based industry standards. Our .NET software makes it possible to exchange and use mission-critical information whenever and wherever needed on different platforms and in different applications. It thus helps partners to integrate their information systems and business processes, making collaboration easier and more effective.

As technology increasingly facilitates collaboration and as a changing economy increasingly demands it, the networked organization with porous walls and many integral partners will become the norm. Today, however, collaborating can seem like a scary leap into the unknown. In these pages you will gain critically important insights into how to collaborate successfully: how to design collaborative relationships suited to your strategy; how to prepare your organization to embrace collaboration; how to mine "tacit knowledge" to benefit collaborations while keeping your intellectual capital secure; and how to evaluate technologies to support your collaborative efforts. If collaboration today is a little like what Kurt Vonnegut described as "jumping off cliffs and developing our wings on the way down," *The Jericho Principle* is a great source of instruction in learning how to fly safely, in the right direction, through all the turbulent change that the future holds.

STEVEN A. BALLMER
Chief Executive Officer, Microsoft Corporation

ACKNOWLEDGMENTS

The Spanish poet Antonio Machado said, "We build the road as we travel." This book starts us on a journey of making sense of the collaborative necessity—the name of our marketplace road.

Over the past several years, many organizations have experimented with differing business models and technology approaches. We have had the opportunity to work with a number of them and this experience, shaped by the insights of the many remarkably talented and dedicated people with whom we have worked, forms the backbone of this book. The ideas and models of *The Jericho Principle* were conceived, shaped, and refined by many gifted teams during this past few years of great uncertainty when the crashing economy forced organizations to confront difficult questions quickly; when companies responded by aggressively refocusing on core values, core assets, and core strengths; as companies have begun to recognize that partnering with others around their core strengths to enhance mutual competitive positions needs to be part of any leading organization's core competence; as companies experimented with different collaborative forms in their attempts to find the right formula of centralization, control, and "ownership" of production and distribution, strategy, and service processes.

Our clients, colleagues, and competitors have helped us to recognize the nascent but ineluctable patterns of collaboration. They have enabled us to begin to sketch these nascent patterns, to highlight their edges with the simple aim of bringing them into relief, and, by so doing, assist them in identifying their underlying dynamics and overriding business potential. We wish to express our sincere thanks for the inspirations and the opportunities to help communicate the emerging patterns of collaborations that we describe in *The Jericho Principle*.

We want to thank Jeff Pappin, one of our most brilliant and insightful colleagues. Jeff's soft-spoken manner belies the loud importance of what he says. "Patterns, patterns everywhere" is one of Jeff's mantras, one that he has used to help numerous clients and sharpen our insights into emerging collaborative models. Trevor Davis, Alex O'Cinneide, and Ben Reichenau, are three more of our brilliant, insightful, and tireless colleagues who were central to many of the client experiences discussed in this book. Dan DiPlacido, Doug Schneider, and Tony Shumskas are the stalwarts of the Collaborative Delivery Framework that has strongly informed our views on how to execute collaboration. We thank Ellyn Raftery, head of Marketing at Unisys Corporation, and Linda Rebrovick, chief marketing officer of BearingPoint, for their support of this project. Others have helped us refine our thinking, including Bill McGee, a person of great integrity and strategic insight, Jeremy Schutte, with his razor-sharp comments, Ted Schadler of Forrester Research with his web services evangelical zeal, and Debin Schliesman with her continual emphasis on architectural frameworks, standards, and role of visual acuity framing actions. We thank, of course, Steve Ballmer for agreeing to write the Foreword and many of his colleagues at Microsoft for their debates, their actions, and their perspectives. To Matt Holt, our editor at John Wiley & Sons, we express admiration for his effectiveness in ensuring that deadlines were kept and momentum was maintained. Appreciation goes to Pam Blackmon and Nancy Marcus Land, our production team at Publications Development Company, who collaboratively pruned meandering paths and kept challenging us to ever highlight the collaborative edges and keep the arguments (relatively) tight.

A special thanks to our families. To our wives Meg Welborn and Darlene Kasten, who are beyond wonderful and whose encouragement, forbearance, support, and understanding have been and are always more appreciated—and more important—than we can express here. To the Welborn children—Nicole, Jeremy, and Jacob—who thought it was pretty funny that dad kept drawing funny pictures, talking about collaboration, and who finally, in their minds, understood what they kept telling him: "Dad, isn't that the same thing as playing together nicely?" To Alex and Nick Kasten who are stitched into a collaborative network with their Pingry School classmates—via instant messaging, e-mail, and cell phone—that would be the envy of any of our clients, and that contributed more than a little to our observations on the nature of collaboration.

Thank you one and all for your role in helping us to build this small stretch of road. We are in your debt.

R. W.
V. K.

ABOUT THE AUTHORS

Ralph Welborn and **Vince Kasten** are partners leading the Global Transformation Team at Unisys Corporation, responsible for market evangelism, thought leadership, and strategic implementation. They have both widely consulted and presented on emerging business and technology trends and business transformations throughout the world. They can be reached at http://www.thejerichoprinciple.com.

Ralph's perspectives reflect an eclectic background including client and consulting organizations in both academic and business environments, as well as a relentless focus on how to pragmatically integrate insights from cognitive science and linguistics through business strategies to organizational needs. His former affiliations include BearingPoint (formerly KPMG Consulting) where he was senior vice president of Solutions Engineering, responsible for global solutions as well as the Innovation Council focusing on partnerships and emerging business models with global clients; Charles Schwab; the Advanced Technology Group at Coopers & Lybrand; and a startup in San Francisco. Ralph has given multiple seminars globally on numerous topics, including emerging business and technology trends, the pragmatics of knowledge, and patterns of organizational transformation. He holds a doctorate in the Philosophy of Science & Technology.

Vince's 25-year career combines leading (sometimes bleeding) edge business experience with deep technical experience, spanning e-business creation and operation, business strategy, research & development, technology training, and commercial software product development. His former affiliations include BearingPoint (formerly KPMG Consulting), where he was global lead for application architecture and Web services; Lucent Technologies, where he specialized in large-scale system integrations; Bell Communications Research (now Telcordia), where he was director of the High Performance Transaction Technology Group; Bell Laboratories; and two technology startups. Vince has published over 30 papers on a variety of strategic, management, and technical topics. He has given numerous seminars on topics ranging from the Internet's influence on business transformation to system and network performance measurement, analysis, and tuning. He holds a masters in Computer Science and three U.S. patents.

CHAPTER ONE

The Jericho Principle: Using Collaboration to Break Down Organizational Walls

Paraphrasing William James, a nineteenth-century philosopher: We live in a competitive world of "big, blooming, buzzing, confusion."[1] For a business executive, this confusion stems from the screeching slow-down of the global economy, the lingering echo of the dot-com busts, the debates over refocusing the business, and the searching cries for answers to these problems that are pragmatic and yet innovative. We seek some calmness and reason within our competitive confusion and just plain market uncertainty. And this suggests some key questions: How do we make sense of the noise; of the fashions and fads; of the press releases; of the continued onslaught of sales pitches, value propositions, buzz words, and new products and services? How do we separate out the important from the merely interesting? How do we acknowledge, embrace, and exploit the competitive uncertainty we face each day?

One of the loudest noises we hear today reverberates around the need for *business collaboration,* which is defined as the alignment of business activities and processes with another business to create mutual benefit.

Business collaboration is an umbrella term for many "hot" phrases: strategic partnerships, key alliances, business-to-business connectivity, supply chain integration, co-opetition, preferred providers, and any number of variations on these words. Yet they all share the same *premise* and address a similar *problem*. The premise is that rapidly shifting economic and technology conditions create dynamic opportunities for mutual benefit through closer alignment of activities and processes. The problem is that sticky *operational-execution-devil-is-in-the-details* question: How *do* we make these opportunities a reality? There is a lot of noise—advice, opinions, examples, and lessons (some effective and some less so)—about the opportunities that exist and the need to take advantage of them. This book is about making sense of the noise that surrounds the notion of business collaboration, and then taking advantage of the revealed opportunities for mutual benefit. We construct models to expose the underlying mechanisms for successful collaboration, then use those models to work through examples, examine emerging business practices and opportunities, discuss lessons that are already apparent, and present some guidelines for actions.

Realizing the benefits of business collaboration depends on making sense consistently and taking advantage of the resulting opportunities. Building on this straightforward statement, this book has three equally straightforward objectives:

1. To make sense of the noise of business acceleration toward collaboration

2. To provide perspectives and lessons for understanding the implications of these collaborative trends and emerging models on how organizations build processes and services to support and drive collaborative partnerships and alliances

3. To offer a framework for action describing how to take advantage of collaborative trends and the specific business opportunities that they create

Examples and lessons from business organizations, systems integrators, and vendors substantiate the perspectives and emerging best practices provided. This focus on lessons from the field (the bottom-up view) in combination with the perspectives (the top-down view) is critical for consistent sense making and action taking.

The rest of this chapter lays out the book's starting points. These provide the foundation and overall structure on which we build perspectives, provide examples and derive lessons. We then describe how each chapter's focus helps weave in details from these starting points.

THE COLLABORATIVE NECESSITY: SOME STARTING POINTS

Four basic concepts are central to understanding emerging collaborative opportunities. We have identified them as follows:

1. The network as a dominant organizational metaphor,
2. Back to the basics as "return-to-the-future,"
3. The competitive Red Queen, and
4. The Jericho Principle.

The Network as a Dominant Organizational Metaphor

There is no doubt that organizations are collaborating more and more. We all see, experience, and read that organizations increasingly combine their efforts around specific business opportunities, that systems integrators are trumpeting their partnerships more aggressively, and that vendors are extending their application suites to support cross-vendor and partnership capabilities. There is also no doubt that the Internet has induced behavioral change as well as technological advances. Manuel Castells aptly observes, "The Internet is the fabric of our lives . . . [it is] the technological basis for the organizational form of the Information Age: the network."[2] As the network has become a pervasive metaphor of individual organizational and market life, so network economies have become a key part of leading-edge strategies.

Great metaphor, but what does it have to do with collaboration between companies? What are the implications of networks as our organizational fabric? Is this focus on "networks" too restrictive to discern the rich dynamics underlying emerging business collaboration? There is no question that the network metaphor surrounds us like air. But we need to do more than simply inhale. We need to analyze the individual particles in this metaphor so that we can identify the real message, and assess its ongoing relevance year after year.

That the network is a useful metaphor for understanding current business behaviors is certain. What is less certain and what we do not yet understand is the changing nature and emerging trends of *networked* and collaborative behavior, along with their likely implications. The very nature of what constitutes networks changes with time, as we have experienced over the past 20 years. So, too, do relevant models and the characteristics of collaboration, alliances, and partnerships—of how companies work together for mutual benefit. We need to examine the *how, why,* and *what* underlying these changes so that we can take advantage of what we are all experiencing and creating, day by day.

In Chapter Two, we describe a framework for collaboration that has at its foundation a simple but powerfully intuitive model based on organizational boundaries, partnerships, and the degree to which transactional costs shape networked economies. Disruptive changes in transactions and coordination costs—as assessed along dimensions such as costs, time, quality, agility, and control—affect how organizations respond both internally and with their partners. Our networked economy is simply the current response to disruptive changes in organizational and competitive cost functions that have been dramatically impacted by connectivity-oriented technologies. Exploring the underlying conditions of these changes allows us both to describe the current business environment and to understand its inevitable evolution.

Our discussion yields a framework for understanding key organizational, operational, and governance implications for companies that are based on, and driven by, collaboration. It provides, as well, tools for anticipating and characterizing disruptive competitive and technological changes in our environment that frame differing degrees of collaborative response with transaction cost implications. Based on this understanding, we identify best practices, models, and tools to guide organizations to more effectively take advantage of their specific collaborative activity.

Having explored these organizational issues, we return to look squarely at the human elements, incentives, and patterns at the core of effective collaborative business activities. These are fully part of the network metaphor, but they have been overlooked in the collective focus on the technocentric view of the network—the TCP/IP networks, Internet commerce, and the World Wide Web. At the intersection of organizational design and technology, we must understand the "people, process, and technology" interaction that impacts the broad landscape of networked and collaborative behaviors.

Back to the Basics as "Return-to-the-Future"

Businesses show a clear trend of getting back to the basics as they digest the economic and technology disruptions of the past few years and incorporate their experiments with emerging technologies and business models into their core business. There is an aggressive focus on governance and processes around business assets that are essential to creating shareholder value. There is an equally aggressive effort to find alternative sourcing—whether outsourcing or some form of managed service—for those business assets that provide necessary functions for the business but are not central to creating shareholder value. Which assets fall into which category depends, at least partially, on continually changing transactional and partnership models. The implication is that back to the basics is actually *continual change* or, maybe more descriptively, *continual innovation.*

This means that investments that the company makes, lessons that are learned, and opportunities that lie ahead depend on leveraging the investments already made and refocusing on core capabilities. It yields a framework for understanding the following important organizational issues:

- Effectively managing innovation
- Recognizing how the characteristics of business assets shift over time and across geographies
- Recognizing, exploiting, and protecting essential intellectual property and business assets in a collaborative structure
- Exploring implications of such emerging technologies as Web services that offer opportunities (or, for some, threaten) to expose an organization's business assets to its customers and partners
- Acknowledging the operational implications of a shifting business asset base

Although none of these is the exclusive domain of collaborative business models, they each raise sharp questions about the viability of strategic opportunities offered by collaboration.

The Competitive Red Queen

Lewis Carroll created a character called the Red Queen in *Through the Looking Glass,* his masterful sequel to *Alice's Adventures in Wonderland.* The Red Queen relentlessly ran, faster and faster, never stopping—merely to keep up—relative to the other fast-moving, seemingly bizarre, and uncertain activities in her environment. Evolutionary biologists have picked up the Red Queen metaphor to explain the dynamic interplay of genetic mutations and adaptations. The biological reality is simple and the metaphor apt: Species must mutate or evolve due to constant competition from other individuals and species and the conditions of their environment. The alternative is extinction. Diversifying, mutating, or innovating in terms of functions and behaviors is a survival strategy, not a luxury.[3] The Red Queen effect applied to business is equally simple, and equally apt: Business models and operating procedures must continually evolve in response to the changing business environment. To not do so is to inevitably fail. Thus, the Red Queen of biology has a direct analogue in implementing business strategy: Companies evolve, whether to anticipate or respond to changes in their competitive environment; the market either embraces or rejects the adaptation, and the evolutionary process rolls on.

The Red Queen effect stems from the very nature of our competitive environment: its uncertainty. Later in the book, we explore strategic uncertainty and the use of collaboration to navigate and embrace an uncertain future. For now, it is sufficient to observe that because the Red Queen effect is engulfing our customers, our processes, our technologies, and our business environment, there is an urgent need to understand its dynamics and to explore how to execute through our never-ending cycles of competitive uncertainty.

The Red Queen runs, and she runs relentlessly. As she runs, she puts significant pressure on what we do and how we do it. As margins inevitably shrink, the nature, source, and number of competitors shift and, for a while, possibly increase as the changes draw in new participants. Thus, competitors continuously battle to exploit high-margin opportunities, while their very existence will always put pressures on attempts to shrink those margins. Changes in technology, business process enhancements, competitive models, and new players will always vie to attack the high-margin market opportunities and thereby arbitrage away those margins with commensurate shifts in competitive positioning. The Red Queen runs, and she runs relentlessly.

Why the Red Queen runs, from a business perspective, is simple: She has to. Her impact on business is equally simple: innovate or die. *Collaborations are a strategic and pragmatic means to help companies innovate, and to do so quickly.* We explore collaborations as an engine that can drive rapid—and if necessary, radical—innovation. As an adaptive mechanism for continual innovation, collaborations are not only nice to have but also are increasingly becoming a critical business requirement. *The collaborative imperative is less a felicitous phrase than it is a strategic necessity.* Exploring this necessity from the vantage point of the Red Queen provides an insight into the dynamic that makes it so.

The Jericho Principle

In the Old Testament, Joshua blew his trumpet and the walls of Jericho came tumbling down. The Jericho Principle uses the implications of the network metaphor to bring down organizational walls. Few, if any, behaviors can be isolated or contained within the walls of their inception. All actions create changes that ripple through interconnected business processes with implications beyond their primary and intended focus. This mirrors what we all observe every day in our organizations: Behaviors have primary and secondary impacts, as do strategic decisions that we make about business and technology architectures and project implementations. A song from the 1920s—with its refrain about the hip bone being connected to the thigh bone, which in turn is connected to the knee bone, and on through the human skeleton—captures this particular aspect of the Jericho Principle. By focusing on understanding this connectedness as well as the inevitable dismantling of organizational walls, the Jericho Principle yields a perspective for understanding the following crucial organizational issues:

- Identifying and then anticipating the extended implications of behaviors and of new applications that may affect a company and its partners beyond the intended scope
- Anticipating and designing these extended implications into the decision-making process, thereby strengthening leadership's ability to respond quickly
- Enhancing capabilities to manage distributed value and risk from the perspective of any participant of a collaborative venture as well as from that of the collaboration itself

These issues become increasingly important as organizational walls begin to crumble and our operational landscape requires us to work more frequently and effectively with our partners.

In the Old Testament account, once the walls came down, Joshua's army dispatched all of the town's inhabitants, took all of the town's wealth, and left it stripped, vacant, and barren. The Bible is silent on possible alternative outcomes for Jericho, but one thing seems clear: If someone at the front of an irresistible force rips down your walls, the outcome is definitely not going to be pleasant. The relentlessly running Red Queen is at the head of a juggernaut against organizational walls, driving the continual market shifts that attract competition into niches where you formerly enjoyed a comfortable position. This requires an aggressive and agile response to defend your turf and to exploit the brief windows of opportunities before new competitors slam them shut. An effective response frequently requires skills, capabilities, assets, and processes that either may not exist within the organization or cannot be marshaled quickly enough to match the speed of the new demand. *Hence, the opportunity and the need to build collaborative capabilities as core competencies.* If, in fact, the Red Queen running with the network economy is a major force, you have only one alternative: Take down your own walls before she, or one of your competitors running along with her, takes them down for you.

These four starting points inform the *Jericho Principle.* We refer to them throughout this book—offering perspectives, examples, and tools to make your collaborations more effective. Collaborations are no passing fad. Nor are they a mere operational tool. They are, in fact, becoming a key strategic tool in your competitive arsenal.

STRUCTURE AND FOCUS OF THE BOOK

This first chapter lays out the arguments, structure, and business value of the *Jericho Principle.* It focuses on why you should care about emerging collaborative business models and suggests how to use the collaborative models, insights, and tools provided throughout the book.

Organizational effectiveness depends on having a clear vision, a passion for execution, and a discipline to communicate that vision and execute activities over and over again. The companies that go from "good to great" tightly align these essential characteristics.[4] And alignment depends on making sense of and taking action on these characteristics consistently. In the current business environment, significant emerging trends are reshaping traditional competitive relationships into collaborative business partnerships, alliances, and business models. To take advantage of the opportunities these trends create, it is important to have both a perspective on and a framework for understanding their implications.

In the beginning, intones the Old Testament, was the "Word." And from the word there emerged, among other things, common ways of speaking and therefore of shared communications and effective actions. Collaborative ventures involve much discussion, much writing, and much activity. Making sense of all of these activities requires having a common way of understanding, discerning, and communicating the underlying dynamics and effective behaviors of these activities. It requires, in essence, a shared vocabulary and understanding to identify the patterns, explore the options, and exploit the opportunities of effective collaboration.

Chapters Two and Three build the collaborative vocabulary used throughout the book to explore the patterns, dynamics, lessons, and implications of different collaborative types.

Chapter Two answers the question "*Why* should we care about collaborative ventures?" It explores the inherent uncertainty in our business environment and the role of collaborations as key strategic tools to enhance company agility when competitive pathways become apparent. It also provides a simple definition of collaboration and builds on this definition to create what we call the *Collaborative Landscape*. Multiple types of collaboration exist. It is both a strategic and operational challenge to align a company's business objective with the appropriate collaboration. The Collaborative Landscape begins to characterize the differences as well as the arguably more important similarities among various collaborative types. Being able to characterize these differences and underlying similarities helps to achieve the alignment necessary for any effective collaboration. Chapter Two then, grounds our understanding of the strategic value of collaborations and of emerging collaborative models and begins to build the frameworks to drive the crucial alignment between collaborative forms and business opportunities.

Chapter Three explores the question "*How* do we build effective collaborative ventures?" The diversity of collaborations often makes it difficult to identify, much less target, appropriate actions to increase effectiveness. Yet, dynamics common to them provide insight into how they work and why. Chapter Three explores these underlying dynamics (what we call the *collaborative DNA*) for effective partnerships.

Collaborations are inherently risky. They combine assets and capabilities from different companies, each with its own value and its own set of expectations, behaviors, and processes. As we have all experienced, building consistent processes and expectations is sufficiently challenging within an organization, much less across distinct organizations. Yet, it is through building such cross-organizational consistency and *codifying* executable and meaningful processes and standards that we achieve the scale and leverage critical for effective collaborations. Different types, or layers of activities need to be consistent to be scalable. Creating such standards which are no more than the shared acceptance of what to do based on shared meaning or "semantics," is what we refer to as *the process of walking up and across the semantic stack*. This semantic stack becomes one of our key explanatory tools for distinguishing among and enhancing effective collaborative actions.

Chapters Two and Three build our collaborative framework and vocabulary to make sense of "buzzing, booming" collaborative activities. They describe the *collaborative necessity* and the underlying mechanics of effective collaborative behaviors. In Chapters Four through Six, the focus shifts as we consider how to take action to engender effective collaborations in the face of the Red Queen and her juggernaut. These three chapters distill the lessons learned and emerging best practices by suggesting pragmatic steps to guide strategic and partnership discussions. They do so from the classic organizational perspectives of process, people, and technology. Each of these perspectives is informed by the principles with which we started this book. These different perspectives serve as tangible windows into the underlying dynamics and specific operational implications of collaborations. To provide a practical set of tools for anticipating and executing collaborative activities, these chapters follow a similar structure: Examples are described, observations are made, and specific implications are suggested.

Chapter Four explores three organizational levers to push, monitor, and drive cross-organizational activity: (1) business processes and their exposure as "business services" for organizational partners and customers; (2) the changing role and expectations of a company's workforce; and (3) the role of leadership to develop, nurture, and sustain collaborative capabilities. Each of these activities puts pressure on organizational walls and thereby challenges our underlying understanding of how organizations work. The Jericho Principle recognizes that organizational walls are coming down and that cross-organizational collaborative work will soon become the strategic norm instead of an operationally expedient exception. We center the discussions and examples of Chapter Four around business processes and their changing form. Once a utilitarian part of the plumbing, business processes are increasingly being recognized and harvested for the value they provide both within and across organizations.

Organizational walls cannot sustain the pressures of business processes. As designed from the customer's perspective, business processes are activities that add value to the customer. Your customers have no interest at all in the operational requirements—in your company or across a series of companies—needed to fulfill their expectations. Whereas it is true that one company's demand chain is another company's supply chain, and so on, the only pertinent issue is how this extended set of business processes supports the objective of meeting customer expectations. If the mechanics of the process become visible to the customer, you have already failed. It is here that processes, supported by the emerging Internet technologies and standard sets of protocols, become juggernauts against organizational walls. We explore this raging force that not only is pounding away on the walls of individual companies but also is accelerating the need for collaborative relationships.

As well as exploring the increasing need for sharing business processes, we consider the obstacles to that sharing—especially the real problems in rationalizing, reconciling, and normalizing data and what we call the semantics within and across organizational boundaries. In this context, we also look at the organizational, partnership, and delivery promises and challenges of emerging services-sharing models such as peer-to-peer technologies, Microsoft®.NET™, Web services, open systems standards that will affect overall organizational design and processes, and business description approaches such as Unisys Corporation Business Blueprints.

Organizational design cannot be isolated from considerations of collaborative businesses or technologies. Nor can organizational design be separated from an understanding of how to identify, filter, and leverage knowledge assets—for example, what people know, which artifacts they use, and how they use them. Chapter Five focuses on the people side of the collaborative equation, on the role of knowledge and the owners of that knowledge—our workforce and our colleagues.

People involved in continual collaboration will come into contact with lots of other people and organizations. At least in some cases, this can lead to split allegiances and identity questions. How we manage the workforce when its loyalty becomes as distributed as does its geographic base is a critical piece of the collaborative puzzle. It raises questions about approaches to management and governance around those knowledge assets—people and their tacit knowledge—so necessary for collaborative success. It becomes, as well, a touchstone to clarify the distribution and valuation of intellectual property, knowledge assets, and just plain knowledge—how it needs to be used, by whom, when, and where. The acceleration of *peer-to-peer connectivity* and *edge computing*, in the context of this chapter, is explored as a technology trend that both is being pulled by these organizational trends and is serving to push new methods of human and collaborative scalability.

As we've said, collaborations are inherently risky. They represent novel business propositions along with often-unproven processes for exploiting them. Developing and market-testing unproven business propositions and processes requires artful experimentation and adaptation to changing circumstances, which in turn requires extensive knowledge, experience, and commitment. At least for the initial stages of any collaborative venture, this inherent messiness creates a bottleneck in that relatively few people can productively work in the sort of ambiguity we have just described. Compound this "scaling" challenge with the need to identify, measure, and value the intellectual assets of the collaboration, and it becomes obvious that the people side of the collaborative equation—the tacit knowledge and resulting intellectual assets involved—is an essential consideration in any collaborative endeavor. Chapter Five focuses on this intellectual asset side of the equation. We explore the rationale and implications in the ongoing battle to identify, capture, and reuse intellectual capital, intrinsic to collaborations. Because intellectual assets play a critical role in the establishment of collaborations, it is essential to manage them tightly. This will ensure that these assets are used effectively within the collaborative venture and are "harvested back" to participating companies.

Chapter Six explores the implications of technology for collaborative behaviors. One approach would be to characterize the type of technologies, survey existing products and services, and list vendors that support collaborative behavior. Although such a mechanical enumeration of technical possibilities might be interesting, it would have little lasting relevance. Consequently, we take a different path. We build on the collaborative DNA lessons from earlier chapters and explore their implications for architectural design and business/technology governance. A key challenge for effective collaborations, as mentioned before, is constructing and using a shared vocabulary, or semantic base, that reconciles different understandings, expectations, and processes. This same challenge exists within the technology domain. Given technology's vital role to enable effective collaborations, aggressively exploiting what we call *architectural semantics* becomes critical to support the ability and scale needed across multiple collaborative ventures.

Chapter Six provides a framework for characterizing relevant technologies around this concept of architectural semantics. It is a focal point for creating business value from technology innovation, and for leveraging information technology (IT) assets within the emerging models of business collaboration. We explore the push-me/pull-me tensions that characterize technology/business investments in emerging technologies and include tools to assess collaborative technology-enabling claims and their potential business impacts. Finally, we investigate some potentially disruptive technology trends and suggest ways to respond to and assimilate them, depending on appropriate collaborative business models. Each of the assessments made and the implications drawn reflect the correlation between differing collaborative models and the competitive dynamics described by walking up and across the semantic stack. Grounding this chapter in architectural semantics cuts through the deafening technology noise around collaborative opportunities.

The final chapter, Chapter Seven, steps backward to go forward. In it, we return to the mapping coordinates that guide the book: the network metaphor, back-to-the-basics as innovation, the competitive Red Queen, and the Jericho Principle. After reaffirming them in the light of the models, lessons, and implications developed throughout the book, we build on these insights to raise some questions—the answers to which will impact collaborative structures and governing principles over time.

Collaborations differ greatly in their focus and structure. Yet, common competitive dynamics and patterns frame the evolutionary path of any particular collaborative form. In this final chapter, we raise questions about trends and issues that could punctuate some of those paths, causing them to veer toward other directions. We cannot provide definitive answers, but by exploring potential future scenarios, we may help you to anticipate and respond aggressively as your competitive and collaborative shapes become more defined.

What we see, again and again, is the overlapping nature of the different perspectives provided. It is neither possible nor desirable to isolate the organizational framework from the process, the process from the people, and the people from the technology discussions. Reality is inherently messy—with overlaps and dependencies from various perspectives. The challenge is to discern basic and useful patterns within that messiness. To simplify the task, each chapter has taken a different vantage point in providing examples, lessons, and implications that highlight and, in fact, celebrate the overlaps so critical for making these lessons understandable and their implications usable.

GETTING READY FOR THE NEXT STEP

While collaborative ventures are inherently risky, they are also inexorably necessary. Therefore, making collaborations a key strategic tool and collaborative skills a core competency is becoming less an option than a competitive necessity. The reason we wrote the book is simple: The Jericho Principle is not to be denied. The Red Queen is leading the horn section and organizational walls *are* coming down. What matters now is that we acknowledge the competitive uncertainty we all face while exploiting collaborative opportunities to deal with it. Collaborative ventures are fundamentally about creating shared value and managing distributed risk. It is that simple. But within simplicity often lies deep complexity. Our objective is to foster appreciation of the complexity while providing a map of simplicity to help you navigate the shoals of multiple collaborations and align your business objectives with the relevant collaborative structure.

We provide a vision of the future that has resonated well with clients across a spectrum of industry segments and that has allowed us to help those clients set strategic direction and drive not only tangible but also pragmatically innovative results. We also draw on lessons and best practices from industries, colleagues, and clients who live and breathe collaboration and who are witnesses to the collaborative imperative. *The Jericho Principle* focuses on creating awareness through a "postcards-from-the-edge" perspective while suggesting pragmatic lessons and operational implications of rapidly emerging opportunities.

"We build the road as we travel," as the Spanish poet Antonio Machado puts it.[5] This book starts us all on a journey of making sense of the Jericho Principle and the collaborative necessity that it spawns.

CHAPTER HIGHLIGHTS

The Issue

Collaborations take many forms. What is driving the focus and increased attention around collaborative forms? Why now? How do we make sense of the emerging and multiple collaborative forms and take action to make them more effective?

The Insight

Simple models to make sense and tangible implications to take action can improve the effectiveness of collaborations. The combination of lessons from the field (the bottom-up perspective) and frameworks for action (the top-down perspective) provides a visceral picture of how to exploit this emerging trend aggressively.

The Phrases

The Red Queen as a competitive dynamic and the critical implications of transactions costs to explain organizational collaborations.

THE JERICHO PRINCIPLE: USING COLLABORATION   15

The Implications

There are multiple forms of collaborations. Knowing that these differences exist is important. Knowing which of these collaborative forms align with your business objectives is, obviously, critical. Yet, what becomes necessary to drive that alignment is less an understanding of collaborative differences than their underlying similarities. And these similarities result from shared underlying dynamics and mechanisms to make each of these forms more effective. Therefore, understanding the underlying dynamics and manipulating the collaborative DNA is more than a mere operational and intellectual exercise; it becomes, instead, a competitive requirement. So, making sense and taking action effectively require understanding and then exploiting collaboration's competitive dynamics and underlying DNA strands.

The Strategic Value of Collaborative Ventures: Emerging Collaborative Models and Why Do We Care?

In this chapter, we define the basic concepts for collaboration that we develop throughout the rest of the book. We develop the notion of collaboration as a specific model for working with others to create innovations so important in uncertain times. Collaboration occurs whenever organizations work together. There are many ways that organizations work with one another. First we examine why organizations want to work together in uncertain times, then introduce a model for characterizing the landscape of the ways companies do so. To do this, we introduce, define, and discuss the following:

- *The need for a strategic approach for uncertain times.* Market dynamics and new technologies have created an environment where it is not possible to predict the future of your business, your markets, or your competition with certainty. Such uncertainty has become one of the only areas of certainty within our competitive landscape. Consequently, answering the questions of how to acknowledge and exploit such uncertainty as well as how to create mutual opportunities and share the risks within such an environment have become key strategic challenges. Collaborative ventures are an emerging and critical strategic tool to address such challenges and work through uncertain times.

▪ *The strategic reasons for collaboration.* Collaborations are an inherently risky yet necessary business option. The uncertainty we face and dynamic pressures with which we all deal require an agility to respond as competitive plates shift, opening up specific market inefficiencies and opportunities that need to be exploited quickly and with alacrity. A problem many organizations face, however, is the difficulty in *responding* quickly and effectively. The processes we've established and the business model that has made our companies as successful as they are often become obstacles when it is necessary to quickly exploit short-lived market arbitrage opportunities. Collaborative ventures are a means around our well-structured processes. They offer an opportunity to build on core strengths of one, two, or more companies in a nascent business environment that can be structured outside of our traditional processes to take advantage of particular market opportunities.

▪ *The vocabulary of collaboration.* In the beginning, intones the Old Testament, was the "Word." And from the Word emerged, among other things, common ways of speaking, shared communications, and effective actions. There is much discussion, much writing, and much activity associated with collaborative ventures, but little commonality in vocabulary or meaning. Making sense of all of these activities requires having a common way of understanding, discerning, and communicating the underlying dynamics and effective behaviors. Building a vocabulary of collaboration is critical to discerning its patterns and exploiting its opportunities effectively.

▪ *Models for collaboration.* We define the *Collaborative Landscape* as a framework to help provide context for the overall approach to collaboration and to be used as a diagnostic to evaluate strategic relationships. Different types of collaborations exist. Any can be effective, depending on the specific business objective. Understanding the different types of collaborations is important. Yet, even more important is understanding the underlying dynamics of collaborative ventures. Across the very different types of collaborations, there exist common dynamics and features. Delineating these common patterns and their underlying competitive dynamics is critical to effectively align your business objective with the relevant type of collaborative venture. The Collaborative Landscape provides the starting point for understanding these underlying patterns. The rest of the book refers to this landscape and explores its underlying dynamics, providing a set of general observations and actionable implications from a number of different perspectives.

- *Necessary conditions for collaboration.* Given the strategic need for collaboration, a vocabulary for discussing it, and a framework for evaluating collaborative relationships, we set the stage for the people, process, and technology requirements for collaboration that will be developed in detail in subsequent chapters. There is no way we can enumerate all of the sufficient conditions for effective collaborative ventures. But we can sensitize you to what we see as the necessary conditions—the underlying patterns, emerging models, and best practices to help you execute collaborative actions more effectively.

This chapter, as do subsequent chapters, weaves together these elements that infuse our examples and directs attention to the critical points necessary to effective collaborative activities. Collaborations are not a passing fad. They are critical strategic tools in our competitive arsenal. As such, understanding how they fit within what we call *strategic imperatives* becomes not merely important but a critical next step. It is the one to which we turn next.

THE STRATEGIC IMPERATIVES: STRATEGY IN UNCERTAIN TIMES

As we mentioned in Chapter One, the Red Queen runs, and she runs relentlessly. As she runs, she puts significant pressure on what we do and how we do it. As margins continuously shrink, the nature, source, and number of competitors shift and, for a while, possibly increase. A key competitive battlefield is over continuously attempting to exploit high-margin opportunities while their very existence creates competitive pressures that drive them toward commoditization and shrinking margins. Technology changes, business process enhancements, competitive models, and new competitive players will always vie to attack high-margin market opportunities thereby arbitraging away those margins. As we said, the Red Queen runs, and she runs relentlessly.

The Red Queen effect applied to business is significant, and for that reason, business models and operating procedures must continually evolve. The business environment for the foreseeable future will be characterized by particularly rapid changes in direction due to:

- The fundamentally disruptive nature of the Internet and related connectivity-based technologies
- The continual introduction of these new technologies to a mass audience
- The continued sorting out of business models to capitalize on the commercial potential of these new technologies

It is not our intention to discuss how you should go about creating strategies. Instead, we concentrate on how the Red Queen dynamics drive your implementation of whatever strategy you have created. We introduce and explain a simple model for describing an uncertain future and for characterizing how to go about creating new business value central to the implementation of your strategy to support the evolution of your business. We examine the notion of collaboration as a means for mobilizing core value from other organizations to combine with your own to create new value. We characterize various forms of collaboration in a *Collaborative Landscape* that provides a framework for weighing collaborative alternatives in differing business circumstances. In subsequent chapters, we use this framework to examine the people, process, and technological conditions necessary to create more effective collaborations. We do so through making observations, identifying implications, and making specific recommendations to exploit the implications identified. We start by looking at some of the strategy background that got us here.

The models that we use for treating uncertainty were developed in the course of strategy work that was done for major financial, telecommunications, and manufacturing institutions during the height of the dot-com hysteria. While many of the emerging business models—and many of the companies formed to explore them—have been discredited in the aftermath of the dot-com bust, the uncertainty of the time caused many of the world's largest companies to aggressively rethink their core business models. The financial services industry was a particularly good place to observe the strategic impact of uncertainty because financial institutions are: (1) acutely aware of how virtual their core business is, and thus how vulnerable it is to disruption by new technologies, and (2) in a position to finance the exploration of strategic alternatives.

Most of the global financial institutions at the time were very concerned that there was a fundamental competitive shift at work. The scenarios that were considered plausible ranged from essentially a steady-state scenario—for example, the Internet as just another distribution channel—to a chaotic view where financial institutions as we know them disappear, disaggregated into many separate entities, each providing one or a small number of services, fluidly interacting in value chains dynamically constructed to meet the needs of a particular customer transaction at a particular time and place.[1]

For now, at least, the impact of the Internet on financial institutions is somewhere in the middle of these two extremes. There are certainly viable companies that seem to have carved out new territory. Examples of these include companies like eBondTrade—that established a viable online model for trading municipal bonds in an industry characterized by entrenched old-boy networks—and Creditex, established for online trading of credit derivatives.[2] Other companies have leveraged the Internet to reshape the way that companies in the market interact. A classic example of this is how Charles Schwab, Inc. has aggressively exploited Internet technologies and opportunities. Charles Schwab, whose offerings of easy Internet access to a wide array of products and services make it easy for independent financial advisors to provide increasingly sophisticated services to an ever wider range of clients, opened up financial planning to people other than extremely high net worth individuals.

Regardless of how the Internet ultimately affects financial institutions, the industry has been a fertile ground for exploring approaches to business strategy in uncertain times because the Internet was, for this industry as for many others, a *disruptive technology*. The concept of disruptive technologies is defined and explored in Clayton M. Christensen's book, *The Innovator's Dilemma*.[3] Christensen characterizes a technology as disruptive when it can provide value to some segment of an existing market that is currently underserved, providing a foothold for subsequent improvements in price/performance that ultimately unseats the incumbent technology. Disruptive innovations are not initially interesting to mainstream markets, usually because they lack some degree of performance or functionality. They are, however, appealing to some group of customers—

typically those with less skill or wealth than the mainstream customers, and thus not interesting to the companies serving the mainstream—because they are easier to use, or cost less.

An example of this is the personal computer (PC). PCs started as underpowered, clumsy machines that couldn't perform many meaningful business functions. However, they were the only alternative for a set of low-end customers to access computing power. These customers were not serviced by the computer providers of the day who were—quite logically—focused on the highly lucrative mainframe and mid-sized market. From this foothold, PCs over the next 30 years took over a large part of the mainframe computer market.

A key insight in *The Innovator's Dilemma* is that excellent companies that dominate an existing marketplace are seldom able to capitalize on disruptive technologies; their planning processes cause them to create innovations that improve their existing products, offering better and better performance to their existing customer base. However, the newer technologies are not sufficiently powerful to be applied to the existing customer base, nor as profitable as the incumbent technology. At the same time, the potential customer base for the new technology is not attractive to the incumbent. This opens a market niche inducing new competition. Once the new technology has become established in the niche, it can invade existing markets and steal the business of existing companies.

The Innovator's Dilemma clearly shows that excellent established companies fail to keep pace when markets change dramatically. This point was not lost on financial institutions during the dot-com bubble. Nor should it be lost on you. What is the lesson to be learned? *During times of uncertainty, traditional approaches to formulating and implementing strategy are not sufficient.*

Traditional strategy approaches are fundamentally grounded on assumptions of continuity and gradual evolution, such as:

- Business conditions are reasonably stable, or at least can be reasonably forecast.
- The future is predictable enough that executives can apply analysis tools to determine how their business will fare in future conditions.
- From the analysis, quantitative measures can be applied that can then be used to choose among alternative strategies or optimize a chosen strategy.

However, when business conditions are unstable, and thus the future is not predictable, traditional approaches to strategy are "marginally helpful, and at worst downright dangerous: Underestimating uncertainty can lead to strategies that neither defend a company against the threats, nor take advantage of the opportunities that higher levels of uncertainty provide."[4] In other words, in uncertain times, it is a mistake to assume that the future is predictable to any reasonable degree.

Thus, in formulating strategy and in implementing the resulting business objectives, it is important to recognize the uncertainty inherent in planning for the future, and to have a model and a vocabulary for articulating *strategic uncertainty*. In our strategy work, we have created a simple model for visualizing the degree of uncertainty facing a company and for articulating the actual events that occur in the subsequent implementation of strategy. Before looking at the model, we need to be more specific about what it means to formulate and implement a strategy.

Collaboration as a Strategic Innovation Tool

As we said earlier, this book is about *implementing* strategy, not about *creating* strategies. Therefore, we have the luxury of being uncomplicated in our description of, and our approach to, strategy. For our purposes, *a strategy is a road map for determining how a company makes its choices about how it creates value over time.* This gets to the heart of what the word *strategy* means to the nonstrategist—that is, to the person who has to make the strategy real for the company over the lifetime of that strategy.

First, strategy is about creating value. If, in biological terms, the Red Queen drives a species to continually evolve new abilities, in business terms, it drives a company to evolve new ways of creating value for its customers and its shareholders. New value is created when a company pursues a business opportunity that is differentiated from its existing business in terms of one or more of the following:

- *Customer.* Where the opportunity allows the business to address the needs of a new base of customers or extend services provided to the existing customer base.

- *Product.* Where the opportunity creates new product or service (generally intellectual property) that can be sold to existing or new customers.

- *Scale.* Where the opportunity allows a company to deliver its product(s) or service(s) in greater quantities or at markedly lower prices across geographies.

- *Positioning.* Where the opportunity repositions the company's brand, for example, a commodity player moves into a higher value brand position, or a service company moves in the direction of a product company.

We refer to the grouping (customer, product, scale, positioning) as the *value-bundle.*

Second, a strategy has to provide some guidance for how the people responsible for operating the company will make choices about which opportunities to pursue, with whom to partner and compete, which customers to nurture and which to fire, which markets to enter and which to leave, and so on. Thus, along with conceptual artifacts like the corporate mission statement, strategic objectives, and so on, a strategy needs to provide for a mechanism of continual innovation, which includes the corporate culture, governance, and funding to find, vet, and finally commercialize opportunities. This package of innovative capabilities, which we call the *Innovation Factory,* is the corporate analog to the biological processes that create and express diversity in a species.

Thus, the Red Queen of biology has a direct analog in the implementation of business strategy: Companies evolve by creating value-bundles, mutations that represent a company diversifying along one or more of the value dimensions. The market either embraces or rejects the mutation, and thus the evolutionary process proceeds.

The more uncertain the future business environment, the harsher the market selection functions will be. A company must trade off between the costs of evolution and the probability of success. The cost of evolution is the cost of innovation—and the corresponding effort that goes into creating value-bundles. The probability of success is basically the likelihood that any particular innovation will be accepted by the market and become profitable.

In uncertain times, there are many different possible future market conditions, so any given new business opportunity has a relatively small chance of success. *Therefore, it is important in uncertain times to have a very active mechanism of innovation,* which, in turn, requires ready access to the raw materials of the value-bundle: customers, product, scale, or positioning. Yet, given the reality of limited organizational resources, this further implies that it is crucial to control the costs associated with innovation—that is, with creating new value-bundles.

Collaborations—with other companies or between organizations within your company—provide both of these benefits. Before we explore how, we need to spend more time characterizing future uncertainty. In the next section, we introduce a simple model for visualizing and discussing marketplace uncertainty. This model becomes part of the basis for our characterization of collaboration as a tool for maximizing innovation while managing its associated costs.

Characterizing Business Uncertainty

Figure 2.1 is a simple depiction of strategic uncertainty, which we call the *three-arrow picture*. The three-arrow picture is a useful way of representing ranges of potential future business conditions and business outcomes in an uncertain environment.

In the three-arrow picture, time moves horizontally, from left to right. The vertical dimension represents the degree of change in business conditions. As a person who owns a business, you are standing at the far left

FIGURE 2.1   CHARACTERIZING STRATEGIC UNCERTAINTY: THE THREE-ARROW PICTURE

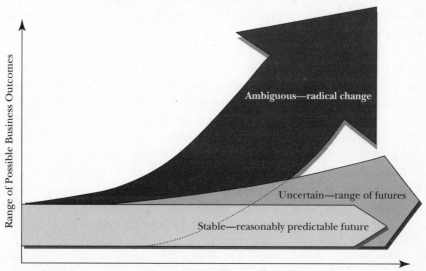

of the picture, looking to the right. The particular path into the future is obscured. All you really know for sure is the path directly in front of you, and the possibilities faced are that the future direction can be pretty stable, very radical, or somewhere in between.

The bottom arrow represents the stable, reasonably predictable future—the future assumed by traditional strategic planning exercises. In the stable business environment of the bottom arrow, very little changes as time goes on. In other words, you basically stay in the same business, producing sustainable innovations that improve your product and increase your penetration of your best customers. This is a mature industry model.

The middle arrow that overlaps the first arrow represents a scenario where markets are changing. This can represent various things—growth markets, businesses where new technologies are creating new business channels, consolidation, and so on—generally things that will change your existing business climate but won't make your current business obsolete. This is the arrow that represents the future of financial institutions in the *Internet as a new distribution channel* scenario that we discussed earlier in this chapter.

The top arrow represents radical change, where the business climate changes so that there is very little overlap with your existing business. This is the scenario that results when a disruptive technology changes the basic rules of the game. It is the arrow that represents the future of financial institutions in the *complete disaggregation* scenario discussed earlier in this chapter.

Traditional strategic planning essentially assumes a bottom arrow future. It tends to be the default strategic assumption for businesses that are inward-facing and thus focusing mainly on operational metrics, and for businesses that are trying to maximize the amount of production they get from a cash cow. Finally, and most damaging, it tends to be the strategic assumption made by many people when they see that the future is murky and posit that, since they cannot reasonably predict the future, they might as well assume a straight line until things become clearer. *This is the worst approach you can take.*

What happens if you plan for a stable future and the future is not stable? This is the environment in which we live. The three-arrow picture visually depicts this unstable environment and resulting options.

On the three-arrow picture in Figure 2.2, you begin at the left and move to the right along the bottom arrow. When you reach point A, the radical future scenario may have already begun to take shape, with

FIGURE 2.2   THE DANGERS OF THE STEADY STATE ASSUMPTION

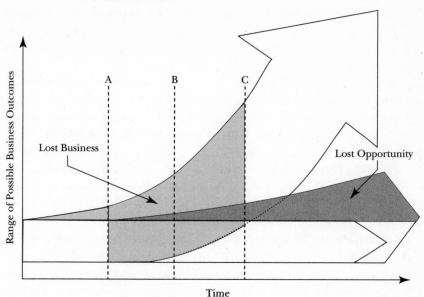

markets forming represented by the lightly shaded area to the left of point A. If you are focused down the path of the bottom arrow—likely if you've made an assumption of future stability—you miss this development (after all, at this point, there's been no real impact on your going-forward business).

When you reach point B, there are two possibilities, depending on whether the future is unfolding along the middle arrow or along the top arrow. If your business has been disrupted and things are radically changing, you are beginning to lose business to the disruption as it emerges from its nurturing niche and starts to invade your markets. This is represented by the lightly shaded area between A and B. Two different pieces comprise the lost business: *opportunities lost,* which is the shaded area above the bottom arrow, and *cannibalized businesses* which is the shaded area within the bottom area. On the other hand, if the middle arrow—future—is unfolding, you have not been disrupted but there have been changes that have opened new business opportunities of which you have not taken advantage. In terms of the Internet examples we discussed earlier, this is the *Internet as distribution channel* scenario, where you are not taking advantage of the new channel. The small darkly shaded area between A and B represents this lost business opportunity.

Continuing to move into the future to point C, if you have been disrupted, you are basically out of business: The market has followed the top arrow and left you behind. If instead you have failed to grow into new market opportunities, represented by the area labeled *Lost Opportunity,* you might become a target for takeover, or at the very least, have missed an opportunity for growth.

What do we take away from this brief analysis? Looking at the pictures, the kind of choices and the kind of dangers involved in focusing on the wrong strategic planning scenario are pretty clear. What really happens is that, as you are standing at the left side of that picture looking to the right, most of the right side is shrouded in fog and there's very little you can go on other than feelings about what the probable future will look like. In this book, we suggest that *you need to pay close attention to how you will move into the future in such a way as to be prepared to recognize and exploit the radical change scenario.* It's not that the radical change scenario is the most likely. By definition, that cannot be known. However, the lessons learned and implications of the more extreme scenarios can easily be modified to fit the actual opportunity set that actually emerges. It is easier to *pull back* and draw from what has already been considered than to attempt to *push into* areas yet anticipated without preparation.

There are significant implications on a company's people, process, and technology depending on the planning approach taken. An assumption of a stable future creates structures and implications throughout an organization that support stability, instead of creating the agility needed to move into the future quickly. The essence of strategic implementation is to create new value-bundles that allow your company to evolve, grow, and prosper, regardless of which scenario becomes a reality. The challenge from the perspective of uncertain futures is to create new value-bundles that encompass the range of future scenarios. Given what we said earlier about innovation and the tradeoffs involved, the real challenge is to innovate quickly and cheaply enough that you can spread value-bundles across the range encompassed by the three arrows while still operating your current business. What is needed, in other words, is an approach that minimizes your degree of planning while maximizing your range of value creation, depending on the type of competitive reality that emerges.

Figure 2.3 shows value creation in the context of the three-arrow picture. Each star represents a new piece of value for your company, that is, a business opportunity or innovation that your company has created and brought to market. Recall that an innovation differentiates in terms of some component of the value-bundle. Therefore, each star could just as well represent a new product, a new set of customers, access to additional

FIGURE 2.3   EXPANDING YOUR OPTIONS

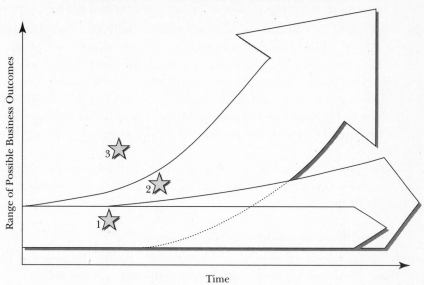

scale, or a change in brand positioning. In Figure 2.3, a company has brought three innovations to market.

The star labeled "1" represents some type of sustaining innovation for your company. This is an innovation—possibly simple, possibly very radical—that improves your offering to your mainstream customers.

The star labeled "2" represents an innovation that is clearly outside of your mainstream business. It represents an experiment and a risk in the sense that it is placed outside of your known "sweet spot." However, as it is shown in Figure 2.3, this innovation sits in the area defined by the middle arrow and thus is in a newly developing area for your business. If you are Barnes & Noble in 1999, this star represents the establishment of a new distribution channel for your book business: The market for online retailing is established so while the new channel is different from a traditional bookstore, this is not a radical experiment. Note that star 2 also lies on the path of the top arrow so, by creating this innovation, you are hedging against the possibility of radical change. Again, using books as an example, had Amazon.com proven disruptive to booksellers—putting all traditional bookstores out of business—Barnes & Noble would be in the path of competing in the new market.

Finally, the star labeled "3" represents an innovation that is outside the known market for your company. It might represent an innovation that in the future will intersect the top arrow. However, from the viewpoint of an established company, it represents an out-and-out *big bet*. An example of star 3 might be a vertical marketplace like Covisint that was created by the Big Three U.S. automakers in an attempt to establish a central marketplace for the purchasing of auto parts from parts suppliers. Covisint was created on the supposition that parts suppliers would flock to a central place that provided demand for their products and a pricing mechanism. At some point in the future, a star 3 created in advance of the market might find itself within the top arrow in which case the bet pays off. In the case of Covisint, the arrows have not yet caught up with the innovation.

In the simplified world of the three-arrow picture, the ideal strategic implementation approach for uncertain times is to create new stars—new value-bundles, or innovations:

- That cover the range of future outcomes
- Quickly enough that you can move even after the arrow gets there—that is, after the market is revealed—as a very fast follower
- With a minimum of cost and risk

Figure 2.4 shows this, representing a company that creates several innovations spread out along the possible futures. An effective strategy

FIGURE 2.4   LEVERAGING INTO THE FUTURE

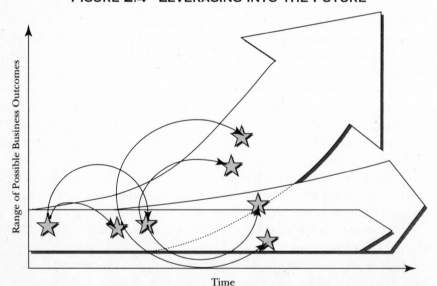

Range of Possible Business Outcomes

Time

provides a conceptual framework for prioritizing and choosing among the many different innovations that might be of highest relevance and potential impact.

There are many ways to drive innovation, but the core dynamics remain the same. Articulated in terms of the three-arrow picture, the vertical spread of the innovations represents a departure from the value created in a company's core business, and therefore presumably a departure from the company's core competencies and the competencies of its people. We are left with the question: *How do we drive innovation when it requires continual, rapid creation of value that progressively moves further and further away from your company's core competencies?*

In terms of the value-bundle, innovation requires differentiating along one or more of the four areas. This builds on Treacy and Wiersema's effective *value discipline* model that has helped companies clearly structure their competencies around one or two of these value disciplines.[5] One important way to do this is to work with other sources of value that are already differentiated from yours. Other companies that are in different businesses and markets—possibly related to your core business, possibly not—can provide the competencies and the value differentiation needed to drive your innovation. You can use another company as a vendor or consultant, where you pay for *access* to their core value they provide, or you can create a relationship where both businesses create and extract new value. Both of these approaches are based on a simple reality: They involve working some form of partnership, alliance, or other cross-company cooperation to create shared value. This is where collaboration comes in.

We are now ready to explore *collaboration* as a means to jumpstart value creation.

The Collaborative Landscape

Collaboration takes many different forms. Each form has different business objectives and different characteristics. Yet, underlying these vast differences are profound similarities. It is from these similarities that we identify what we call the *collaborative DNA*—or underlying dynamics—of different collaborative forms. By understanding these underlying dynamics, we can begin to more effectively exploit collaborative ventures. But first, we need a shared understanding of these different collaborative forms. In addition, we need a vocabulary to frame our understanding and engender shared communications about what we mean by collaboration.

This section provides a definition of collaboration. We continuously build on and use this definition to delineate different types of collaborations and their implications. It is only by building our collaborative vocabulary now that we can clearly focus later on implications for collaborative actions.

Collaboration, as we use it in this book, is defined as *two or more entities working together to create mutual value.* To make it more tangible, collaboration involves two or more companies, departments, customers, regulatory agencies, or whomever that combine their competencies to create new shared value while, at the same time, managing their respective costs and risks. The entities can combine in any one of several different business relationships and for very different periods of time—ranging from some duration needed to exploit a particular innovation or business opportunity, to a much longer term ongoing relationship.

As you can see from this brief definition, collaboration is conceptually simple. It comprises two main parts: *creating value*—that is, creating differentiated value-bundles, and *creating relationships* that allow people to work together to create that value. Let's look at a concrete example from the securities industry to illustrate the point, discuss some of the implications, and introduce a model of collaboration. This example, which we will use several times in this book, requires some background.

Straight through Processing: GSTPA and Omgeo[6]

When you choose to buy a security for your portfolio, or more typically when the manager of a fund in which you have shares decides to buy shares for the fund, the *buy* request begins the execution of a series of actions, collectively referred to as the *trade life cycle.* Generally, trading activity involves three groups: investment managers, broker/dealers, and custodians. Investment managers focus mainly on the performance of their investments, which positions they hold in which securities, and how the securities in the portfolio are allocated to the various accounts that make up the portfolio. Broker/dealers focus on the fulfillment of the buy and sell orders that come from investment managers. Custodians focus on the actual securities involved in the trade. The trade life cycle begins with the placing of the order, called *Initiation,* and ends with *Settlement and Clearance* when the buyer's funds end up in the seller's account, and the seller's securities end up in the buyer's account.[7] The fulfillment of a particular buy or sell order is *Execution,* which happens on an exchange. Millions of trades happen each day across multiple exchanges, and individual securities transactions are grouped into larger executions that may take place in different exchanges. The step between Execution and Settlement and Clearance called *Trade Matching* is where the parties involved cross-check information related to each trade, including the specific security, price, and quantity for each trade to ensure that all parties involved in the trade are on the same page.[8] This step is time consuming as messages flow among all the parties involved. Due to a lack of standards and a proliferation of proprietary processes in the major global financial institutions that are typically the parties to the trade, there is a high failure rate in the Trade Matching step, consuming time and requiring expensive manual rework.

In a typical U.S.-only securities trade, three business days elapse between Initiation and Settlement. In 2002, a typical day's trading volume was approximately $300 billion. Therefore, on any given day, the dollar value of unsettled trades—that is, trades where the order has executed but the funds and securities have not changed hands—can be close to a trillion dollars. This represents a risk to the trading community because events can happen during those three days that can affect a party's ability to actually settle the trade—for example, one of the parties could precipitously go out of business. As an additional incentive, in 2002, approximately 70 percent of all cross-border securities trading involved some form of foreign exchange.[9] The foreign exchange activity adds time to the Settlement process, creating even more risk to the parties involved due to additional risk factors such as changes in foreign exchange rates for the currencies in which Settlement will occur, or problems due to political factors.

Largely because of the risk factors, but also due to the savings that a more efficient, hands-off process would bring, the securities industry has been motivated to shorten the trade life cycle. Taken as a whole, the goal is to compress the time frame of a trade, from Initiation through Settlement and Clearance, to one day. The securities industry refers to this goal of a one-day life cycle and the initiatives to achieve it as T + 1. There are two major components to achieving T + 1. One component is the creation of a common *utility* that participants in securities transactions can use to facilitate the information and process flow among the participants. The other component, which must be individually undertaken by each company involved in securities trading, is the reengineering of internal business processes to provide rapid, error-free execution of all of the in-house portions of the securities transaction, including connection to the utility. The story of how securities companies moved to create such a Settlement and Clearing utility is a great example for our ongoing discussion of the risks, rewards, and implications of collaborations. The way individual companies have approached the reinvention of their internal process provides some useful examples as well on how individual companies work with a collaboratively developed innovation and supporting business model.

To create the Settlement and Clearing utility, major industry players combined to form a not-for-profit organization called the Global Straight Through Processing Association (GSTPA), an industry association that includes broker/dealers, custodians, and investment/asset managers—the participants in a securities transaction. It is focused on creating and promulgating the standards, architecture, business rules, workflows, and technology necessary to allow the processing of equity trades—especially trades that cross national borders—from Initiation through Clearing and Settlement with little or no human intervention.[10] Formed in 1998, in 2002 there were approximately 70 members of the association, representing some of the largest financial institutions and most influential financial services technology and service providers in the world, as well as many other affiliated organizations.

According to GSTPA, the challenges in creating a true straight-through processing utility included lack of standardization, incompatible manual procedures, a multiplicity of service providers, incompatible databases, and generally a high rate of trade failures.[11] GSTPA members have worked together with technology and business partners to address the challenges and create standards and processes that will let them handle the problematic trade matching processing that occurs after the trade and before the Settlement. Additionally, the GSTPA created and launched a new company, Axion4, to build the utility, envisaged as the GSTPA Transaction Flow Manager (TFM). Axion4 has conducted a broad selection process for partners to help build the utility. It was due to be piloted in 2002 contingent on the state of the economy and the availability of members to participate in the pilot.

Let's stop here to interpret some of this in terms of the collaborative terms we've defined so far. The GSTPA's defined standards, process, and the TFM utility together address issues that have existed in the securities industry for years. Yet, do they constitute an innovation in the sense that we use the term in this book?

Recall that the core issues that drove the formation of GSTPA were the risks inherent in long Settlement times with large volumes of money outstanding and the costs associated with the extensive manual processing and rework in trade matching. Both of these drivers are issues of *scale:* the financial system as a whole cannot take on more risk at the scale implied by a long life cycle and the trade volumes that exist now and are projected into the future, globally. Implementation of GSTPA allows for larger scale in the numbers of transactions processed by reducing the exposure for any particular company at any given scale. Similarly, the capability of financial institutions to trade is limited by the inherent nonscalability of highly manual processes as well as by the costs of those manual processes. In value-bundle terms, then, GSTPA provides a differentiated value-bundle in the scale dimension.

GSTPA also arguably provides its participants access to new *customers*. In cross-border trades especially, due to the hassles of the foreign settlement process, small firms tend to rely on in-country full-service firms to handle the Settlement and Clearance. With the GSTPA utility, small firms will potentially be in a position to economically offer such services in a borderless manner providing them access to these new customers. Lower costs also might help open cross-border trading to a wider audience, providing differentiation in the *customer* dimension. Given the lower costs and easier access to cross-border trades, GSTPA will probably serve as a means for smaller equities companies to provide an international trading capability, that, depending on how they choose to present it to their clients, can be a change in *positioning* if used as a brand differentiator, or a new *product* if presented as a new offering for clients.

GSTPA is an example of collaboration—of companies working together to create shared value. It's a good example on which to build as we further develop our collaboration model, particularly from the perspectives of:

- The degree to which the members of the association exposed and shared core competencies, value, and intellectual property in the formation of GSTPA, and the creation of the utility
- The degree to which the members "feel" committed to the association in the long term

Several years ago, the capability to process through the trade life cycle was a differentiator for GSTPA members, particularly those with global reach and transactional capabilities, but that is no longer the case. The lowering of technology transaction costs, the encroachment by new competitors into the once-closed world of Clearing and Settlement, and the increasing requirements for cross-border Settlement capabilities squeezed the margins of these capabilities, reducing their viability as a competitive differentiator. As Steven Crosby, the first CEO of GSTPA put it, they become mere *table stakes* to play the game, no longer the *rule makers* of the settlement game.[12] *The Red Queen runs, and she runs relentlessly.*

Yet, GSTPA members have made enormous legacy investments in their internal processes and systems that supported equity trading, and they faced having to make still more enormous additional investment in what has become a low-margin, commodity part of their business. The option? *Collaborate.* And collaborate by establishing a *utility* pulling from best practices and competencies from multiple companies that would create mutual value at reduced costs for all parties involved. Thus was born (and borne) the business rationale—the value proposition, and the innovation—of GSTPA.

GSTPA members contributed to the requirements and design of the standards, architecture, business rules, workflows, and technology for global trade Clearing and Settlement to provide value for all GSTPA members. The members contributed intellectual property that represented a major sunk investment, representing an important, though typically no longer differentiating, part of their business. The high-margin battlefield would continue in other areas among GSTPA members, but no longer in this area. The Red Queen changed the course of the competitive race.

Interestingly, the issue of contribution of intellectual property caused some potential participants to not participate in GSTPA, and, in fact, to create an alternative to GSTPA. During the GSTPA technology selection process, some of the participating vendors already had working products and/or businesses that addressed some of the key GSTPA challenges. As the story goes, the position taken by GSTPA on the ownership of intellectual property used in the GSTPA solution was unacceptable to some of these vendors who felt that if they participated in GSTPA they could in effect be giving away important parts of their business, and so they opted out of working with the association. One of these companies was Thomson Financials. Thomson, a leading provider of software solutions in financial services, had a robust product called electronic trade completion (ETC) and a growing business with many customers using ETC to help facilitate information flow in the trade life cycle.[13] Thomson chose to not participate in GSTPA. In fact, Thomson teamed with some other players in the industry to create a competitive offering to GSTPA, called Omgeo. From the perspective of GSTPA, the existence of Omgeo represents competition where they could have otherwise had an uncontested market. From the perspective of the industry as a whole, Omgeo represents a second "standard," creating additional costs and reducing the efficiency of return on the investments of GSTPA members. Consequently, securities firms must either (1) choose sides between GSTPA and Omgeo, which introduces the risk that they might choose a losing platform with the attendant damage to their market position, (2) support both, which means that they have to connect to both, raising the costs of business, or (3) inveigle GSTPA and Omgeo to inter-operate, which requires investment by both GSTPA and Omgeo to create and maintain interfaces.

For the purposes of this book, the GSTPA/Omgeo story highlights a crucial element of collaboration: To create value, companies must realistically come to grips with the value that each brings to the relationship and the concerns that each will have about how losing control of that value will impact their business. We explore the role of intellectual property and its critical role within collaborative ventures in Chapter Five. For now, two points are important:

1. *Collaborations are inherently risky.* By design, they attack new areas of business value and opportunity. Managing that risk that accords to both the participating company as well as to the collaborative venture becomes a critical requirement for any effective collaboration—a topic covered in Chapter Three.

2. *Meaningful collaborations require that each participant exposes and shares important parts of its key competencies and core value to other participants—* possibly competitors. We call this the *intimacy* of the collaborative relationship. Over the course of this book, we explore intimacy implications, one being that a high degree of intimacy, equivalent to putting something of high value to the company at risk, requires a high degree of comfort. The other GSTPA participants did not provide that degree of comfort to Thomson, so Thomson could not participate in GSTPA, and GSTPA therefore spawned a competitor.

To be successful, GSTPA will need stability in its membership over a reasonably long period of time while the requirements and standards are put into place and the utility is created and launched. Until the utility is operating and the membership is receiving value from its investment, GSTPA remains a cost. Therefore, members need to be committed to GSTPA as a basic condition of their participation. In a collaborative situation, there will always be a period of investment where the participants are committing resources and value has yet to be created. Over time, participants individually assess whether their investment will generate reasonable returns, but as a starting point for collaborating, participants need a shared notion for how long they will have to work together in creating the new value for which the collaboration was formed. We call this the *dynamism* of the collaborative relationship.

The notion of how long members of any collaboration expect it to last is an important one. Earlier, we mentioned eBondTrade as a viable business created out of the Internet. At about the same time in early 2000 that eBondTrade was launched, Goldman Sachs, Merrill Lynch, and Morgan Stanley Dean Witter, joined within the first few months by Deutsche Bank, started BondBook, an online bond trading system intended to address "the market's call for a more open structure, improved transparency, and greater liquidity."[14] BondBook closed in October 2001: To be successful, BondBook required a fundamental change in the behavior of bond traders, and the participants did not see such a change happening in a reasonable time frame. It is possible that BondBook is simply an example of an unsuccessful business proposition. It is also possible that BondBook represented a potentially successful collaboration that failed because the participants did not accurately assess the time commitment that would be required. Generally speaking, the longer it takes for a collaborative relationship to generate value, the more likely it is that one or more participants will lose their appetite, threatening the investment for everyone.

A major goal of this book is to identify ways to make it easier for companies to collaborate and create value. Later, we return to these examples to explain how some of the lessons, models, and best practices we explore could be used not merely to explain but to anticipate both the success and challenges of these and other collaborative ventures.

First, we need to continue building vocabulary around collaboration. We do so by characterizing what we call the *Collaborative Landscape.* As we mentioned earlier, collaborations differ broadly in form and function. They do, however, live in a common space characterized by the two dimensions discussed earlier: *intimacy* and *dynamism.* These form the basis for our characterization of collaborative relationships and therefore the grids of the Collaborative Landscape.

The Collaborative Landscape: The Model

Figure 2.5 shows the Collaborative Landscape, one of the models we use to discuss collaboration and place it in context. The two dimensions, intimacy and dynamism, form its axes.

Intimacy is a measure of the degree to which participants of a collaborative effort expose their core competencies and value to one another. For our purposes, a company's core competencies and value take the form of one or more of the elements of the value-bundle—product, customer, scale, or positioning.

FIGURE 2.5 THE COLLABORATIVE LANDSCAPE

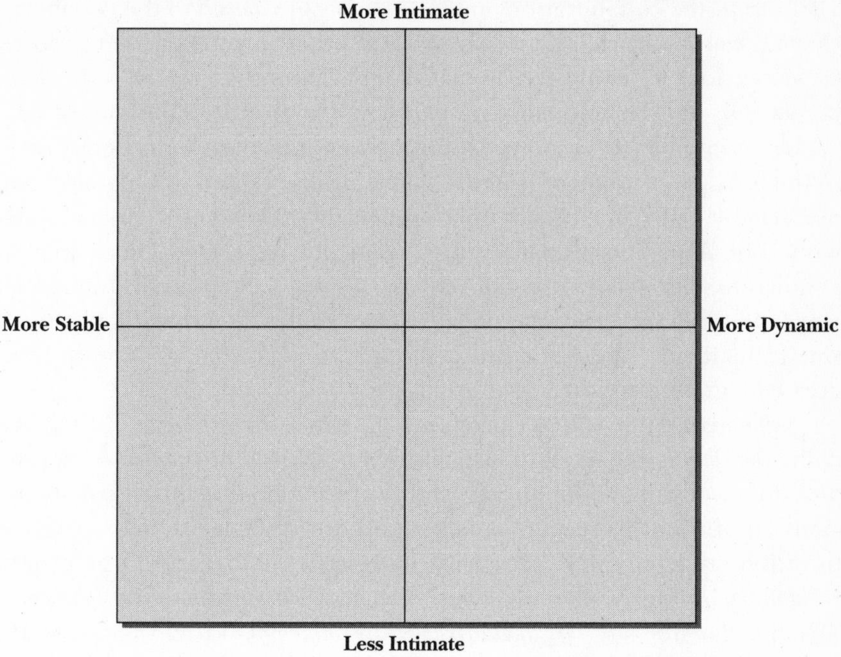

An example of a high-intimacy collaboration is one where two vendor companies, who in some instances compete with one another, work together to bid on a contract. In our recent experience, two global services firms, A and B, came together to respond to a large and complex Request for Proposal (RFP) from a company that is a client of both. Firm A has a deep understanding of the client's business and operations and an excellent reputation for managing large, complex programs. Firm B has an excellent reputation for technology development, especially in the target client's industry. Firms A and B compete regularly for work in business and operations—A's strength—and in technology—B's strength. By choosing to collaborate on this opportunity, each firm was contributing from its strength, and each firm was able to observe—close up and in detail—the other's offering. Realistically, at the end of the proposal process, both A and B had learned a lot about each others' strengths, strengthening themselves and putting each in a better position to compete.

An example of low-intimacy collaboration can be found in any of the numerous e-marketplaces, for example, eBay, the world's largest online auction and exchange site. In eBay, the important collaboration occurs between eBay and the seller. In terms of the value-bundle, a seller brings a *product* to the collaboration, and eBay brings *customers* to the collaboration (as well as a pricing mechanism and other infrastructure to create the conditions for commerce to take place). The value created is the marketplace itself. The collaboration between eBay and its thousands of sellers has created billions in wealth through appreciation in its equity and, in the process, income for its sellers. The intimacy is low in the sense that neither the seller nor eBay have a significant risk exposure in the individual collaborations that make up a seller putting something online for an auction: The seller does not see any of eBay's core intellectual property, and eBay sees only the item for sale. Each collaboration creates a small amount of value, but taken in the aggregate, the collaborations have created a giant business.

Dynamism, as we stated earlier, is a measure of the length of time the collaboration is expected to last. Going back to the three-arrow picture and the discussion about an uncertain future, we argued that collaboration is useful in that it gives access to resources needed to help drive innovation, and provides that access more quickly than could be grown internally. *In highly uncertain times, then, where innovation must take place rapidly and continually, the capability to create collaborative relationships quickly and efficiently is not merely desirable but critical.* All things being equal, the more quickly a collaborative relationship can be formed, the more quickly you can innovate. If you can quickly form highly intimate relationships, then you can innovate quickly and with high value. In more certain times or markets, it is not as important for a collaboration to yield value rapidly, and more stable relationships might be appropriate. Later on, we'll explore how collaborations tend to evolve over time, from less to more stable relationships as either the business environment changes, or as the target of the collaboration becomes an established, reliable market.

Stated differently, as the initial business proposition on which the collaboration was formed becomes successful, competitors enter the market, creating downward price pressure and thus shifting the competitive basis from high-margin innovation to low-margin commodity—today's successful innovations are inevitably tomorrow's commodities. With this natural competitive dynamic, the business proposition shifts, as does the purpose and likely form of the collaboration. We seed this thought now, and return to harvest it in subsequent chapters.

The eBay example we used earlier is a highly dynamic collaboration in that each collaboration with a seller lasts for only the length of an auction (a few days). GSTPA is an example of a stable collaboration where members expect to be involved with GSTPA conceptually "forever." The collaboration between firm A and firm B is somewhere in between.

With the axes defined, we can walk through the quadrants of the Collaborative Landscape (see Figure 2.6) and discuss the characteristics of each. The bottom two quadrants are characterized by relatively low degrees of intimacy—little core value is exposed among the participants. Consequently, the collaborations are focused on aggregating value across multiple low-margin transactions. On a whole, we expect collaborative forms in these zones to yield relatively low value per transaction.

The lower left quadrant is for highly stable, low-intimacy collaborations. We label it *Country Clubs* because of its similarity in terms of a stable set of members who know one another socially, but not necessarily intimately. An example of collaboration in the Country Club Zone is the New York Stock Exchange (NYSE). To trade on the exchange you must be a member. Membership is controlled, with approximately 400 members at the time of this writing. In this sense, the collaboration between the NYSE and its members is very stable. The exchange provides a place for members to transact trades and mechanisms to facilitate the transactions—for

FIGURE 2.6   ZONES OF THE COLLABORATIVE LANDSCAPE

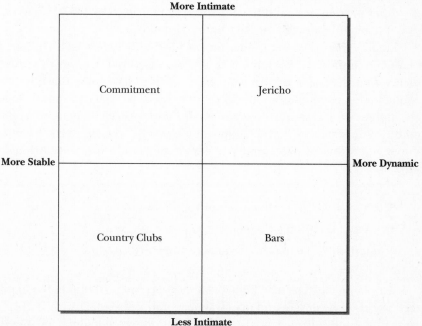

example, mechanisms for pricing and for providing liquidity. The exchange interacts with its members, and the members with one another in the roles of buyer and seller, transacting using the abstraction of a share of stock. Through the mechanisms of an impersonal exchange and shares of stock, the members of the exchange interact with one another and with the exchange with a minimum of intimacy.

The lower right quadrant is for highly dynamic, low-intimacy collaborations. We label it *Bars* because of its similarity to the active social life that is anchored by a fashionable bar or nightclub in a city, where relationships come and go, and generally don't mean all that much. We've positioned eBay as an example of collaboration in the Bar Zone. Unlike the NYSE with its guarded member list, eBay sellers come and go. Like the NYSE, sellers and buyers interact in a highly impersonalized manner.

The upper two quadrants are characterized by relatively high degrees of intimacy—substantial core value is exposed among the participants. With high value shared, we would expect high value to be created, and thus that these collaborations would center around high-value, high-margin transactions.

The upper left quadrant is for very stable, highly intimate collaborations. We label it *Commitment* because participants in these relationships have made a substantial decision to share important, valuable assets with the other participants, and to stick with the relationship. GSTPA is as an example of collaboration in the Commitment Zone.

Finally, the upper right quadrant is for highly dynamic, highly intimate collaborations. We label it *Jericho* because operating in this zone means that the walls around your organization have come down to accommodate the collaborations. In the Jericho Zone, you can rapidly create high-value collaborative relationships with other companies. Based on everything that we have seen in this chapter, operating in the Jericho Zone means that you and your partners have found rapid and efficient ways of:

- Quantifying the value each of you brings to the relationship
- Controlling the risks associated with high intimacy
- Equitably sharing the rewards of the collaboration

An example of a Jericho Zone collaboration can be found in the high-tech world of the design and manufacture of mixed-signal integrated circuits.[15] A standard integrated circuit, as found in a computer or stereo system, is either all digital or all analog. For a number of reasons, mostly the proliferation of wireless handheld devices, there is a rapidly growing demand for small, low-power implementations of circuits that include analog, digital, radio-frequency (RF), and, increasingly, micro-mechanical components. For example, a cell phone has analog components that interface with the microphone and speaker, digital components that implement the features of the phone, and RF components that transmit and receive the cell signal. To keep phones small and costs down, cell phone manufacturers want to minimize the number of individual components in a phone. Ideally the analog, digital, and RF components needed in a cell phone would be on a single integrated circuit (chip).

A chip that includes digital, analog, and/or RF circuitry is called a mixed-signal chip. Creating mixed-signal chips is problematic: Each design is innovative, requires design skills that cut across multiple disciplines, needs to be completed quickly because of time to market pressures, and needs to be of high quality because of the brutal penalty extracted by any problem discovered after the chips are made in volume and, in the worst case, distributed into the hands of millions of demanding consumers. In terms of our framework, designers need to create new value (chip designs), quickly and creating those chip designs requires skills and knowledge outside of those possessed by any one designer.

Based on what we have said, this should be a ripe environment for collaboration, and, interestingly, the industry has organized a collaborative model that lies directly in the Jericho Zone.

In this market, when a new mixed-signal chip is needed, the product manufacturer contracts a designer. The designer creates the new design, which is then contracted to a chip manufacturer for production. Numerous freelance designers with specialty skills in RF, digital, analog, and micro-mechanical circuitry have chosen to support this supply chain. They create intellectual property by designing and testing designs of specialty circuits that are suitable to be used as building blocks in the design of mixed-signal chips. They then make their single-mode building blocks available to designers of mixed-signal circuits. The mixed-signal chip designers use this pre-created intellectual property in the creation of their own intellectual property—the design of a mixed-signal chip. Lessons learned in the mixed-signal chip design are often used by the building block designer to improve a building block circuit or to create a useful variant.

The challenges in this environment have been those predicted by the models we have developed in this chapter. The innovations must be rapid. Consequently, it is important for a mixed-signal chip designer to be able to find new intellectual property and, more importantly, to get the permission and business terms needed to put it to use in a new chip, quickly and efficiently. The relationship is highly intimate in that the providers of new intellectual property expose everything in digital form—the designs are expressed using design tools that create and store the designs digitally—so they are potentially at extreme risk of their intellectual property being copied and used without their being properly compensated. The relationships are temporary, with a lifetime measured in terms of a given chip's production cycle. The response to these challenges has been to create an environment for Jericho Zone collaborations between the designers of mixed-signal chips and the designers of the building blocks. The industry has created an intellectual property (IP) clearinghouse to help mixed-signal chip designers find the right building blocks and to connect the mixed-signal designer with the building block designer if modifications are necessary. The industry has also created standards and practices to mitigate the risk that the intellectual property of the building block designer will be misused, stolen, or compromised. Finally, pricing models are emerging that help quantify the value created by the different participants in the collaboration.

From these individual examples, Figure 2.7 shows the Collaborative Landscape overlaid with different business relationships that we see today. We will take one more pass through the Collaborative Landscape to introduce some of the themes that we further explore throughout the rest of this book.

The Jericho Zone includes the IP clearinghouse described in the integrated circuit example, and, to a lesser extent, partnerships (an agreement to work together within some scope) and cooperation. In each of these business relationships, the parties know that they are committing to it not for the long haul, but rather are exploiting a particular opportunity by creating a collaborative relationship. In each of these relationships, the parties know that there will be significant sharing of some valuable corporate assets with the risk of its being co-opted and leveraged by the other participant(s). We saw this in the example of firms A and B working together on a proposal—an example of partnership. Practically, what does it take to create such a partnership?

Recall that we determined that creating a successful collaborative relationship requires:

- Quantifying the value each of you brings to the relationship
- Controlling the risks associated with high intimacy
- Equitably sharing the rewards of the collaboration

FIGURE 2.7   DIFFERENT FORMS OF COLLABORATION

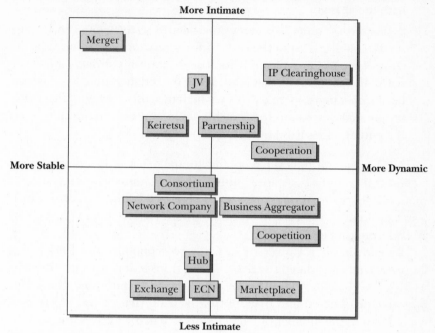

From personal experience in firm A, partnership collaborations:

1. Happen through negotiation and consensus building in the participating organizations

2. Are achieved through nondisclosure agreements, confidentiality agreements, and often "no poaching" agreements regarding the participants employees

3. Are realized through some sort of partnership agreement

Each of these takes time and resources to negotiate, and they make up an important piece of the costs associated with collaboration: the transaction cost. There are two implications of these transaction costs:

1. The amount of time needed to create the needed agreements constrains the dynamism of the relationship, slowing down your ability to form collaborative relationships. Thinking back to the three-arrow picture, if the top arrow prevails, it might be difficult to

create relationships fast enough to innovate quickly enough to cope with the change.

2. The cost required to create the needed agreements can be substantial, adding cost to the collaborative relationship. Intuitively, the costs of establishing the collaborative relationship directly affect the size of the opportunity that is attractive for collaboration. For the partnership relationship we have described, the costs are high. Therefore, it only makes sense to form such a collaborative relationship when the potential rewards are sufficiently high.

A key lesson follows. Much organizational behavior can be explained by how transactions costs are handled. Organizational size and, as we'll show, collaborative options are greatly impacted by the degree to which it makes sense to internalize or collaborate to share these transactions and coordination costs.

Ronald Coase, a University of Chicago economist and 1991 Nobel laureate, first articulated the dynamics of transaction costs in 1934. His writings on the nature of the firm asked the basic question: "If markets optimize production and distribution, why do firms exist?"[16] He concluded that as the number of participants in a market grows, the costs of finding a source for what you seek and negotiating the transaction grows. Past a certain point, the cost of a market transaction exceeds the cost of doing it inside your firm. From that initial insight, he asked the next logical question: "Why, if by organizing we can eliminate certain [transaction] costs and in fact reduce the cost of production, are there any market transactions at all?" Here he concluded that as a firm grows, its efficient governance is subject to decreasing returns and the internal cost of management and coordination increases. There is a point at which the cost of the market transaction and the cost of the internal transaction are equal. That equilibrium point governs the optimal size of the firm.

Oliver Williamson, Edgar F. Kaiser Professor of Economics and Law, and Transamerica Professor of Business at the University of California at Berkeley, has built on Coase's insights creating what is now known as *transaction cost economics*. Williamson's work has found its way into executives' everyday life in terms of the commonplace *build-or-buy* decision.[17] Much of the business uncertainty (in terms of the three-arrow picture) of the e-commerce bubble is traceable to the possibility that the Internet, by providing ubiquitous connectivity between businesses and also between consumers and businesses, fundamentally changed the transaction cost equation. If such connectivity can drive down transaction costs radically, then—per Coase and Williamson—it can radically affect the size of the firms engaged in those transactions. Global giants, the argument goes, exist because their internal transaction costs are lower than market costs. If the transaction costs go down, the giants become dinosaurs, and they must *vertically disaggregate*—that is, make their core value accessible in smaller pieces that can be assembled into market transactions. Since the global giants were able to mark up their internal transaction costs when selling their services to the market, and that markup no longer exists if disaggregation occurs, they face huge reductions in revenue.

How does this apply to collaboration and the Collaborative Landscape? Through recognizing that *innovation is a particular case of a transaction that can occur either inside your firm or with other firms in a market environment.* Firms have long understood the need to make the goods and services that they create available to the market. However, innovation has been treated as mainly an in-house activity: Given the intimacy incumbent in innovation and its attendant risks, the cost of creating transactions around innovation have been high enough that it has been reserved for special cases where the expected return has been large enough to justify the high cost of the transaction.

But, as we discussed when we introduced the three-arrow picture, uncertainty forces us to reexamine the role of innovation. When business uncertainty requires you to innovate into areas that significantly extend your core competence or the costs of extending them are greater than the time allowed to take advantage of the innovation, then collaboration with other firms who possess the needed competence is not merely pragmatic, but becomes a strategic option. When business uncertainty requires companies to innovate rapidly and continually, a company needs to find a way to do it quickly and cheaply. Stated differently, in times where uncertainty is the rule rather than the exception, we must find ways to drive down the transaction and coordination costs of innovation. This is the Jericho Zone.

Jericho Zone collaborations require agile responsiveness and capabilities to quickly plug in and out of different collaborative ventures. In Chapter Three, we discuss the creation of *value ports* and the key capabilities critical to "plug-and-play" quickly into these value ports and collaborations. We also explore the underlying dynamics of *how* to make collaborations more effective, regardless of where they might live within the Collaborative Landscape. As we mentioned before and will again, there are many different types of collaborations; yet there are similarities—basic competitive dynamics and patterns to them—that are necessary to exploit them and their resulting collaborative forms more effectively.

Jericho Zone collaborations require minimizing the time and costs of establishing the necessary relationships. In terms of transaction cost economics, this means that, for transactions involving the sharing of core value, we need to internalize a shift from a *build* posture toward a *buy* posture. In turn, this means we need to shift innovation activities from what transaction cost economists call *firm governance* toward *market governance*. Firm governance is characterized by employees transacting in customized, complex ways, where the ambiguities inherent in the employee interaction are reduced by large amounts of context and tacit knowledge (i.e., they know each other and have worked together over and over again thereby creating mutually shared expectations regarding performance and recurrent ways of working together). In other words, the interactions are complex and not very efficient, but the cost is manageable because smart, motivated employees with a shared system of values and trust can work through the complexities. Market governance is characterized by buyers and sellers transacting on standardized goods and services, Here, buyers and sellers each have access to the same information regarding the transaction. Markets are efficient when the participants can easily describe the object of the transaction, and are confident that they know as much about the transaction as everyone else involved.

Moving from firm to market governance requires simplifying the interaction and standardizing the object of the transaction. For innovation, this means that we need to codify the value brought to the collaboration by each party, the risks that each party faces in exposing its value to the others, and the rewards that will result. How do we do this? By establishing a standard vocabulary and process for quantifying the value, controlling the risk, and sharing the rewards.

We've said it once and we'll say it again and again: Collaborative forms differ and they differ greatly, as we've seen in the Collaborative Landscape. Discerning the common competitive dynamics across them and, more specifically, building the common vocabulary to express them, becomes a critical first step to exploiting them and their underlying processes more effectively. So far, we've introduced a number of definitions, or what we call *grammar tools* that are necessary to clarify what we mean by collaborations, including the Collaborative Landscape, the role of transactions and coordination costs, and our definition of collaborations. We continuously use these grammar tools to delineate the best practices, some lessons learned, and tangible implications of collaborative opportunities. So far, and stepping back, the common elements of collaborations are the need to:

- Share the value
- Manage the risks
- Share the rewards

This simple statement has significant implications on organizational behaviors, on business processes, and on the technology used to engender and sustain collaborations. The more quickly, cheaply, and effectively you can implement these three elements, the more you will be able to innovate using collaboration. The rest of the book concentrates on establishing the people, process, and technology conditions for this to occur, and the implications for your company of making collaborations one of your core and necessary competencies.

SUMMARY: FROM THE WHY TO THE HOW OF COLLABORATIVE EFFECTIVENESS

Strategically, the changing business environment—changes in markets, competition, customers, and technology—drives companies to continuously evolve. The imperative is the same as the Red Queen principle that drives species to evolve in response to constant competition from other individuals and species. Plants and animals that do not evolve become extinct. Similarly, businesses must constantly evolve or they will inevitably shrink and die.

Businesses evolve by creating new value. In this chapter, we've seen that collaboration is one means for creating new value that has the benefit of mobilizing value from other businesses into the value creation process for all participating parties. In the process, participating parties share the value created, in a sense, combining organizational DNA in the creation of that new value. Without doubt, there are both risks and costs of any such DNA collaborative combinations. These risks and underlying costs must be managed, from the perspective of each participating party, or shared equitably along with the value created from the perspective of the collaboration.

There are many different collaborative forms. These different forms can be located within the Collaborative Landscape and characterized by:

- How *intimate* is the relationship—how much of your core value is being shared with the partner.

- How *dynamic* is the relationship—do you expect the collaborative relationship to be long lived or do you expect to have more, shorter relationships.

Effective value creation requires sharing of value by each party in the collaboration. Greater intimacy therefore implies greater potential for value creation. The cost and risk of forming and breaking a collaborative relationship dictates how much value must be created to justify the collaboration. More dynamic relationships therefore implies—all things being equal—the need for good management of the costs and risks of creating and breaking collaborative relationships. As we see in the next chapter, this implies a sharing of vocabulary that allows the collaborative partners to communicate and agree on the value and risk components of the relationship.

The combination of highly intimate and highly dynamic results in a powerful strategic concept we have called the Jericho Zone. The Jericho Zone characterizes an environment where companies can come together quickly to create high value in response to strategic imperatives, at low cost and low risk. The conditions for operating in the Jericho Zone are:

> Agreed vocabulary, which give you and your prospective partners the ability to articulate, discuss, and agree on how to create and share the rewards, while managing the shared organizational, technology, and people risks inherent in the intimacy needed for meaningful collaboration.

Yet, while Jericho Zone collaborations are particularly compelling, they are not the only effective collaborative form. All collaborations share common elements and dynamics. Understanding these commonalities are as important as exploiting their differences. A key strategic requirement is aligning a company's specific business objective with the appropriate type of collaborative form. Yet, such alignment requires "making sense" of the different types of collaborations that exist and the resultant opportunities. It requires, again, having a shared understanding through a common vocabulary and methods to create that understanding from which effective action can be derived. This takes us back to the overall objective of this chapter which is to explore *why* collaborations are becoming such a strategic imperative.

Collaborations are inherently risky. They are also intrinsically costly. Yet, while these risks and costs are real, so too is the strategic imperative for collaborations. Our competitive environment is uncertain. Building capabilities to exploit this uncertainty becomes not an issue of operational interest but of competitive necessity. Uncertainty by its very nature cannot be dictated or predicted. What is needed is a mechanism for increasing your organization's capacity to adapt and aggressively exploit fast-moving market opportunities and business propositions. Collaborations provide such a mechanism, giving you a strategic tool to extend your core competencies into the worlds of the competitive unknown. *Thus, the "why" of collaborations is the need to enhance strategic agility and competitive relevance. What we need to explore next is the "how" of collaborative effectiveness—exploring the mechanics and the underlying mechanisms of different collaborative forms.*

Chapter Three explores this question of "how." Chapter Three extends our vocabulary and begins to operationalize the collaborative models, giving an understanding of the underlying DNA of effective collaborations. Subsequent chapters shift gears. We build on the collaboration models and language provided to suggest specific implications of these different collaborative forms and their dynamics—their "hows"—from different perspectives: from organizational, people, and technology.

CHAPTER HIGHLIGHTS

The Issue

Marketplace uncertainty is our only competitive given. How do we exploit this uncertainty as a competitive asset? What transforms collaboration from merely an operational option to a strategic imperative?

The Insight

Recognizing that uncertainty infuses the competitive environment in which we live requires that we acknowledge that no simple or single answer exists to navigate through that uncertainty. How can we embrace this uncertainty with respect to emerging collaborative

(continued)

business opportunities and thereby begin to manage that uncertainty as we acknowledge its ubiquity? Simply put: Through exploiting collaboration. At their essence, collaborations are *innovation engines* designed to exploit fast-moving business opportunities. They are a means to create new "genes" in your organizational DNA to enhance organizational capabilities and thereby more effectively harness the power of competitive uncertainty. Thus, the "why" of collaboration is the need to enhance strategic agility and competitive relavance.

The Phrases

The Collaborative Landscape; collaborations as *innovation engines*.

The Implications

Collaboration is a set of business activities that create shared value while managing distributed risk. They are strategic mechanisms to exploit fast-moving business opportunities. Consequently, exploiting collaborations as a strategic innovative engine is critical to maintain competitive agility and relevance. With one key implication: the unmitigated, absolute, and critical need to make collaboration core to organizational and managerial skills. Building the capabilities to "plug-into-and-out-of" collaborations becomes critical to exploit the dynamics of these fast-moving opportunities. Why? Because what is today's competitive advantage becomes tomorrow's mere table stakes to play in that marketplace game.

CHAPTER THREE

Collaborative DNA: Exploring the Dynamics of Effective Collaborations

Collaborations are inherently risky. They are difficult to operationalize, hard to maintain, and even harder to realize value from. Yet they are increasingly a strategic necessity for ongoing competitive relevance. In Chapter Two, we explored the strategic necessity for collaboration—addressing the question: Why should we care about collaborations? *Bottom line: We care because collaborations are pragmatic responses to continually drive innovation in uncertain market environments*. Simple and critical. The three-arrow picture provided a simple model to visualize this future uncertainty. The value-bundle—of product, customer, scale, and positioning—was defined as a simple means to concretely characterize what type of value is created in innovation. We introduced the *Collaborative Landscape* as a means to characterize various collaborative forms.

Finally, we applied the notion of transaction costs to collaboration to raise a key issue about the absolute criticality of building capabilities to minimize the time and cost of establishing collaborative relationships.

Market conditions change both unpredictably and quickly, opening windows of specific business opportunities. Taking advantage of these often fast-moving business opportunities requires an agility and alacrity—of process and capabilities—fully internalized by few and capable of quick exploitation by even fewer. The market waits for no organization. Consequently, an active adaptive mechanism—constructed from a variety of organizations, skills, products, and processes to attack very specific business opportunities—is a core asset, a key requirement and a critical capability. The ability to effectively, and efficiently, collaborate is just such a mechanism. It is for this reason, as we demonstrate throughout this book, that collaborations are not simply execution expedients. Rather, they are becoming strategic tools in the corporate arsenal. This is the answer to the question: Why should we care about collaborations?

Re-summarizing this critical initial message, market uncertainty forces us to reexamine the role of innovation:

- Uncertainty runs with the Red Queen and forces organizations to innovate into areas that stretch the bounds of an organization's core competence.

- When organizations need to innovate rapidly and continually, they must find a way to do a lot of it, quickly and effectively.

- As innovation drives businesses into new territory, internal costs of innovation rise, and collaboration with other firms who possess the needed competence becomes a critical strategic option.

- Therefore, organizations must drive down the transaction and coordination costs of collaboration to cost effectively innovate and therefore organizationally evolve and competitively survive.

So much for the *whys* of collaboration. Now the hard part—that pesky *how* question: How *do* we build effective collaborative ventures? The remainder of the book explores this operational question. This chapter builds the framework we use to pose, and then, in subsequent chapters, answer this operational question; it provides some perspectives and some tools with which we draw specific observations and operational implications in subsequent chapters.

As we know from experience, and demonstrated in Chapter Two, there are many different forms of collaborations. It is this very diversity that often makes it difficult to identify, much less target, appropriate actions to make collaborations effective. Yet, there are competitive dynamics common to them all that provide insight into how they work and why. There are also common elements underlying effective collaborations—what we call their underlying *collaborative DNA*. Identifying these common elements and knowing how to assess and then manipulate them effectively are critical to increasing collaborative effectiveness. This chapter characterizes the collaborative DNA, so that, in subsequent chapters, we can discuss specific means and implications of manipulating it. Taking effective action requires first making sense of the collaborative patterns, their underlying dynamics and their underlying DNA elements. This chapter, like Chapter Two, is a *sense-making* chapter; subsequent chapters rapidly move to the implications of *action taking*

In Chapter Two, we said that the three key elements of effective collaboration are to:

1. Create the value
2. Share the rewards
3. Manage the risks

Chapter Two focused on defining the value to be created in a collaboration and the rewards to be shared. In this chapter, with our focus on the operational elements of collaboration, we derive a blueprint for the structures and capabilities important to have in place to reduce the transaction and coordination costs of collaboration. We examine in more detail how collaboration takes place, discussing the value, cost, and risk associated with two companies working together intimately. We examine the fact that innovation involves people working together to produce something new, which concentrates key company value *at the edges of your organization* and therefore entails the risk of intellectual property *leakage*. From this we see that a key element needed for effective, efficient collaboration is the ability to manage distributed risk.

We carry out the notion of collaboration as a transaction where intellectual property (IP) is traded to create innovative value for each participant. This leads us to considering collaboration as part of your core business process, exposing parts of your business through the concept of a *value port* with capabilities that allow other firms to plug-and-play quickly with you in collaborations, driving down the transaction cost of collaboration while also reducing the time required to create collaborative relationships. As we all know from experience with technology systems, plug-and-play interfaces only work when the interface—the characteristics, definitions and "semantics"—are well-defined and agreed to by the parties on either end of the interface. Following this simple but powerful lesson of "shared semantics," we introduce the notion of the *semantic stack* as a means to explicitly communicate the maturity and readiness of an organization to rapidly exploit collaborations. From this we see that another key element needed for effective, efficient collaboration is the ability to blend the semantics of collaborative behaviors, that is, to get a well-developed, shared vocabulary for the participants in a collaboration.

Let's explore this last point briefly, given its importance in subsequent discussions. At some point in the distant past, peoples began expressing themselves using words, first spoken and then written. From these words emerged common ways of speaking, shared communications, common viewpoints, shared behaviors and culture, and hence the ability to mobilize people to effective action. What made actions effective was and is the shared understanding of what is expected, of what to do, of how to do it, and of measuring and realizing the value of those actions. This sharing of what is intended and then realized is what we mean when we use the term *shared semantics* or *shared vocabulary*. The semantic stack, as we will see again and again, becomes a critical means to identify, to assess, to anticipate, and to prioritize where and how to exploit both marketplace dynamics and collaborative opportunities.

How so? Because of the following statement that we develop in this chapter: *Shared knowledge and understanding becomes more scalable and cheaper when knowledge is codified, so the degree of codification is an important measure of the readiness of the organization to collaborate often, rapidly, effectively, and efficiently.* The semantic stack is a tool to help us identify, assess, anticipate, and exploit different areas of knowledge critical for sustained and effective collaborative activities—hence its critical role and characterization as underlying collaborative DNA.

Exploring the collaborative DNA strands requires defining and discussing the following:

- *The collaboration model.* A framework for describing and understanding the generalized dynamics of organizations engaged in a collaborative relationship, and the creation of the resulting value.

- *The semantic stack.* A framework for characterizing the state of shared knowledge critical for effective collaboration.

- *Intellectual property at the edge.* Innovation always comes down to people working with other people, which means that the intellectual property both being employed and created in the collaboration ends up in the heads of a relatively small number of people at the cutting edge of innovation. This creates pressures and a need to scale the knowledge of these few people to others throughout the organization and the collaborative effort.

- *The collaborative risk scale.* A simple tool to identify and assess what type of value and corresponding risk is brought to any collaborative venture.

Each of these topics has implications for your organization, its processes, and its technology strategy that we build on in detail throughout the rest of this book.

Taken together, Chapters Two and Three build our collaborative framework and vocabulary to make sense of the buzzing, booming activities that are collaborative activities. They describe the *collaborative necessity* and the underlying mechanics of effective collaborative behaviors. Chapters Four through Six shift the focus. They focus on how to take action to engender effective collaborations in the face of the Red Queen and her juggernaut. They build on the insights, examples, and frameworks of Chapters Two and Three and explore collaborative implications from different vantage points: the classic set of process, people, and technology.

OPERATIONALIZING COLLABORATION

Collaborating effectively requires being able to create shared value, share the rewards of the value created, and manage distributed risk. It's that simple. Yet, it is also extraordinarily complex as we've all experienced and as we explored in the previous chapter. Collaborating extensively and cost effectively is even more complex, yet necessary given fast-moving business opportunities and our extant market uncertainty. Taken together, this means that operating in the Jericho Zone, with the Red Queen running apace, places some specific requirements on both you and your partners to keep up with the pace of change in uncertain times. We examine these requirements, and the resultant operational implications, in terms of the semantic stack, a construction that helps describe the amount of vocabulary shared by the participants in a collaboration across seven operational areas. For this, we draw heavily on lessons learned in making computer systems interact to create new value.

This requires a significant digression to discuss the drivers and enablers of effective technology integration. We'll use the discussion for three purposes:

1. Lessons from effective technology integration provide an analogy to our approach for organizational collaboration overall.

2. Lessons can be generalized to provide examples of and an introduction to the role and conceptual power of the semantic stack.

3. Not incidentally, this digression lays some groundwork for Chapter Six where we focus on specific technology implications of collaboration.

Collaboration among Computer Systems: the System Integration Analogy

Companies have been driving a specific form of internal collaboration for the past decade. In its simplest form, system integration (SI) is about taking computer systems that were never intended to work together, and making them do so to create additional business value. There can be many reasons that applications don't work together, but the most common include:

1. The business process that incorporated the system was itself a standalone process and didn't require much outside interaction (this is the most common case for older applications), or

2. The applications were purchased as vendor packages in a best-of-breed selection process that valued specific business functionality more than it did the capability to work well with other applications.

Over the years, companies have made an enormous investment in computer software that implements specific, isolated pieces of business functionality. Innovative pressures have driven companies toward the recognition that standalone business units and systems create barriers to value creation. As competitive pressures continue to drive them to create new business functions, companies have relied more and more on integrating existing systems—either those that they created in the past or those purchased from vendors—to provide the newly needed functionality. The rationale is that an existing system represents sunk investment, and has a proven track record of reliability in supporting a business function.

By leveraging such systems, you get the benefits of their functionality and reliability.

The first commercial computer systems were created to automate repetitive, error-prone tasks like tabulating the U.S. census, and calculating the range tables used by artillery gunners in figuring out how to elevate their guns to hit a target. This progressed to the automation of specific business functions such as assigning telephone company switching gear to a particular pair of wires coming in from the street, or keeping track of the connectivity of that pair of wires from big feeder cables through various connections and splices, and finally to the pair of wires that brings phone service to your home. During these early stages of automation, it was not unusual for a person, as a part of the process by which the business delivered value to its customers, to take data provided by one system, for example, the system that knows which pair of wires actually connects to your home, swivel their chair around to another system, such as the system that decides which piece of switch gear should be used to provide your service, and re-key the data.

Integrating systems basically began as a way to automate such "swivel chair integration," using computer interfaces between existing applications to increase productivity and reduce cost. At the outset, most of the people doing the integrating thought that integrating systems was a stop-gap measure, preparatory to building new applications that had all the needed functionality. But over time, it became clear that the pressures to automate more and more of the business, coupled with how difficult it is to reengineer an application that has existed for a long time and has been modified and enhanced throughout its lifetime, meant that integrated systems would have a long life, and systems integration (SI) became a particular specialty within IT. Systems integration focuses on creating interfaces between computer systems to create new business functionality, and therefore new business value. Arguably, one of the hottest examples of this currently is the area of Customer Relationship Management (CRM), which we will use here to provide some context to the drivers of system integration activity.

Customer Relationship Management has driven an enormous amount of investment in technology and business process over the past few years. Companies realize that customers interact with a firm to satisfy some particular personal need. The successful firm is proclaimed one that can marshal its resources to meet that customer's need. Traditionally, customers conformed their interactions to a company to meet the company's internal business processes—for example, by filling out the XYZ form, understanding that their bank deposit would not be posted until the next day (after the evening computer batch run put all of the deposit transactions into the deposit system), and so on. Today, with customers increasingly taking the power of their business into their own hands, companies go out of their way to provide a customer-centric experience. Especially challenging in this era of consolidation when companies have been created from repeated mergers and acquisitions—they also try to make sure that the customer has a uniform experience regardless of which part of the company the customer interacts with, or with whom in that company the customer is working. Examples include trying not to have the customer reenter their account number multiple times when interacting with a customer service hotline, being able to automate most of the data needed when a customer applies for a new service, or ensuring that the most valued customers automatically get VIP treatment in all interactions with the company. Clearly, creating a customer-centric experience requires that the various internal organizations in a company, organizations that often have been very independent with their own business processes, record-keeping systems, and customers, work with a common view of the customer. Given that there are existing computer systems that have, for example, customer account data, or information on a customer's transactions with a particular part of the business, it makes more sense to leverage those systems to provide that data to the common customer view than to try to reengineer all of that system functionality in a new application.

A system integrator creates new business functionality by leveraging existing systems, crafting interfaces between them that facilitate communication, information flow, and business process. The cost of creating the new functionality is the cost of the integration. The value of the new functionality is made up of the value added in the integration plus the value represented by each of the systems included in the integration. To create new functionality at the rates that the market requires, companies must efficiently leverage building block assets that they and others have created. In 2001, companies were rating system integration investment as second only to maintaining and enhancing existing applications, with the top three business drivers being (1) time to market for new business needs, (2) improving employee productivity, and (3) providing better service to customers. A new category of software products, Application Integration Software (AIS), emerged, targeted specifically to integrating applications both within a given company and with applications external to the company.[1]

Hopefully, the analogy to collaboration is reasonably clear. Each system to be integrated provides value, much like individuals in any collaboration. The isolated system functionality, focused on serving relatively narrow needs within an organization, is similar to the organizational characteristics and business process in a company that are focused internally on the company, not on the company's interaction with other companies. The integration of systems is roughly analogous to the collaboration of companies, and the new value created when systems are integrated—the new business functionality—represents a new value-bundle to the company. For example, when integration is used for customer relationship management, the new business functionality can potentially create a value-bundle differentiated on customer (CRM is after all about retaining customers), scale (efficient CRM can allow a company to service more customers with the same number of representatives), or positioning (providing better service can enhance a company's brand position, moving to a higher "touch" company).

Given that system integration activity has become such a large part of corporate IT activity, the IT industry has focused heavily on ways of doing more integration for less money—more effectively and efficiently. In the analogy where systems are the individuals in the collaboration, the IT industry is working hard to operate in the Jericho Zone. If we understand what the IT industry had to do to get to its own Jericho Zone, especially in the areas of lightweight interactions and managing risk, we will see how the lessons of system integration lead to implications on Jericho Zone collaboration on organizations, people, processes, and technology.

Because this book is not specifically for an IT audience, we do not belabor the technology aspects of integration. However, we first create the shared vocabulary needed for this discussion that we use throughout the rest of the book.

Figure 3.1 shows the essentials of an interaction between two computer applications. The familiar scenario to most readers is probably application A as the Web browser on their personal computer, and application B as the Web server sitting on a physical computer somewhere on the Internet. This is a useful scenario in that the World Wide Web exhibits most of the behavior—in machine terms—that we require of a company operating in the Jericho Zone. By looking at what the IT industry did to get to the point where applications can work in the technological Jericho Zone, we can expose the key human, organizational, process, risk, and technology elements needed for you to work in the Jericho Zone.

FIGURE 3.1   APPLICATION INTERACTION

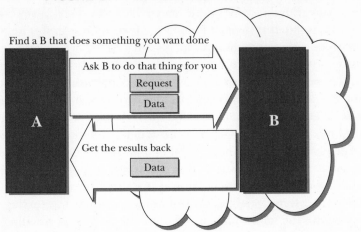

Let's look at this straightforward interaction between applications and machines in terms of some of the key dimensions that we discussed in the last chapter, namely managing both costs and risks. We'll look at these in terms of how early system integration efforts worked, and how the industry has evolved in ways that have moved it toward the system integration version of the Jericho Zone.

At the most basic, creating the depicted relationship between A and B requires interactions at four levels:

1. *Finding the resource that you need.* Identifying the provider of the functionality from among the large amount of software that is already built and running. The analogy with collaboration is finding a collaboration partner who can contribute meaningfully to creating a new value-bundle.

2. *Exchanging information.* Getting the bits (the ones and zeros of computer data) reliably from one system to another. The analogy with collaboration is having the business process and culture in place to enable individuals on both sides to engage productively.

3. *Operating on the data.* Each system needs to understand what the data represents, what it is expected to do with it, and what its responsibilities are with respect to its interaction with the other system. The analogy with collaboration is a shared understanding of the role to be played by each side in creating the new value-bundle, and confidence by each side in the mutual fulfillment of their roles.

4. *Returning the results.* Once B has operated on the data (added its value), A expects a result back that it then uses for its own purposes. The analogy with collaboration is, from A's side at least, the sharing in the value created, and presumably its reward.

In the early days of integration—the late 1960s and early 1970s—each of these four activities was performed using very experienced business and technology people who would essentially handcraft each solution. Such a person would be able to determine, from a description of the newly desired functionality and an encyclopedic knowledge of the existing suite of systems, what applicable existing systems might be available to be reused. When the selected systems were to be integrated, the development teams from the two systems would meet, and they would work through the rules and the technology for physically moving the data between the systems, for how the data would represent business information, for how the request/response interaction would take place—for example, which system had the responsibility for making sure that a request was fulfilled, how to handle the condition when one or the other resources became unexpectedly unavailable, who had responsibility for making sure that all data was updated and self-consistent across various business and failure scenarios, and so on. The reality was that there were few if any standards in place, and even fewer generally agreed-upon models or practices for how such interactions should work. Literally, everything was up for grabs. As a result, each case of integration took a great deal of effort by highly skilled people to identify the systems and create the needed interfaces. Since each of these was essentially a custom creation, each required a specialized workforce to operate and maintain it. As you can imagine, the resulting high cost and lengthy time limited integration efforts to the clear cases where there was a very large payback to be gained over a long system lifetime. This is exactly analogous to the discussion in Chapter Two about the limiting effects of the present high cost of collaboration.

Over the years, system integrators have concentrated on engineering approaches to reduce the time and effort in integrating systems. System integration remains a field where talented people have to grapple with hard problems, but the field has made real progress in reducing the cost and time involved in making applications work together. At the writing of this book, the state of the art in creating functionality by combining applications is Web services.[2] In contrast with the system integration environment described in the preceding paragraph, in a Web services environment applications advertise their availability in a place that everyone knows about, and knows how to interact with.[3] Each application describes what it does, what it expects from a request, and what it will send for a response, in a language that everyone understands.[4] An application can make a request to another application irrespective of where it is on the Internet (with some qualifications that don't concern us here), and regardless of which hardware platform it resides on or language in which it is written.[5] Finally, neither of the interacting applications—nor, crucially, the developers of those applications—need know anything of the existence of the other, either before the interaction, or after the interaction beyond what we just described.

In other words, at the forward edge of software development, we have the ability to find resources that can add value, and know what we need to do to interact with them to create value, in a manner that is highly dynamic, lightweight, and low cost. Substitute organization for software and the previous sentence describes collaboration in the Jericho Zone. We'll spend some time looking at how we got from the 1960s system integration environment to an environment where Web services is a reality.

If system integration is a good analogy for collaboration, then the current promise of the Web services environment is a good analogy for an environment that supports fast-moving collaborations. If you are a non-technologist who harbors thoughts that business process and organizational behavior are immensely more complex than making new applications from old ones, we will try to give you a flavor for the ugliness involved in making applications talk to one another, and leave you to decide on your own whether there are lessons to be learned from technology integration.

There are major challenges to the general problem of integrating applications that were implemented at different times, by different people, using different programming languages, on different brands of computer systems, separated by some sort of network (yes, separated by, not connected with). We examine a few of them to provide a sense—especially for non-technologists of the complexity of the problems involved and for the variety of approaches used to manage the complexity in hopes that this will convince you that the analogy of application integration extends to organizational collaboration. We are hitting only a few of the high points, but the discussion might be more detailed than you want. If so, you can resume reading at the section "Lessons Learned from System Integration," on page 73.

Finding the Resource That You Need

When application A wants to find a desired application B, there are two basic pieces of functionality that need to be available to application A:

(1) having a way of expressing what you want B to be able to do (or the complement of that, of B displaying what it *can* do), and (2) the ability for application A to refer to application B by a name, independent of the physical location of application B, but that somehow gets resolved to a physical reference to application B that allows A and B to communicate. Recall that we said that in the earliest days, (1) was achieved through smart experienced people, clearly not a scalable model, so some automated capability to perform these activities is critical. The importance of (2) has to do with the maintenance burden of the integrated programs. In general, the more that application A's operation depends on aspects of application B that might change, the more expensive the maintenance of the integrated application. In human terms, the maintenance burden varies significantly among locating me by my home address (which changes every time I move), home phone number (which may stay the same if I move two doors down the street), my mobile phone number (which I might keep constant over a long period of time), or my social security number which follows me to the grave. Over the years, there have been different approaches to solving pieces of these two problems. We describe some of them briefly here.

LIBRARIES   A library bundles pieces of application functionality in a way that allows an application A to refer to a name, and allows other software to resolve that name into a particular reference to a program, say application B. There are many details to the way libraries function, but one important one for the purposes of discussing the evolution of how we got from there to here, is the distinction between static and dynamic libraries. In a static library, the association between the name *application B* and the actual program implementing application B happens when application A is created (generally during a step in the program creation called *linking*). If application B changes, then at the very least, application A must be relinked (as must every other program that uses application B). Conversely, in a dynamic library, the association between the name *application B* and the actual program implementing application B happens when application A is executed. If application B is changed, it is only necessary to distribute a new library with the updated application B, and application A (and every other program that uses application B) will automatically use the new application B.

Libraries were an important first step toward providing some sort of location independent naming—the early precursor of the sophisticated functionality provided in Web services that we discuss soon—and continue to be an effective way of bundling and distributing software, and of allowing multiples 'application As to access an *application B*. They are restrictive, however, in several ways: Application A's use of the name *application B* is hard-coded into application A when it is created. Consequently, if an application C comes along that is a better implementation of application B's functionality (that is, in the opinion of application A, but not necessarily so perfect that all of the other applications that use application B want to switch), application A must be rewritten to use it. Libraries are more-or-less confined to one particular computing environment and/or vendor. There are few if any rules for naming applications in libraries, so practically speaking, a library is only useful within a fairly restricted domain. Otherwise, the same names get used for very different applications, and mayhem results.

DIRECTORY SERVICES   Directory services broadly provide the next step in the capability to locate resources. The term *directory service* refers to a specialized application that provides multiple machines in a network access to a common pool of information about entities on a network—for example, applications, printers, and so on. A network can be very large, and applications tend to rely heavily on directory services when they are available. So, along with simple access to common data, a practical directory service provides for such things as *replication*—that allows multiple copies of the directory service to exist for reasons of security, performance, and reliability—for the *automatic propagation of changed data* throughout the directory system, for *security and management* of directory data, and for *access protocols* that define how to locate, and access information in the directory. The Domain Naming System (DNS) is a simple directory service specifically created for looking up the IP addresses associated with Internet domain names. Most specifically, DNS provides the underpinnings for the resource locators that provide access to resources on the Internet. An International Standards Organization (ISO) codification of directory services concepts and capabilities existed in the so-called X.500 series of standards that today form the basis for providing network-based information look up and retrieval by programs on the Internet.

UNIFORM RESOURCE IDENTIFIERS   A Uniform Resource Identifier (URI) is a string of characters that is used to identify resources—documents, images, services, files, and so on—on the World Wide Web. The URI (most commonly seen as the Universal Resource Locator (URL) used by your Web browser to find Internet sites) can represent a resource on any machine in the Internet along with the method used to access it—for example, a Web page, and the HyperText Transfer Protocol (HTTP) used for transferring Web content to and from your computers Internet browser, or the File Transfer protocol (FTP) used for downloading or uploading files. The concept of a URI is straightforward. However, its actual realization depends on basically everyone in the world agreeing to using the Domain Naming System (instead of X.500, or any other directory system), which, in turn, depends on that same group agreeing to the hegemony of the organizations that administer domain names and Internet addresses, and all of which would be academic were it not for the fact that the hardware and software vendors have also all agreed to support a common communications protocol. This amazing consensus, basically representing the agreement among all of the users of and vendors to the Internet, is codified in a pile of standards and white papers from the Internet Engineering Task Force (IETF), which is a large open international community of network designers, operators, vendors, and researchers concerned with the evolution of the Internet architecture and the smooth operation of the Internet.[6]

UDDI AND WSDL   If a URI allows you to associate a name with a resource, the Universal Description, Discovery, and Integration (UDDI) is a registry of Web services—a directory service where the entries are programs that are intended to be accessed and executed via the Internet—and the Web Services Description Language (WSDL) is used to define Web services and describe how they are accessed, that is, how to make requests and what to expect for responses. UDDI provides a place where programs on the Internet—the application As—can find the resources—the application Bs—that they need, and WSDL is the language that tells application A how to interact with its application B.

Exchanging Information

Exchanging information requires a shared communication channel and a shared vocabulary for communication.

SHARED COMMUNICATION CHANNEL   Computer networks exist to create shared communication channel between machines.[7] As with naming and locating a resource, computer communication has also moved from homegrown, custom-engineered solutions to a fully codified, standards-based capability:

- *Homegrown protocols.* A protocol is just a well-defined model for the interaction between senders and receivers of data. In the late 1960s and early 1970s, there were few standard protocols available, so engineers created many specialized protocols to provide pairwise connection between systems that they were integrating.

- *Open Systems Interconnection.* Protocols based on the Open Systems Interconnection (OSI) standard, such as X.25,[8] provide connectivity using a standard protocol—this provides the same advantage that interchangeable parts offers to manufacturers, namely that different vendor implementations of a standard protocol should all be able to interoperate. It provides an additional benefit—by codifying the form of communication in a widely reviewed document, the OSI standard gave technologists a workable model for implementation and a common vocabulary for expressing new ideas.

- *Proprietary vendor network technologies.* This includes products such as IBM's Binary Synchronous Communications (BSC) protocol, IBM's Systems Network Architecture (SNA), and Digital Equipment Corporation's DecNet. These provided (and continue to provide) robust enterprise-level connectivity, but in the context of a specific vendor. The resulting models and vocabularies are useful, but in an audience limited to the customers of the vendor.

- *Internet technology.* The network technology used in the U.S. Department of Defense Advanced Projects Research Agency Network (ARPANet) project was well-received and eventually became the de facto standard for the industry. ARPANet, a multihost network that was created to study network survivability in the face of massive unexpected disruptions (like those that might occur in a thermonuclear attack), transitioned to the now-ubiquitous Internet Protocol (IP) family in 1982, including the Transmission Control Protocol (TCP). These protocols have been accepted virtually unanimously as the standard way to move data among distributed computer applications. Like the OSI, they have codified the models and vocabularies into the underpinnings of the Internet, forming the basis for numerous associated standards and protocols that define, for example, how to send data from one machine to another independent of the physical machines or particular network topology that exists between them (Domain Naming), how one application can invoke another application and receive the response (Remote Procedure Call or RPC, Simple Object Access Protocol or SOAP), or how an application can communicate with a user independent of physical location or computer system (HyperText Transfer Protocol, HyperText Markup Language, Extensible Markup Language).

As the technology for protocols has progressed, the effort required to create connections has decreased dramatically. As standards for networks were proposed and codified, engineers created protocols that could interoperate, breaking down the walls between vendors. *As the codified standards became more prevalent in the network, it became possible to plug in or out of the network at more and more points.* With TCP/IP having become ubiquitous, we've come to expect the ability to plug into the network anywhere we go.

It is difficult to comprehend the accomplishment represented by this massive coming together of standards, programmers, users, and vendors. The sunk investment in those proprietary technologies represented—and represents—an enormous investment by its owners, well in the billions in today's dollars. The programming community who signed up to this model represents one of the most fractious communities of people you'll find anywhere (one of the authors is a 25-year legacy member of this community, and the other author will attest to the fractious characterization), and *they* all signed up for this codification. The result? The single largest sustained period of economic growth and productivity gains recorded since anyone has kept records.

SHARED VOCABULARY   The vocabulary *spoken* among applications consists of an understanding of how data is represented and what the data means. Data representation concerns how to interpret the ones and zeros flowing between the machines, whether, for example, the bit pattern 00001010 represents the number 12 or the linefeed character that tells a display or printer to space down the page one line. Over the years, system integrators have created increasingly abstracted data views to create data representations that are useful independent of computer architecture, hardware vendor, system software (e.g., UNIX or Windows), programming language, database, and so on. This effort has been generally successful; we'll discuss some of the high points, touching on the representation of individual characters, the abstract notion of a computer display, and on the data exchanged between two applications. Again, the import here lies less in the specific lessons from the data representation than the analog problems faced with how to make sense of multiple collaborative options that exist and the methods of how these particular lower level technology issues were resolved.

Different computers have different ways of storing the ones and zeros that comprise their internal data—in different groupings (8 bits, 9 bits, 32 bits, 36 bits), and in different arrangements of bit order to number place-value. Humans don't read ones and zeroes, so with the different internal representations there have been multiple ways of mapping the computer's internal representation to readable characters. There were, and remain, two different ways of mapping computer data to a human representation of a character, for example the letter A—the American Standard Code for Information Interchange (ASCII) and the Extended Binary Coded Decimal Interchange Code (EBCDIC)—referred to as *character sets*. Over the years, ASCII has become the dominant character set in use, and essentially all traffic over the Internet is in ASCII representation.

While computer displays may not seem particularly relevant to a discussion of common vocabulary, the ability to control the computer display has driven the codification of a huge vocabulary, specifically the language by which computers interact with humans. One of the nastier battlegrounds over the years has been the human interface, as engineers have struggled with thorny problems, including:

- The look and feel of a good human interface
- The performance requirements for an acceptable interface
- What constitutes a terminal device
- The volume of data that flows back and forth

Predictably, the responses to this partial list created quite a variety of approaches. One example is the familiar "green screen" of IBM's 3270-based networks. The 3270 terminals performed well with efficient use of bandwidth by using a forms-oriented interface, where the traffic between computer and terminal was generally held to just data that had changed on the form. Another example was the terminal used by Western Union where the work was less about filling out forms, and more about keying in large quantities of data. These terminals were organized into 24 rows of 80 characters each. These two types of terminals created very different user experiences, offered absolutely no interoperability, and were incapable of displaying graphics. Graphics displays are capable of displaying the rich interfaces that we are used to seeing on personal computers and when we surf the Web. As is the pattern with everything we've discussed, displays have moved from custom, special purpose devices to a set of common standards. There were two incompatible graphics approaches—vector graphics and raster graphics—that competed for primacy. Raster graphics—where the screen is divided into rows and columns of picture elements, or pixels, emerged as the clear preference for general purpose displays. Driven by the massive consumer computer market, raster-graphic computer displays widely interoperate among different computers.

A Brief Recap

We are discussing some background of the computing environment in which we find ourselves today. Why is this important? For a simple reason: The history of systems integration has very much been about traveling a path from small numbers of highly skilled people using specialized skills understood only among a relatively few creating innovation on a case-by-case basis, to our current environment where large numbers of people with highly available skill sets create innovation in a highly scalable manner. To be sure, the world of computer software remains beset with real, significant, even intractable problems.[9] But the gains in productivity, scale, and accomplishment have been enormous, and it has been largely due to the codification of the way computers interact with one another, the way people interact with computers, and the way that programmers put it all together.

But we're ahead of ourselves a bit right now. So, back to the story.

Architectures Enabled by Codification

TCP/IP created a common shared communication channel between machines. This provided the basis for data to be moved across machines via network applications such as e-mail, for groups of machines to share common data on network-based file servers, and for users to share files on their machines with users on other machines via the network. In terms of Figure 3.1, application A might be your word processing program requesting a file from a network file sharing utility application B. In a general way, in this sort of environment, application As are rich, complex, expensive programs implementing some set of business functionality for a single user on his or her machine. In this sort of architecture (the word *architecture* in this context refers to the description of services and the way those services interact with one another) shown in Figure 3.2, the users' machines are referred to as *clients* and the machines that provide common services—typically in a data center environment—are called *servers,* hence the label *client-server.*

In client-server architectures, the servers can provide simple file service as in the one in Figure 3.2, or they can provide application functionality to be shared among multiple clients. Generally speaking, the clients are fairly powerful machines running a rich set of software. If they are the same type of computer running the same type of system software, then applications can be installed on a network server and each person can run it from there. If, as is often the case, there is a mix of machines and operating systems, or users need application A even when they are not on the

FIGURE 3.2 CLIENT-SERVER ARCHITECTURE

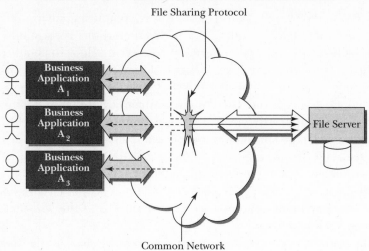

company network, then application A must be installed locally on each machine. If a group of people wants to collaborate, they can do so through a single data file that sits on a network file server. They can do this because the file-sharing protocols provide the abstraction of a file as a name and a string of data that different machines can operate on according to their own specific rules. However, if a group wants to collaborate, they need to make sure that they all have the same version of the client application installed. If some of them don't, they need to buy it and install it, adding cost and time to the collaboration.

Figure 3.3 shows a very different architecture, a so-called *thin-client* architecture. In this architecture, the functionality of the applications has moved to the server side, sitting on an application server. The application server interacts with the file server, analogously to the client-server interaction between users' machines and the file server. The application interacts with the user using an abstraction that allows it to interchange various elements—text, graphics, audio, and so on—with the user's machine, and to describe how those elements will be placed on the user's display. The abstraction is called a *Web page*. The Web browser on each client machine renders the Web page appropriately according to the specific requirements of the client machine. This allows access to the same application functionality across a variety of client machines. Thinking of the group of people we discussed earlier who want to collaborate, as long

FIGURE 3.3 THIN-CLIENT ARCHITECTURE

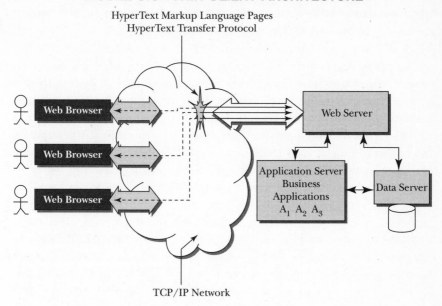

as each has a Web browser on his or her machine, they can collaborate around common data using the functionality of a common application.

The key enabler for thin-client architecture is still further codification, in that the abstractions of client server are extended through the abstraction of a web page, created through a language, the HyperText Markup Language (HTML), and the agreement on a protocol, the HyperText Transfer Protocol (HTTP). Thus, in Figure 3.3, we see that the ubiquitous TCP/IP network provides connectivity between all the elements, and the ubiquitous HTTP provides transport for HTML data to flow between each client and the Web server. The resulting system architecture—the thin-client architecture—is lightweight, provides for people to make and break connections easily, and allows them access to applications with minimal setup and administration.

Lessons Learned from System Integration

A challenge we face is how to harness the variety of activities and collaborative options available. How we make sense of this variety will influence where we enter and how to exploit—by narrowing—the collaborative options. Our rapid walkthrough of computing integration challenges highlights the same collaborative challenge we're addressing here: How to provide scale and rapid adaptation to specific requirements—read *business opportunities.*

The Red Queen has accompanied this very technology story. The enabling technology of the Internet and increasingly other connectivity-based technologies have changed the way businesses work—internally and with one another—and have contributed to disrupting business models, creating uncertainty. Working through that uncertainty and enabling rapid adaptations to equally rapid business requirements shifts required the means to quickly share, collaborate, and exploit common technology elements—*through codification, through shared language, through shared semantics*—that could be and were built into competing products, applications, and services. The upshot: *Scale was realized,* and the nature of competition shifted away from *which* of the standards and supporting products would prevail to *how* to use those products for specific business purposes. And this *is* the Red Queen story: What was once a highly fractured, high-margin competitive environment, drawing in multiple competitors, becomes less so as standards are established, margins are reduced, competitors are consolidated, and the focus of competition shifts to new arenas of rich and as yet sufficiently scalable, untapped high-margin opportunities. We've seen this in parts of the technology integration history and we'll see it again in this and subsequent chapters.

The examples from the field of system integration demonstrate the value of codifying the contributions of scarce, specifically skilled people so that much larger groups—with different skill sets—can innovate on a much larger scale. It is not that people involved in system integration and software development today are less skilled than those years ago; they are highly skilled, but with a different skill set. In the 1960s and 1970s, the people who identified themselves as software engineers were writing applications such as the telephone company inventory system we discussed earlier, and the people who identified themselves as computer geeks wrestled with data representation, connectivity, and application-level communication. In the 1990s and the 2000s, the people who identify themselves as software engineers are writing business applications such as global equities clearing and settlement systems (the system we discussed earlier, being created by GSTPA), and the people who identify themselves as computer geeks are wrestling with the standards for SOAP, UDDI, and WSDL.

The people who are innovating are still solving thorny technology integration problems; they have just moved away from low-level computer things into higher level, more human-understandable things. At this higher level, they can create more value for less work, and therefore more cheaply and more quickly. The activity that allows them to do that is the codification of standards, processes, and practices that has provided solid platforms for them to build on—to paraphrase Sir Isaac Newton, if they see further than others, it's because they stand on the shoulders of giants. As we will see soon, this process of codification is a process of taking knowledge—in the abstract, intellectual property—that can be understood only by way of substantial shared context among the people trying to understand it, which we will term *tacit knowledge* to a form that is thoroughly specified, allowing a large group of people to meaningfully exchange and operate on the information. We will see also that the Red Queen drives a natural migration in innovation in a given area, from more foundational layers to more human layers, the set of which we call the *semantic stack*.

Codification is king, and our abbreviated characterization of system integration shows that there are broadly two parts to effectively codifying some area of intellectual property: *abstraction* and *agreement.*

Abstraction, in the case of systems integration, is an application of the so-called *Inventor's Paradox.* This paradox asserts that if a particular problem is too difficult to solve, try to find a simpler but more general problem of which your specific problem is a special case, and solve *that* problem. Look at data representation: Different computer manufacturers still represent data differently within their own family, but the existence of standards like ASCII creates a common layer that masks those differences. We could ask, "Why don't all manufacturers just settle on a common way to organize the ones and zeros?" They could, but there are many valid reasons why there are different representations. One reason is historical—computer manufacturers need to maintain stability in product lines because their customers demand it. Changing the low-level data representation in a family of machines might cause older applications to stop running that would not be acceptable to their client base. Another reason has to do with the focus of the vendor. IBM has historically focused on the business market, and so it's not surprising that their internal machine architecture, including the particular way that they choose to organize the bits, might be different from, say, the architecture of machines built by Silicon Graphics whose target has been high-performance computer graphics and whose machines are used widely to create computer generated images (CGI) in Hollywood. There are usually valid reasons for people to do things in some unique way. Abstraction, then, allows for the creation of a common representation that admits many specific instances of implementation. By reconciling the differences between different implementations, abstraction creates regularity and promotes commonality.

Agreement to use an abstraction is the key to what in this book we refer to as *codification*. Take networks for example, and look specifically at IBM's SNA and the ArpaNet's TCP/IP. TCP/IP has become the standard for the Internet (where, by the way, ASCII is the standard character representation involved in data interchange). Now, unlike ASCII, TCP/IP is not an abstraction; it does not create a common layer in which another protocol, like SNA is just one particular instance, and, say, Apple's AppleTalk is another. Instead, TCP/IP is a communications protocol that is good enough for most computer-computer communication, and, for a variety of reasons, some technical and some not, it is the one that the market has chosen as the standard that has to be complied with if you're going to do business on the Internet. Vendors who want their machines to be able to participate in the Internet have no choice but to figure out how to make their proprietary material work with TCP/IP.

When a population has generally agreed to use some set of abstractions, that population has a *shared vocabulary* with which to communicate. As the population grows, the shared vocabulary becomes a common language. At some point of critical mass, the common language becomes the *lingua franca* for some domain. When all the people in the domain can speak the same language, innovation can run unfettered, and massive progress can be made—witness the economic boom we discussed earlier, for which the Internet technologies we have discussed here can take a certain amount of credit. Or, so the story goes.

But now, let's reintroduce the Red Queen perspective.

A common language, a shared vocabulary, a shared set of standards solves particular technical problems. But it introduces profoundly new business ones—namely, competitive ones. As we'll explore in subsequent chapters, the very nature of scale shifts the nature of competition. As codified technologies become fully accepted and increasingly exploited, competitive differentiation can only come from one of two sources: one, from having the lowest manufacturing costs or two, shifting the very nature of the competition. By no means does this mean that innovation is fettered. On the contrary. It does mean, however, that the focus of innovation must change. As standards emerge, competition and enabling innovation must shift away from the *best* technologies to create a standard to the *most relevant* ones to enable the use of those standards. This is a competitive shift with significant implications on the semantic stack— which we'll soon explore.

The Collaboration Model: Innovation at the Edges

Systems integration creates new value as disparate systems are integrated engendering new business functionality and resulting in a new value-bundle to the company. The analogy to collaboration is apt and lessons directly relevant between creating what we characterized as lightweight systems integration and effective collaboration. For systems integration, we discussed abstractions and agreements that together smooth the way that systems interact. Now we apply these concepts to collaboration.

Figure 3.4 shows two companies, A and B, collaborating. In the analogy of computer systems interacting, we've represented each company interacting with the collaboration, where each provides and receives components of a value-bundle. In fact, the value each company provides to the collaboration is provided in terms of the value-bundle as embodied in the people working in the collaboration. Collaborative effectiveness depends on those people being able to begin rapidly sharing value. Rapidly sharing value requires that people are able to *mind-meld* around the elements underlying the collaboration. This mind-meld, as seen from the examples of effective systems integration, requires codifying the key aspects of the interaction, that is, in developing a common vocabulary for expressing the key aspects of that collaboration. In sharing the value, managing the risks, and sharing the reward in the Jericho Zone, we need to have a common vocabulary for finding partners, creating the collaborative relationship, actually collaborating to create value, and closing out the collaboration.

Having a vocabulary is in itself insufficient for effective collaboration, but, it *is* necessary. Without shared understanding, little if any consistent or effective action can result. So far, we've explored a process of

FIGURE 3.4 INNOVATING AT THE EDGES

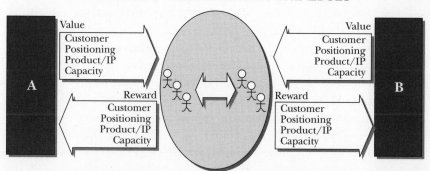

codifying technical information, from which we've drawn some lessons. The question is: Does this process and its dynamic work only with technology? Or, are their other sets of activities and processes subject to the same dynamics, activities, and processes that, if understood, could be exploited for effective collaborative activities? The answer is undoubtedly yes—hence a key premise and purpose of this book. Understanding what are similar underlying diverse activities—whether technical or business processes, or a wide range of collaborative forms—is what comprises underlying collaborative DNA.

It is this similarity that we aim to explore, building on the lessons from technical integration to describe key means for creating efficient, effective collaborations. The semantic stack is one of our key tools for this exploration.

THE SEMANTIC STACK: CREATING MARKETPLACE SCALE

Again the key lesson to draw so far from this chapter is the following: *Given that shared knowledge and understanding becomes more scalable and cheaper when the knowledge is codified, the degree of codification of relevant activities is an important measure of the readiness of the organization to collaborate often, rapidly, effectively, and efficiently.* The semantic stack characterizes what makes up the relevant activities for collaborative behaviors.

As we saw in the earlier discussion about the system integration analogy, and as we know from real life, things build on one another. Children, for example, first learn their mother's face, then simple words, then simple sentences, building upward in accomplishment—being able to understand more words and more sentence constructions—but also in abstraction—such as being able to empathize with the ennui felt by a character in an existentialist novel. A word is a symbol that refers to something meaningful; it is an abstraction of the item to which it refers. The word *mother* to a child is an abstraction of the face he or she recognizes. For a while, the word mother actually means *my mother*. Over time, the child understands the abstraction that mother refers to a type of person with a particular relationship, which is yet another abstraction. On and on goes the cycle of semantic understanding and of how we make sense of the world.[10]

In systems integration, we saw how Web services builds on Uniform Resource Identifiers that builds on DNS and TCP/IP that builds on ASCII as the base data representation. Of course, Web services also builds on

UDDI that builds on directory services that builds on . . . and on and on. You get the idea. There are clear, but interconnected, hierarchies of abstractions—like the relationship of word to sentence, or the relationship of DNS and directory services. Things at the higher levels build on the things at the lower levels.

Collaboration is more efficient and effective if the participants can connect easily and work well together in the innovation process. In practical terms, this means that their organizations can communicate, and match up to one another in various ways, some of them similar to the things we've seen in the system integration analogy, some of them uniquely human, for example:

- Shared experiences in the general field where the collaboration is occurring
- Similar cultures, or an understanding of what is similar, and what is different; cultures that at least embrace collaboration
- Similar sorts of measurements of success that account for innovation and collaboration
- Business processes that work together and support interorganizational process
- Shared applications—for example, everyone using the same version of Microsoft Word™
- Similar technologies
- Shared communication channels

We've identified seven areas where organizations interact during a collaboration, and for which there needs to be the capabilities to share knowledge and understanding—to have a shared semantic understanding critical to effect fast-moving action. Our systems integration analogy showed clearly that shared knowledge and understanding become more scalable and cheaper when the knowledge is codified. Therefore, once again, *given that shared knowledge and understanding becomes more scalable and cheaper when the knowledge is codified, the degree of codification in any of these areas is an important measure of the readiness of the organization to collaborate often, rapidly, effectively, and efficiently.* Putting these things together, we get to the semantic stack, shown in Figure 3.5. The semantic stack figures heavily throughout the rest of the book, so we will take some time to explore it.

As we explore the stack, we should keep in mind the spirit in which it is offered. There are many different types of collaborations; we characterized

FIGURE 3.5   THE SEMANTIC STACK

	Tacit	Framework	Standards	Executable
Environment				
Behaviors/Values				
Roles/Metrics				
Business Processes				
Applications				
Architecture/Platforms				
Connectivity				

many of these differences within the Collaboration Landscape of Chapter Two. There are as many reasons organizations collaborate as there are business conditions that drive organizations to choose to collaborate or not. Making sense and thereby taking action effectively regarding which type of collaborative form fits which type of specific business opportunity requires a means to align this fitting or mapping process.

That is the role of the semantic stack. It is a useful tool to help us to think about collaboration differently. It is a means to align business opportunities with the appropriate collaborative form. It is also a useful tool to stimulate innovative thought about collaboration. Looking at the actual layers of the stack, we feel comfortable with the seven layers we have identified, but that's not to say that the seven layers or domains we have identified are the last word on the topic. What is important is less the specific labeling of the layers than the concept of domains of interaction, at higher and higher levels of abstraction. As a tool, the semantic stack works just fine with three, and probably with two levels of codification. *What is important is the notion that knowledge in a domain can, should, and, as we see in a later chapter, will inexorably move toward greater levels of codification with significant implications on with whom to collaborative, how to do so and consequences on the nature of competition as that codification occurs—as you walk up and across the semantic stack.* Now let's explore the semantic stack.

The horizontal dimension—Tacit, Framework, Standards, Executable—refers to the state of codification of the stack's layers to which it is applied: *the further right, the more the codification and hence the more scalable and executable by many.* The vertical dimension—Environment, Behaviors/Values, Roles/Metrics, Business Processes, Applications, Architecture/Platforms, and Connectivity—refers to the sets of activities, what we call domains, performed by participants in a collaboration. Together, these elements of the semantic stack provide a means to quickly assess possible issues, and opportunities, to make any collaborative venture more effective.

Next, we explore each element of the semantic stack and discuss the dynamic process of what we characterize as *walking up and across* the semantic stack—the inevitable result of competitive dynamics. Let's explore this assertion further.

Competition results from different companies attempting to exploit a sufficiently attractive market opportunity. Initial market opportunities are usually high margin and/or high revenue opportunities, the results of their underlying value propositions being novel and consequently relatively unexploited or difficult to replicate. Over time, these margins tend to get arbitraged away or shrunk as new competitors, recognizing the potential of those market opportunities, enter the competitive fray. What shrinks those margins are processes, technologies, and other activities that bring down their operational costs and allow them to become more scalable, hence executable by many. And, as we saw using the systems integration analogy, the means of driving scalable activities is the enabling codification of those activities into frameworks, into standards, into executable and repeatable activities. According to the semantic stack, there will be inexorable competitive pressures to move both up and to the right—or, of walking up and across the stack—as business activities and technologies become codified, themselves the result of rigorous competitive pressures.

As activities become more codified, the very nature of competition shifts. This is a simple but profound implication of walking the stack. Competition for high-margin activities is vastly different than those of low-margin activities. Geoffrey Moore has described how the nature of competition shifts as companies *cross the chasm* a result of increasing market acceptance, itself a result of more codified business and technology processes.[11] As we see over and over again throughout this book, this is a natural part of the Red Queen at work: The high-value interactions between participants in any subject domain become over time generally understandable through an incremental refinement process that creates shared semantics within a community of practitioners, and eventually across a population of casual users.

Thus, as subsequent chapters explore in much more detail, the semantic stack can be used to anticipate how collaborative forms change over time: Margins fall as competitors enter; activities become codified as communications and coordination costs decline; the nature and sources of competition change as these competitive dynamics play out. We can both anticipate and assess how these dynamics will play out as we walk up and across the semantic stack. Through this assessment and with this semantic stack, we can perform the critical steps of both aligning specific business opportunities with appropriate collaborative forms and anticipating how to evolve or end the collaboration, as appropriate, as competitive dynamics play out over time.

This is the power of the semantic stack; and this is the reason that understanding the similar competitive pressures underlying the diverse collaborative forms is less an analytical luxury than an operational necessity. But we're a little ahead of ourselves here. Subsequent chapters explore the dynamics of walking up and across the semantic stack from different perspectives, identifying operational implications of how to more effectively exploit particular collaborative forms. The rest of this chapter continues to build the vocabulary and the tools underlying these implications.

We'll start by describing the horizontal dimension.

Tacit Knowledge

We use the term *tacit* to refer to something that can be shared only in the presence of a substantial amount of shared context or experience. Practically, what that means is that if the value that a person or organization brings to a collaboration is embodied in tacit knowledge, that person will spend substantial effort and time in communicating that knowledge—and hence its value—to their partner(s) in the collaboration. Most knowledge at the leading edge of thought is tacit knowledge, locked up in a person's head.

Executable Knowledge

Executable knowledge has so much built in context, typically in the form of widespread and standardized usage within an organization, industry, or population, that its meaning is readily understood and machines can act on it. For example, in the very large population of Internet users, the three letters URL convey instantly a measure of understanding, and Web applications can readily transact on URLs. Knowledge that is interesting and valuable across a large audience generally moves away from tacit toward being more codified. Knowledge such as network standards or application interface standards moves to *executable* when they are accepted by a wide population and implemented in a wide variety of software.

Frameworks and Standards

These are intermediate stages of codification. We use the term *framework* to refer to an attempt to structure the thought around the knowledge in a domain and begin to move it beyond tacit. For example, the semantic stack is itself a framework for thinking about collaboration. We use the term *standards* to refer to widespread agreement on the structure of knowledge in a domain, where someone or some group has taken the time to write the descriptions, and some other members of the population have reviewed what is written and agreed to it. Standards as a written codification are often an important step toward many programmers creating code to implement something, moving it to being executable.

The information technology industry is especially dependent on the existence and acceptance of standards because computers have little tolerance for ambiguity. Standards have become explicitly imbedded in the thinking of technologists as a fundamental quality for stable interactive products. The first question technologists ask of any component is: Can it speak to other products? This cannot be considered without standards. This is true also in knowledge-based businesses such as financial services, where there is little physical product. The financial services industry is keenly dependent on computer technology as its main means of defining and conducting its business.

As we discussed earlier, the complex system integration problems solved by small numbers of scarce, highly skilled people eventually led to the creation of organizations such as the IETF, and to codification of the standards that today enable much larger groups of people to innovate on a larger scale, attacking bigger problems. As we see over and over again throughout this book, this is a natural consequence of the Red Queen at work: The high-value interactions between participants in any subject domain over time become understandable through an incremental refinement process that creates shared semantics within a community of practitioners, and eventually across a population of casual users.

Standards bodies, such as the International Standards Organization (ISO, who created the OSI standards we discussed earlier) and organizations such as the IETF shepherd processes in which tacit understanding becomes increasingly codified. As a kind of working model, we can think of standards bodies as expert facilitators of collaboration techniques, and expert creators of codification. We discuss in this chapter, and in numerous other places in this book, the need to "walk up and across the stack," moving to higher levels of abstraction and greater degrees of codification. Although they would not describe their work this way, standards bodies have been walking across the stack—usually working with a fairly unruly bunch of participants—for years. This process of recognition and refined communication, which is at the heart of every standards body in the world, has accelerated, formalized, and proliferated the habit of standardization in most disciplines, and in doing so has become a basic part of doing business.

Now on to the vertical dimension, the layers of the stack.

The vertical dimension of the stack depicts seven sets of activities (domains or layers) where people and organizations interact in a collaborative venture. As we move up the stack, the domains both build on one another and create higher level abstractions, moving from relatively low-level enabling things, like *connectivity* up to distinctly human things like *behaviors/values*. As we introduce in this chapter, and then examine in some depth in Chapters Five and Six, *moving up the stack* can mean moving toward more abstract, more tacit, and therefore more valuable intellectual property. As we talk our way through the stack, we refer to Figure 3.6, which is the same semantic stack, but with the gray bars indicating our assessment where that domain currently stands with respect to codification.[12]

FIGURE 3.6   THE SEMANTIC STACK: WHERE ARE WE NOW?

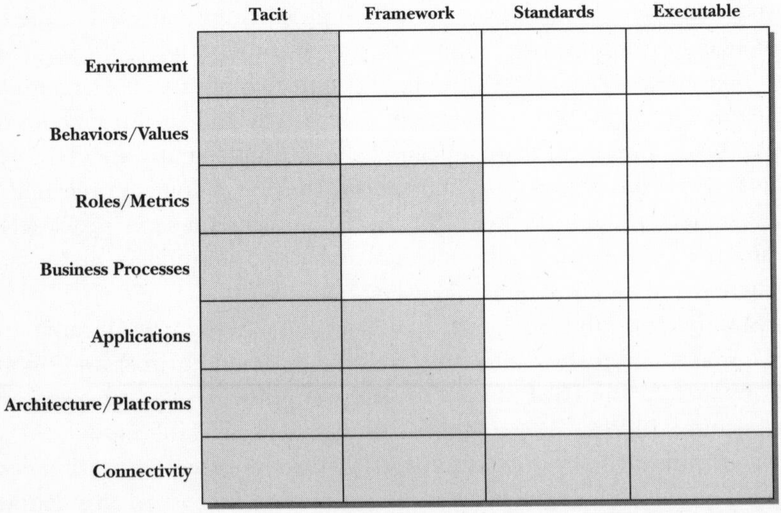

	Tacit	Framework	Standards	Executable
Environment	▓			
Behaviors/Values	▓			
Roles/Metrics	▓	▓		
Business Processes	▓	▓		
Applications	▓	▓		
Architecture/Platforms	▓	▓	▓	
Connectivity	▓	▓	▓	▓

Connectivity Layer: Enabling Ubiquitous Communications

Some parts of the semantic stack have been driven into highly codified states and are executable. In terms of technology, the success of the technology standards embodied in the lower parts of the semantic stack has created an environment where software and hardware vendors can make products in a virtually transparent market. Networks based on the Internet protocol (IP) are a clear example. Connectivity via an IP-based network is essentially a universal prerequisite to modern business. This highly codified knowledge is consequently embedded into commercial technology by most commercial vendors.

The ubiquity of IP networks has made IP the definitive universal connectivity medium and has defined the semantics by which we refer to connectivity. This has been reinforced by widespread business acceptance of the standard, and business' consequent dependence on the Internet.

The *connectivity layer* is the fabric that enables ubiquitous communication among potential participants in collaborations. As we see in Figure 3.6, this is the one domain that we call *executable*. This is very much a technology-oriented layer. Further, connectivity by its very nature assumes that there are at least two ends to the technology—yours and the end that you're trying to connect with—and that the two ends have to agree on some common vocabulary to work together. If you follow this logic through, where you want to communicate with many other ends and each of those other ends wants to communicate with still other ends, it becomes clear that connectivity is a place where ubiquity is important.

As we discussed earlier in this chapter, the TCP/IP networks based on the codification that has been driven by the IETF are a clear example of fully codified activities at this bottom part of the semantic stack. The acceptance of TCP/IP has driven the creation and acceptance of other standards based on TCP/IP that have themselves been universally accepted largely because of IP's universal acceptance. As a result, the intellectual property in this space is executable. These include things like:

- MIME: The encoding standard that allows a single e-mail to contain different types of content—text, embedded pictures, audio, and so on.

- HTML and HTTP: The standards for representing and transmitting Web pages across the Internet.

- URL: The uniform resource locator used to uniquely identify a Web-based resource such as a Web page.

Each of these provides functionality across a range of software products from various vendors.

A fully codified set of practices by no means implies that innovation is less vital than it is in other areas of the stack. It does mean, however, that the focus of innovation and resulting competitive pressures change; competition over the establishment of standards has significantly different implications than does competition over how to use those standards—or any degree of codified intellectual property—competitively. To provide a brief preview: Competitive pressures at each layer leads to a "blurring" of the stack layers; as codification proceeds at the connectivity layer, the margins tighten, as does the reliance on operational excellence and strategies to drive increased volume at lower margin thereby resulting in changes of how and with whom a company competes. Merely look at Cisco Systems and SUN Microsystems as two examples of how their market focus and partnership structures have and are currently changing to reflect the full codification of this layer of the stack with the resulting implications on how and with whom they compete, and collaborate—as they move up the semantic stack into a new competitive arena—by necessity.

The Red Queen runs, and she runs relentlessly. We'll provide more detail and implications on this blurring of the semantic stack and the nature of collaborative competition in subsequent chapters. It is this blurring that becomes a critical insight into how to identify and assess where to anticipate the evolution/mutation of specific business opportunities and collaborative forms. Such blurring is the natural result of the process of codification—of moving from tacit to executable, hence, scalable activities. Further examples of this inevitable blurring follow. For now, it is important merely to keep this inherent blurring of the lines in mind when reading through the rest of the stack.

Architecture and Platform Layer: Semantic Understanding through Patterns, Not Just Products

Recall that *architecture* describes services (or equivalently, components) and the way those services interact with one another. Thus, an organizational architecture describes, at some level of detail, the parts of an organization, the responsibilities of each of those parts, and how the parts are supposed to work together. A business process architecture describes, at some level of detail, each business process and how those business processes interact with one another. Finally, a technology architecture describes technology components and the interaction among them. Technology people have been using the concepts and techniques of architecture for a long time. Business people have come to recognize architecture more recently for a simple reason: It has been demonstrated in the numerous mergers and acquisitions that have taken place as part of industry consolidation that organizations that share similar architectures can more easily assimilate.

Architectures are basically a way to build abstractions that make it possible to comprehend larger and larger pictures. For example, it is not possible to meaningfully understand the details of how every activity in a business relates to every other activity—the mass of detailed data and interactions exceed the ability of a person to comprehend, much less understand, and then act on that understanding. However, by chunking the activities of the business into discrete business processes—sets of related activities that produce some outcome—it is possible to represent each of the chunks as a box, and to comprehend how these relatively few boxes relate to one another. Or if not, the process can be repeated again, chunking the initial set of boxes into sets of related processes, creating an even more abstract view of even fewer boxes. Eventually this process leads to a level of abstraction that a person can comprehend, and thus work with.

Figure 3.6 puts the architecture and platform domain at the framework level, because, while there remains a great deal of tacit knowledge and areas of lively discussion (read disagreement), this domain is no longer a free-for-all. From the perspective of architecture itself, there have been two major influences: the emergence of standard approaches to architecture from the top down, and the impact of the Internet.

Architecture and the work of the architect have been tacit activities for a long time. The emergence of open architectural standards through initiatives like TOGAF[13] has started to bring some regularity to the way architects think about and express architecture. There has also been emerging agreement on architectures based on loosely coupled cooperating services (services-based architecture or equivalently component-based architecture). For example, Unisys Corporation's Business Blueprints and supporting business and technology architectures are targeted to the integration of components from multiple vendors, and have been used in a number of the Global 2000 organizations. These sorts of architectures would not be feasible were it not for some amount of agreement on services-based architectures. This agreement has emerged largely from the influences of the

Internet which, as we discuss in more detail in Chapter Six, has forced technologists to begin the alignment of architectural patterns—the common models used to think about architecture—to handle the large scaling requirements driven by the unpredictable work load of the Internet. In Chapter Six, we discuss further how the influence of the Internet has permeated the architectural thinking of companies and is leading to an emerging focus on *architectural semantics*. There has emerged a common pattern of how technologists partition and share the processing load of Internet business through the creation of specialized functions, and this has driven some degree of semantic convergence. This has not been via a singular market adoption of a standard product, but rather through the market's agreement on a set of common abstractions—as we discussed earlier, the so-called thin-client approach to creating application software that can use multiple platforms on the client side, for example, Windows, UNIX, Linux, or Macintosh.

From a platform perspective, this domain has been the target for many commercial offerings competing for market share and specialization. This is the domain of operating systems (Windows™, UNIX), devices (for example, in the storage arena disks, storage arrays, network attached storage), processors (Intel's Pentium, Sun's SPARC, DEC's Alpha) and protocols (queued messaging, request/response, publish, and subscribe) all contending for a piece of the business that occurs in supporting this layer. While there has not been wide standardization, there has been a major shaking out of vendors, and there have emerged a small number of platforms. For example, the Windows operating system dominates the desktop, while UNIX-based or UNIX-like (Linux) operating systems have a large share of the Internet server market. Using another example, the database market is dominated by a common database model (the relational model) and a common language for accessing databases (the Structured Query Language or SQL). No doubt, there are clear differences and incompatibilities among various database products from competing vendors, but the similarities outweigh the differences.

The architecture and platform domain has experienced enough codification that there are meaningful patterns emerging, and there is enough shared understanding in the form of frameworks, market leaders, and emerging standards that practitioners in this domain can rapidly close communication gaps and get on to discussing core value. Since the domain is not standardized, practitioners will have to work through some thorny areas of disagreement, for example, which operating system to use.

However, the grounds for the disagreements are generally understood, therefore, the process of resolving them is a process of competing for and creating specific business value.

The Application Layer: Patterns and Best Practices

Applications provide chunks of useful capability, through a combination of software and manual means. Application, as we use it here, can equivalently be called *service, capability,* or *functionality.* Our focus here is on applications such as computer programs enabling specific business processes.

The same type of codification via agreement on the partitioning of functionality rather than on common standards or product that we found in the platform/architecture domain is driving the application domain of the semantic stack. This is a natural occurrence because the components and services that are the "stuff" of architecture are the business and technology applications that exist in this domain. It should be no surprise, therefore, that we show this domain to be in the framework stage of codification as well. Recall that we defined two parts to codification—abstraction and agreement. The application domain has benefited from agreement on good practices for developing applications that meet the needs of a set of stakeholders, principles of how to design robust applications, methods for integrating applications, and a commonly used set of programming languages for actually implementing applications.

There is still an enormously tacit aspect in determining exactly *what* a given application should do. There are practices that guide technologists regarding how they should go about finding out what they need, and so forth. However, the actual description of what an end user wants the application to do involves business people communicating with technology people across a significant language gulf. There are some development approaches, such as the methods used with the Unified Modeling Language (UML) that facilitate bridging the gulf, but generally it takes knowledgeable people working together to make effective applications.

However, the codification of the architecture/platform layer has created a set of reasonably common services to support applications. Consequently, the applications, once written, tend to have certain common features—some of which we discuss in Chapter Six—that make it reasonably straightforward to understand what they do and how to work with them. Interface languages, such as XML, common programming environments such as .NET, and common types of platform services used by applications create a common semantic layer that practitioners can leverage when the time comes to collaborate. Looking at this from the point of view of practitioners in a collaboration, the current state of the application domain is such that technologists working in a collaborative venture have built in common context for discussing the applications in each of the participating organizations. It is therefore likely that the applications themselves have enough common structure that making them work together is less an exercise in messy technology and more of an exercise in creating value.

What would executable look like in this layer? It would mean that an application could seek an application that performed some desired functionality, exchange information with that application, and work with the result of that application's functionality. This is very much the promise of Web services, though as we will see, providing this sort of capability for anything but the most rudimentary sorts of functionality, say calculating an exchange rate or getting the current time in Bangkok, requires an enormous amount of codification to occur in higher levels of the stack as well.

While we are describing the characteristics of each layer in isolation, there is continual competitive pressure to blur the distinctions among these domains. Organizational focus requires clearly delineated core competency. This core competency results from the pooling and leverage of relevant skill-sets around specific value propositions of an organization relating to specific layers of the semantic stack. The greater the tacit knowledge—the more the proprietary the nature of these skill-sets and the business value they engender—the greater the barriers to entry into their targeted competitive space. Why? Because the very nature of tacit knowledge involves a specificity and particular investment that makes its leverage by others difficult to copy, much less scale. Conversely, the greater the openness and the greater the codification of that knowledge, the lower the barriers to entry. Which results in what? Simply a changing of the competitive landscape as more and more people leap over the once high barriers therefore shifting what was differentiated and forcing a reconsideration and movement of what is high value. What was a highly differentiated offering becomes a mere competitive commodity. This is the competitive dynamic underlying movement across the semantic stack. What is the implication of this? A simple one, namely the competitive need to walk up the stack to attack high-margin opportunities thereby extending an organization's core competency while, in parallel, moving across the stack attempting to realize as much income as possible out of an increasingly pressured and margin-shrinking marketplace. We'll provide an example, that we return to in subsequent chapters, from different perspectives.

Microsoft has built an extraordinary marketplace through exploiting its core competencies on building hardware and software to support specific business applications. However, even Microsoft, with the massive marketplace power it wields, cannot bend the Red Queen to its will. The strategic brilliance of Microsoft is recognizing this fact and the recognition that as the layers which it dominates, or at least, competes with relentlessly, becomes increasingly codified, its future dominance depends on leveraging what it does best—building on its people and their tacit knowledge—and not merely walking, but running up while darting across the semantic stack.

We walk through this dynamic, again and again in Chapters Four through Six, citing examples from many firms and many industries. However, at this point, we want to highlight again the dynamic for blurring the layers as we describe their characteristics.

The Business Process Layer: A Common Need to Understand Variation

The business process domain is where the activities of people, working with technology, are combined in a defined way to create a particular business outcome. Some business processes are focused internally to create things that the customer never sees (e.g., HR processes for developing new employees) and some business processes interact with the customer (e.g., the processes followed by customer service representatives on the customer hotline). Everyone is very value-conscious, so business processes are expected to create value. (Value is not a new focus as evidenced by Henry Ford's adage, "if it doesn't add value, it's waste.")

If a business process and a collaboration are both supposed to add value, then it seems reasonable that business processes should support collaboration, and that at least part of the value created in a collaboration will be found in the business processes of the participating organizations. Since the collaboration will, to some extent, blend the value propositions of the participating companies, the business processes will probably have to come together. That gets us back to the principle that we have been stating repeatedly, this time in terms of business process: If organizations are to collaborate often, efficiently, and effectively, they must have a shared vocabulary around business processes.

Figure 3.6 shows the business process layer in the tacit category, meaning that little codification has yet taken place.

What sorts of things would move the tacit scale toward the right? Efforts that would help an organization articulate its business processes in an unambiguous way using a common representation and vocabulary help a business clean up its internal act, so that the organization's employees all know what they are supposed to do and how to do it, and more importantly for this book, know how to communicate their business process to a collaborative partner. Of course, if they shared a vocabulary with the collaborative partner so that the communication was smooth and efficient, the two collaborating partners could move quickly past the explanation phase and on to the value creation activities so important to collaboration. That brings us to the most important thing that needs to happen to achieve meaningful codification of business process: Common models, practices, and vocabulary across a broad population of organizations need to be created.

The business process domain is still finding its way through the abstraction part of codification, with agreement still distant, though efforts to do so are increasing aggressively. With that said, there is action in the space that should help "walk across" this part of the stack to the right. While we discuss the implications of business processes on collaboration in much detail in Chapter Four, we discuss some of the emerging efforts at codifying business processes here.

MODELING AND BENCHMARKING   Many businesses in many industries have undertaken projects to create models of their business processes. There is no broad consensus on practices or tools, and so the space is something of a free-for-all at this time. There are, however, some rapidly emerging practices and approaches to representation that will become part of the overall approach. One emerging practice is to externalize business rules and the workflow of the business process. Another is to capture the results of the modeling effort in some generally agreed form that can serve downstream engineering. We'll discuss each of these briefly in turn.

To *externalize business rules* means that most business processes have embedded, often tacit, rules that are key to the outcome of the business process. For example, an underwriter for property and casualty (P&C) insurance might have a checklist to determine whether or not to approve a new insurance policy. Surprisingly, but probably inevitably due to the consolidation in the insurance business and the tangled regulatory environment that surrounds insurance, underwriters in one office might not use the same checklist as the underwriters in another office, and it's virtually certain that the life insurance underwriters have a different checklist than the P&C underwriters, even though they might have many of the same considerations. To externalize the rules, in its simplest terms, requires lifting the responsibility for maintaining the checklist to the corporate level, and creating an explicit set of rules—not necessarily uniform across the entire company, but, if not, then different by design, not happenstance.

Similarly for *externalizing workflow*. The P&C underwriter interacts with other people in other departments as the policy flows through the system. When the underwriter's work is finished, the work passes to other people. The flow of paperwork through the organization often happens as part of the organizational consciousness, passed on by tradition and lore to new employees. Externalizing workflow lifts the flow of the policy to the corporate level as well, where again, explicit workflows are create for specific conditions.

This is more than just an exercise in control; it is a crucial first step in codification. Organizations like Unisys work with many clients and those clients know one another through things like industry group meetings. Once rules and workflow are externalized, people can compare themselves with others, often using organizations like Unisys or industry analyst firms, to provide insight, or to *benchmark* organizations against one another. As a result, best practices emerge. These best practices help guide organizations toward some degree of commonality in the way they break work down, and in the steps and sequencing of the work: Everyone emulates what are considered best practices, and so the business rules and workflows tend to start looking similar from company to company. This has obvious advantages when two companies collaborate. It also creates a market for products and services as a highly fragmented and custom environment turns into a more regular market. For example, languages for expressing business processes, such as the Business Process Modeling Language (BPML), and eBusiness Extended Markup Language (ebXML) have begun to emerge as ways for organizations to express their business processes to a wide audience.

MONITORING: BPM AND BAM   Business Performance Monitoring (BPM) and Business Activity Monitoring (BAM) are, as their names imply, targeted to the monitoring and management of business processes. The notion is to use technology to monitor individual business processes and workflow events, and roll up the resulting data into higher level dashboard views that give management the information that they need to make good decisions. Vendors like Systar[14] and Kintana[15] are active in this area. As organizations begin to use products like this and encounter the disciplines needed to make them work effectively, a drive toward more externalized business rules and workflow results, and there is a general trend toward codification.

The Roles and Metrics Layer: Judging Performance Quality

The roles and metrics domain is concerned with understanding what organizations and people do, and then measuring how well they do it. Roles and metrics can apply at the level of the company, an organization within a company, or people within that organization. This domain is where the company's performance is judged as reflected in its share price, where incentive plans are created, and where employee performance reviews happen.

Why is this important for collaboration? Because people in organizations tend to do what their job description says they are supposed to do—those things for which they are rewarded. Figure 3.6 puts the roles and metrics domain in the framework category. There are some common sorts of job titles and job roles, but the major codification that has happened in this domain has come from some of the collaborations that we introduced on the Collaborative Landscape—managed services and outsourcing. Each of these has driven the need to objectively specify roles and responsibilities across organizations, and to specify equally objectively the levels of service that are expected, and to monitor the service that is provided. As a result, a company entering, say, an outsourcing relationship must, for all intents and purposes, externalize those parts of its organization that have to interact with the outsourcer. This has had two impacts.

First, outsourcers quickly understood that to be scalable they could not have different relationships with each customer. Therefore, they standardized a set of roles and responsibilities that matched up reasonably well with the roles and responsibilities of their largest clients at the time—government agencies—who just happened to have a well-codified set of roles and responsibilities in the GSA rating system and the various military grades. More recently, as outsourcing is being pursued ever more aggressively in the commercial sector, outsourcers are using external standards to define their roles and responsibilities. Thus, major Indian offshore development companies base their processes on accepted industry best practices approaches like the Capability Maturity Model (CMM) we discussed earlier. It should not be too surprising that the CMM was heavily influenced by the dominant consumer of software and software services—again, government agencies, so the CMM roles have some common ancestry with the roles that have been used by outsourcers for years. The net result is that there are some fairly widely agreed-upon roles and responsibilities in providers of outsourcing services.

Second, given that the organization has to match up with a set of roles and responsibilities, the organizations of the outsourcers and the processes and practices they employ are often adopted, at least partially, by the technology organizations that use outsourced services. This has also had a codifying effect.

There are no commonly accepted standards for describing roles and metrics. Consequently, when two organizations get together to collaborate it is not uncommon for people with the same role to have different job titles and very different incentives, or for people with similar titles to have different roles. This slows down efforts at collaboration, where people working in the venture have to engage in a dance around their roles, their levels, and so on. In our experience with collaboration in professional services we have found that, in working with another firm, we always need to go through an exercise of matching titles and levels so that people on our team can understand roughly the roles played by the people on the other team, and then we continue to learn over the course of the collaboration how the other team members actually relate to their organization. This leads to miscommunication, misconception, and missed opportunities. For example, in our firm, a managing director in charge of a client relationship has broad authority and power to marshal resources and support for that client as well as to control the overall communications with the client. In one of our recent collaborations, where we partnered with another services firm to jointly pursue a client opportunity, we assumed that our counterpart with roughly the same title had roughly the same authority. He didn't, several conflicting messages got to the client because of lack of control within our partner, and as a result we lost an opportunity.

Remember that our goal is to create the environment for collaboration to occur efficiently and effectively. The roles/metrics layer directly affects our ability to create the working human relationships needed to innovate at the edge of collaboration.

The Behaviors/Values Layer: Making Visible Invisible Actions

The activities in which we engage and the networks of colleagues we share comprise the glue of organizational behaviors. These activities are more often invisible than they are the result of clearly defined processes or functions, becoming routine over time because, frankly, they are proven to get the job done. Many of these activities result in a cohesion of activity resulting from friendships, colleagues, and workarounds establishing an informal network of activities and support, a cohesion that cannot be isolated within departmental boundaries or managerial spans-of-control. One reason: It is not physically or psychologically possible to specify in advance behaviors required to respond to and redress all combinations of possible contingencies. There is thus no way to contain the spill-over across individuals or behaviors with the requisite knowledge, interests, and positions within one, two, or even more departmental boundaries. Behaviors cannot be controlled. Their activities are like water—upon facing an obstacle, a constraint, an outdated policy or procedure—it fights not against it, but surges around or over it. We all know and experience this process of adaptive actions, of behaviors invisible to formally stated processes but critical to actually getting work done. Such behaviors are not marginal to organizational activities; they are their fundamental and foundational nature. They are not peripheral manifestations of everyday behavior; they are its genes. Consequently, describing *actual* as opposed to proscribed behaviors, describing the informal activities performed and how those invisible actions have visible impacts becomes critical as we seek to explore effective collaborative actions. Identifying and making explicit the behaviors that actually occur, as opposed to those that merely ought or need to be followed, becomes particularly critical as cross-organizational activities become established. One question remains, though: How do we make these invisible behaviors visible?

Individual behaviors often result from rational responses to, and navigations of, established incentives and proscribed values. Consequently, understanding incentive programs and values as they are executed as opposed to merely articulated becomes a critical focus of this layer of the stack. The former is certainly easier to grab hold of than the latter, yet both result in both expected and unintended—and often invisible—actions.

Often, *culture* is drawn on to explain both visible and invisible behaviors. Too frequently, however, culture is perceived as a fuzzy category—hard to define but useful to explain away unseen or otherwise unexplainable actions. Culture, in this sense, becomes a residual category, one in which fuzzy guesses and hunches can be dumped. However, rigor can be and has been added to cultural explanations. Our purpose is certainly not to explore the richness of organizational cultural explanations. But our purpose is certainly to highlight the criticality of using such tools to make behaviors that are invisible and tacit, visible and codified.

Organizational behaviors are manifestations of tacit values and assumptions. Therefore, we can look at behaviors not as significant in themselves but as what they can tell us about the fundamental reasons for their occurrence. We can drill down toward their essence, which takes us to the cultural assumptions and orientation of the organization. The essence of a culture lies in its patterns of basic assumptions. Having identified that there exists basic assumptions and having delineated what those patterns are, it is possible to interpret their behaviors, give credence, and make explicit the actual as opposed merely to the articulated values. Uncovering these structures of assumptions between collaborating organizations, while no doubt difficult, remains critical to reconcile, to align, and to exploit the value each brings to the collaborative entity. We will not spend any more time on this topic in this book. It is sufficient merely to highlight that making clear the behavioral "structures" and working to uncover their tacit nature among collaborative partners remains as critical as any other layer of the semantic stack.[16]

The Environment Layer: The Competitive Context of Tacit Actions

All businesses exist within a competitive context that both informs and is informed by organizational actions. Understanding this context and the boundary conditions that frame actions—such as political, economic or social entities, or activities that impact any particular organization—are the focus of classic strategy work. A tremendous amount of work and dollars are spent in attempting to make sense of the competitive environment in which any organization finds itself. Our intention is not to delve into this layer in any detail but merely to highlight that shared semantics are as critical at articulating, identifying, and agreeing to specific market opportunities, strategic bets, and the environmental context as any of the other layers.

Many strategy approaches exist, approaches geared toward making explicit one's competitive environment. The challenge many of them face is the following: While conceptually clear and analytically rigorous, they are often operationally useless. Billy Crystal's adage that it is better to look good than to feel good comes to mind but is far from sufficient here. Making explicit the overall goals of the business, how the business relates to the marketplace, and how the business relates to the various economies with which it deals becomes a difficult though critical activity. One reason for the difficulty stems from the inevitable difference of perspectives, of assumptions, and of heritages each participant of a collaboration brings to bear. And this doesn't even begin to capture the difficulty of creating a tangible and effectively executable environmental strategy. One effective means of getting insight into the environmental domain is through the development, with supporting operational plans, of scenarios. Yet, even these require establishing an explicit set of shared assumptions from which to build. Now, compound the difficulty of this highly dynamic domain across collaborative partners, and it becomes pretty evident that codifying this layer will remain a challenge. No doubt tools and approaches will continue to emerge and become more operationally relevant, but the very dynamisms inherent in any environment will place a premium on the tacit nature of this layer of the stack.

The environment domain is where the Red Queen is most active. The Red Queen, as we will see in Chapters Four and Five, is constantly churning the environment, and in that context we discuss the constant movement of ventures within the collaborative landscape, or equivalently, how the collaborative landscape, under the influence of the Red Queen, is always in motion up and to the right. While there is relatively little that a business can do to increase the codification of the environment domain, the natural movement of the marketplace will drive that codification aggressively as yesterday's innovation is today's commodity and becomes tomorrow's obituary.

Walking up and across the Semantic Stack

We have mentioned the notion of walking up or walking across the semantic stack. The semantic stack goes from familiar technology things, like *connectivity,* at the bottom, to very abstract and human things, like *behaviors,* as you move up. To walk up the stack means to explicitly recognize and embrace the impact of the humanity involved in connecting two organizations. Left-to-right, the stack moves from *tacit,* meaning understood only by way of substantial shared context among the people trying to understand it to *executable,* meaning so thoroughly specified that computers can meaningfully exchange and operate on the information. Therefore, to walk *across* the stack on a given layer means to codify the information relevant to that layer.

If you are walking up and across the semantic stack, you are codifying more and more complex and human behaviors. We have introduced the semantic stack to introduce some of the necessary structure, the *DNA,* of creating and operating collaborative ventures. We have begun the discussion, which will be carried out in the next three chapters, that codifying domains in the stack, especially some of the more complex, human domains, would help us lower the friction, and thus the cost and time, in setting up and tearing down collaborations. By analogy with systems integration, we discuss soon the notion of a *value port* where the mechanics of creating a collaborative venture are sufficiently codified that setting one up to pursue a particular opportunity is simple, quick, and efficient.

It is important to note, however, that we are not talking here about codifying the innovation process itself, nor about codifying the value created in the innovation. Innovation is a uniquely human activity. At its essence, innovation depends on humans working together with other humans, applying their intelligence and unique talents to create something new. The value created, if it is to be high value, will also be unique and human and therefore not amenable to codification. Codification of the value created is roughly equivalent to making that value into a commodity, and thus reducing its value. The Red Queen does that soon enough, and she doesn't need our help!

Most of what we have discussed in this chapter and will discuss in this book is the framing around collaboration—how to recognize when it is appropriate, how to streamline the set up and tear down, how the structure might evolve over time—so that we can make those efforts easier and mechanical, freeing the humans involved in the collaboration to concentrate more on that uniquely human enterprise of innovation. We want the valuable human assets thinking and interacting to create new ideas, new approaches, new avenues. The set up and operational details add no value; they are important, because without them the collaborative venture won't exist and cannot work. However, ultimately, we want to make this supporting stuff automatic and mechanical, so that the humans, the stars of this particular show, can get on with the innovation and the value creation.

Value Ports: Collaborative Plug-and-Play

Extending the analogy of the network in system integration, we introduce the concept of a *value port*—a conceptual way of exposing business process and knowledge at some layer of the semantic stack and thereby enhancing the speed and efficiency of collaboration—*collaborative plug-and-play.* If we think about technologies like Web services, there is a definite trend toward greater end user control through self-configuration, and empowerment at the edges. Combining Web services with the greater codification of business processes that we discussed, and some of the technologies that we discuss in future sections, we can envision being able to build collaboration-oriented services that enable us to walk up the stack, link up the human things at the top of the stack with collaboratively oriented business process, and measurement of services, delivered by IT components in the highly codified lower layers of the stack. This amount of technology support for the frameworks of collaboration is what is needed for a value port. The value port concept is focused on providing enterprise-level higher value collaboration and collaborative services, focused at externalizing the layers of the semantic stack in a reasonably codified way, and enabling innovation at the edges.

People, in your organization, working with the collaborative framework, can identify opportunities and determine whether collaboration is a good approach. The two organizations can connect through value ports. Then people, working at the edge of your organization—wearing your company badge, carrying your company's business card, and so on but working in another organization, the collaborative venture, that is really separate from your organization—do that thing that only humans can do. They think and innovate and, from their efforts, they create a new business proposition. This is where the value of the collaborative venture is created: at the edge of the organization, by people holding enormous amounts of tacit knowledge, applying that knowledge in novel ways to address a business opportunity.

So far, we have explored one of the collaborative DNA elements—that of the semantic stack, and more importantly, the inexorably competitive pressures to walk up and across the semantic stack. The semantic stack is a simple tool—a tool to think with—to understand both the focus of any collaborative effort and the competitive pressures that collaboration will face. It is thus as much a tool for *taking action* as it is one for *making sense.* It provides a simple mechanism to perform a critical step for effective collaborations: namely, assist in aligning specific collaborations with fast-moving business opportunities. In this chapter, we sketched the structure of the semantic stack and hinted at its implications. In subsequent chapters, we delve into the implications derived from its use. Before doing so, however, we need to briefly describe the third collaborative DNA element—that of managing distributed risk.

MANAGING DISTRIBUTED RISK

Risks are inherent in any collaborative venture, irrespective of the specific collaborative form. As we saw in the Collaborative Landscape, there are different types of collaborative ventures, each with different value propositions, business objectives, underlying risk profiles, and, correspondingly, different strategies to manage those risks. This section suggests a simple method first, to articulate the differing types of risk that underlie differing collaborative ventures and, second, to evaluate and balance the risk elements comprising any particular collaborative approach. This simple method, or diagnostic, helps clarify the operational requirements and, hence, strategies to help manage the distributed risk of your collaborative ventures.

There are a number of ways to think about risk, but they all start with the premise that one person's risk is another person's opportunity. At its most basic, the key issue to evaluate distributed risk in any collaborative venture is to evaluate who brings more of what to the collaborative equation. The participants in a collaborative venture bring particular and needed elements to the relationship—organizational skills, intellectual property, customers, and so on. The value-bundle comprises four elements that are key to the value proposition of the collaborative relationship, and next we identify some others that are involved in the operational aspects of the collaboration.

For each of these elements, one of the organizations will be in a position to contribute disproportionately to the others. This leads to a straightforward characterization where, for each valuable element in the collaboration, more risk is borne by one organization, let's call it organization A—the one that brings more of a particular element to the relationship—than by the other organization in the collaborative relationship, say organization B (there might be more than two organizations in the relationship). Conversely, more opportunity avails itself to organization B. Thus, for any particular collaborative element, there is a simple opportunity/risk equation that needs to be balanced, and reconciled, and taken across the set of key collaborative risk elements. There are a number of collaborative risks that need to be balanced, and reconciled. Thus, there is less a *science* of examining any one key risk element and evaluating its trade-off than an *art* of mapping the set of these elements to determine your risk/reward profile for any particular venture.

The Art of Managing Distributed Risk

The beauty of art is its accessibility to many and the different emotional impacts and interpretations it engenders depending on your background, interest, and proclivities. So, too, with identifying and assessing collaborative risk. The steps for doing so are:

1. Identify the risk elements, their characteristics, and their risk/reward opportunities depending on which organization, on balance, tends to bring more of that element.

2. Evaluate which organization brings what risk element to the party. Again, while both—or possibly N number of—organizations may bring customers, intellectual property, or so on to the collaborative venture, on balance, identifying which organization, on average, brings more of that element keeps this diagnostic simple and pragmatically easy-to-use.

3. Assign a weight to these values, depending on your view of the collaborative venture's business objectives and of the relative values of the core competencies brought to the collaboration by the participating organizations with respect to your view of your organization. This is similar in concept to Treacy and Wiersema's market discipline for market leaders model where they characterized organizations as having a proclivity and set of core competencies around one of three market disciplines: customer intimacy, operational efficiency (cost and operational excellence), and product innovation.[17] Assessing the value and opportunity cost of any particular risk element will be impacted by the relative value of that element to your organizational key competencies and market positioning. For example, Procter & Gamble has one of the world's most valued brands. Consequently, any collaborative venture in which it engages needs to ensure that its brand and market positioning are well protected and, at best, enhanced and, at worst, have no impact on its brand and market positioning. Procter & Gamble, therefore, gives great weight to the brand risk element. Conversely, for a small start-up with, arguably, minimal brand yet

powerfully innovative intellectual property, the opportunity for partnering with a brand leader is high, while its opportunity cost, from the brand perspective, is low.

We'll explore how these three steps have been and can be implemented later. For now, we need simply describe the process just outlined.

Step 1: Identify the Collaborative Risk Elements

Table 3.1 suggests a set of risk elements that need to be identified, evaluated, and managed in any collaborative venture. For each element, it also

TABLE 3.1   COLLABORATIVE RISK ELEMENTS OF COLLABORATIVE VENTURES

RISK ELEMENT	DEFINITION	OPPORTUNITY	RISK
Customer	Buyer of services and focus of collaborative venture	Customer acquisition	Customer disintermediation or "theft"
Brand/ reputation	Market perception of capabilities and core competencies	Enhanced market positioning	Diminished market positioning
Governance	Decision-making process and leadership commitment	Incremental degree of decision-making authority/control	Inability to effect significant change
Quality	Perception and reality of enhanced reliability	Enhanced market satisfaction	Perceived reduction in value
Financial	"Hard" and "soft" dollar commitment underwriting venture	Access to resources needed for the collaboration	The "free rider" issue, opportunity cost
Execution	Capabilities and discipline to achieve stated objectives	Positioned to determine platforms and processes underlying venture	Loss of best practices
Capacity/cost of production	Ability to create the products of the collaboration at scale and cost	Access to enhanced scale	Exposure of key practices, trade secrets, or supply chain capabilities
Intellectual property (IP)	Assets (products, services, knowledge) underlying venture's value proposition	Scaling intellectual property	IP "leakage" or loss of control over its use, hence value capture

depicts the type of opportunity and risk involved for any collaborative venture. The following section then describes the art for managing this set, based on the three steps.

These risk elements comprise an initial set of evaluative indicators for the collaborative venture. The risk elements in Table 3.1 are not offered as the last word on the topic, but rather as a good working list to guide a discussion. Other elements could be identified, combined with, or supplant this particular list. The specifics of what comprises a set of risk elements is less important than an identification of some particular set to begin the evaluation. Having a common set on which both Organization A and Organization N agree is critical—the raw paint strokes— to interpret the collaborative art form.

Steps 2 and 3: Identify Who Brings What to the Collaborative Party and Assign Relative Weights

Agreeing on what elements to use for evaluation is the first step. The next step is to begin crafting the risk profile through identifying which organization brings what to the collaborative venture. Again, the elements we've identified are illustrative of the process; the actual elements and the level of detail into which each organization needs to delve will differ and, most assuredly, be more detailed. However, the risk elements of Table 3.1 are the relevant categories of risk elements critical to perform a quick evaluation.

Figure 3.7 provides a quick diagnostic of what each organization brings to a particular collaborative opportunity. It depicts, on balance, which one brings more to the venture and the resultant opportunity and risk that needs to be sorted through. Figure 3.7 provides a quick visual snapshot to assess whether or not there is even any value in continuing a collaborative discussion.

In Figure 3.7, the initial customer base for this particular collaborative venture is seeded from Company A. For this customer risk element, Company A faces the risk of having Company B disintermediate or steal its customers while, conversely, Company B has a much greater opportunity of customer acquisition for this collaboration than does Company A, at least initially. Is this a concern? It depends on the risk profile, the timing of when additional customers are expected to be obtained, and the entire set of risk elements and how the risks and opportunities are shared between the two companies. If all of the "sliders" are on your side of this collaborative scale, then it is very likely that there is not a good collaborative fit, at least in the way the collaboration has initially been designed.

FIGURE 3.7   THE COLLABORATIVE SCALE (WHO BRINGS WHAT
               TO THE PARTY)

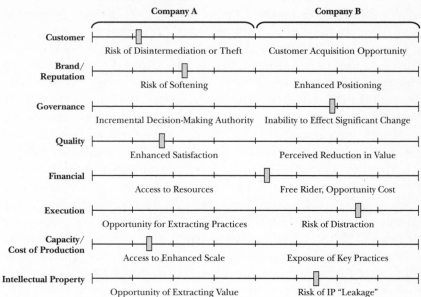

A classic example of this disproportionate contribution to a collaborative venture—that carries an equally disproportionate burden of risk, from one company, and a corresponding disproportionate opportunity from another—is one of a very large company relying on a small software company to provide some core technical functionality. Here, the large company becomes the life-support for the smaller company that tends, as a result of its association with the larger company, to gain a disproportionate share of branding, market equity, and other positive externalities than does the large company.

Yet, here again, the seemingly apparent disparity in terms of who brings what to the party may be irrelevant depending on the relative weight or value one company places on any particular risk element. Is such a disparity a concern? Again, it depends. This takes us back to the discussion about how to value or assign a weight to the particular risk elements and competencies brought to the collaborative venture. A company that is well positioned around customer intimacy is likely to assign a higher value to customer-oriented risk elements and assign lower values to those in which it, comparatively, has a lower set of capabilities. Consequently, having an imbalance in the scale in terms of who brings what to the venture may be sufficient if the weights applied to the element, overall, balance out.

The challenge—and the art—becomes balancing the opportunities (and its resulting value to Company A) and the risks across the set of risk elements. Stated differently, the degree to which the collaborative scale balances across its risk elements means that the cost of any particular risk element is relatively low because there is a relative wash of value and opportunity to risk. Conversely, if there is an imbalance in the scale, each company needs to provide the business case of each proposition thereby creating a never-ending dynamic of individual nit-picking that will drive the collaborative venture far away from its intended collaborative benefit.

There are a number of ways to think about risk, but at their essence, as we've said, they all start with the premise that one person's risk is another person's opportunity. That both companies involved acknowledge, adhere, and agree that balancing the distributed risk portfolio is necessary becomes a critical step at working through and making any collaborative venture a success. Yet, managing the distributed risk of any collaborative venture is only one of the collaborative DNA elements. As with any type of interaction, particularly across companies, a key challenge is how to communicate consistently and effectively and even more importantly, make sense of those communications. This is the focus of the second collaborative DNA element—that of the semantic stack. And the first element entails the creation of mutual value.

No one strand of the collaborative DNA works alone. They are inextricably intertwined. In this and the previous chapters, they require, however, being teased apart to isolate their function. Manipulating them effectively requires exploiting them as sets of activities, but also knowing how to separate them as needed. In subsequent chapters, the lessons we draw and the implications we suggest recombine these elements into specific, practical, and pragmatic actions to make collaborations more effective. Before continuing, however, we need to step backward to go forward.

SUMMARY: WALKING UP AND ACROSS THE SEMANTIC STACK

Collaborative ventures are inherently risky. Yet, they offer powerful opportunities for agility and value creation. And herein lies the rub: They are, intrinsically, unique organizational entities, challenging the once dominant juggernaut of internalizing all functions and capabilities. Collaborative forms are less a sideline of organizational strategy than a competitive necessity. As companies get clearer about what their core strengths are, they are increasingly recognizing the benefits and necessity of collaborating. And emerging technologies are making this collaboration much easier—with Internet protocols, XML, Web services, and the ever-prevalent and multiple flavors of managed services/hosting as key enablers of this collaborative necessity. The essence of what is happening is that companies are becoming increasingly intertwined—or integral participants—in each other's value chain as the organizational dynamics of Coase meets the technology principles of Metcalfe. The result? An explosion of collaborative forms, each with differing value propositions, operational models, and underlying risk profiles. And yet, while initially complex, there is a simplicity, an elegance, a pragmatic approach to parse through these multiple collaborative forms to assess, and to exploit, the collaborative forms most relevant and effective for particular needs. In this chapter, we've described models and diagnostics around the DNA for effective collaborative behaviors that allow you to think and act on how you will share the value and the reward, manage the distributed risk, and walk up and across the semantic stack.

Together, these three DNA strands shape the effectiveness of collaborative ventures. They explain the *hows* of increasing the effectiveness of collaboration, irrespective of its particular form. All collaborative forms must work through how to share value, how to manage distributed risk, and with what speed, where and how to walk up and across the semantic stack. The means to do so differ, depending on the type of designed venture. Yet there are patterns regarding how to manipulate these DNA strands, patterns that can be identified and used to increase the effectiveness of any particular form. These patterns are reflected in the different quadrants of the Collaborative Landscape we initially discussed in Chapter Two. Each quadrant of this Collaborative Landscape has a different profile of these three DNA strands and hence differing operational implications. Chapters Four through Six explore these implications from different perspectives—from that of organization business process and leadership, people and their underlying knowledge, and technology enablers. Yet each of them is structured similarly: Identify emerging business trends and operational patterns, then suggest specific implications that can be exploited to accelerate effective collaborative behaviors. It is to these implications that we soon turn. But first, let's step backward to go forward.

In this chapter, we explored how organizations and people interact in creating innovation. We introduced the important notion of shared semantics in collaboration. Some degree of shared semantics is necessary for productive interaction among people, more so for people who are collaborating to innovate, and still more for companies who need to dynamically create collaborative relationships.

We introduced the notion of differing degrees of semantic agreement, putting at the one extreme tacit and at the other extreme, codified. We also introduced the semantic stack that applies the semantic spectrum to the different areas in which organizations interact. Codification of the knowledge around the key areas involved in collaboration—related to the value-bundle or the relationship—increases the speed and accuracy of the communication that has to take place for collaboration to occur. This applies to the setting up of a collaborative relationship, where codified knowledge helps each side to articulate the value, cost, risk, and reward involved in creating the relationship and thus helps increase the dynamism of the collaboration. It applies to the innovation process itself, where the people involved can communicate much more easily with a common semantic view of the world. It applies to the value that is created at the edges of your organization during a collaboration, where a better codification makes it practical to capture and retain knowledge more efficiently, increasing the return of the collaboration, and reducing the risk of intellectual property leakage. Understanding the role of codified knowledge profoundly impacts how you approach your organization and people, your technology, and your business process.

Collaborative forms differ greatly, as we've seen in the Collaborative Landscape. Yet, discerning the common competitive dynamics across them and, more specifically, building a common language—a vocabulary—to express both these differences and their commonalities becomes a critical first step to exploiting them and their underlying processes more effectively.

Our argument so far can be summarized by the following: Collaborations result from efforts to exploit specific market opportunities—or market inefficiencies in the sense that a high margin exists for some specific opportunity. The high margins result from the barriers or, in classic economic terms, asymmetries of information, knowledge, or capabilities that exist to exploit that opportunity. Over time, however, as the opportunity becomes demonstrably successful, the high margins will be squeezed as the processes, the technologies, the capabilities, the information—in short, the knowledge underlying all of these—becomes more codified and hence more available, reusable, and scalable. Thus, the very process of codifying knowledge is at the crux of sharing the value and sharing the reward of collaborative activities.

Two points jump out of this summary. First, the criticality that the process of codifying tacit knowledge becomes, arguably *the* critical operational challenge and need for sustained collaborative success; and second, the role of the semantic stack to help identify where and how to assess your organizational capabilities, to anticipate competitive trends, and to prioritize actions to make your collaborative response more effective.

Chapters Two and Three built our Collaborative Framework and vocabulary to make sense of the buzzing, booming activities that personify collaborative activities. They described the collaborative necessity and the underlying mechanics of effective collaborative behaviors. Chapters Four through Six shift the focus to how to take action to engender effective collaborations in the face of the Red Queen and her juggernaut. They build on the insights, examples, and frameworks of Chapters Two and Three and explore collaborative implications from different vantage points: the classic set of process, people, and technology. It is to these implications that we turn in Chapter Four.

CHAPTER HIGHLIGHTS

The Issue

Different types of collaborations exist. How do we determine which ones align with business goals and how do we enable that alignment to occur most effectively? How do we make collaborations more effective?

The Insight

The DNA strands underlying effective collaboration are: sharing the value—the reward; managing distributed risk; and walking up and across the semantic stack. These DNA strands ground the "hows" to enhance the effectiveness of collaboration, irrespective of its particular form. Understanding the underlying dynamics of these strands provides tools to help increase the effectiveness of any particular form.

Given that shared knowledge and understanding becomes more scalable and cheaper when the knowledge is codified, the degree of codification of relevant activities is an important measure of the readiness

(continued)

of the organization to collaborate often, rapidly, effectively, and efficiently. The semantic stack is a simple tool to help align business opportunities with the appropriate collaborative form. The semantic stack can also be used to anticipate how collaborative forms change overtime. Through this assessment, we can perform the critical steps of both aligning specific business opportunities with appropriate collaborative forms and anticipating how to evolve or end the collaboration, as appropriate, as competitive dynamics play out over time.

The Phrases

The semantic stack; distributed risk scale.

The Implications

What part of the semantic stack you target, support, and exploit determines the type of collaborative form most relevant to align with your strategic requirements. Also, the nature of competition changes depending on where you are in the stack. Understanding how to exploit the underlying dynamics of the semantic stack becomes a critical strategic requirement and operational focus.

Walking up and across the semantic stack and understanding how collaborations in the different parts of the Collaborative Landscape evolve, get sustained, or die across time are key strategic requirements and challenges to instilling collaborative capabilities as core competencies.

CHAPTER FOUR

As the Walls Come Tumbling Down: Emergent Organizational Implications

Certainty, as defined by *Webster's Dictionary*, entails a high degree of likelihood about an outcome, set of activities or direction. Achieving certainty in business processes—forecasting, execution, production, results, and so on—is an objective to which many organizations aspire, and it is the intended goal of their planning, metrics, and operating procedures. With such certainty, comes predictability, assurance of continuity, and consistent operations—all attributes of a stable business. Yet, such certainty has rarely if ever been a reality of competitive life. In fact, the opposite is true. Arguably one of the most important strategic and leadership challenges is precisely how to make the most out of uncertainty, rather than the chimera of certainty—how to stand at the left side of the three-arrow picture introduced in Chapter Two, and confidently navigate to the right in full knowledge that the arrows are going to bend beneath you. By no means does this mean that attempting to create degrees of certainty through structured and standardized means is either futile or a misappropriation of scarce attention. But it does mean that a disproportionate amount of attention, from a leadership perspective, needs to focus on how to use the reality of uncertainty to your advantage.

We could cite multiple studies of chaos and complexity theory that explore the dynamics of how to ascertain order and rules of behavior within complex adaptive systems, such as weather patterns, the formation of ice crystals, and a bewildering range of other physical systems. Much of the recent explorations into physical and natural sciences has been driven by models of chaos and complexity that are built on exploring simple rules underlying complex actions, all focused on understanding how to make sense, identify hidden order, and take advantage of uncertain behaviors.[1] Many recent management practitioners and thinkers have brought lessons from the fields of chaos and complexity into the business domain. Yet, we need not go so far afield to witness, observe, and viscerally experience the pressures of uncertainty on our businesses and our business decisions.

In Chapter Two, we explored some of the dynamics driving uncertainty: the never-ending accelerations toward the *real-time economy,* globalization, the (only temporarily fettered) unfettered capital markets, the recurrent technology tsunamis. These, and any other of a myriad of new buzzwords, concerns, and pressures do, however, result in *one* certainty: namely, that ever-higher degrees of uncertainty continually rewrite our definitions of opportunities and risks. What this means is that, as a McKinsey report has put it, strategic questions we ask and decisions we make have morphed into a more complex and high-stakes dilemma.[2] The competitive reality we face is that no simple answer or single answer exists, nor can any decision be constant or unchanging for any substantial period of time. Attempts to simplify strategic directions or to create certainty are bound to be undermined.

Richard Foster and Sarah Kaplan, in their insightful book, *Creative Destruction,* point out that there are few if any companies that continually outperform the market.[3] Certainly, there are companies that have gone from good to great over time and their value has endured more than the majority of their competitors. However, the lessons to draw from both the few *great* and the vast majority of *good* companies remains similar: Building constant management philosophies, standardized procedures, control processes, and other managerial tools based on the premises of continuity and consistency only deadens the organization to the creative impulses and need to embrace the market forces of "creative destruction."[4] As we also discussed in Chapter Two, the *innovator's dilemma* makes a complementary observation, namely that companies get *locked into* their success and underlying processes, incentives, and structures that made them so, thereby making it difficult for them to adapt to new opportunities.[5] What worked for them once no longer does and what, in retrospect, appeared certain, no longer is. This folds us back to how we started this chapter and indeed this book: The seductive and ultimately futile pursuit of certainty in an ever-uncertain competitive world.

This leads us to a simple observation and an equally simple question. First the observation: Once we recognize that uncertainty permeates—in fact, characterizes—our competitive environment, we must acknowledge that no simple or single answer exists to navigate through that uncertainty. That's the lesson of the three-arrow picture presented in Chapter Two, and that's the reality we face. Now the equally simple question: How can we embrace this uncertainty with respect to emerging collaborative business opportunities and begin to manage it even as we acknowledge its ubiquity?

This chapter explores this observation and suggests some answers to the question. All simple. All built on what we've discussed before. Let's start from another vantage point, by exploring not what we do not (or cannot) know about our uncertain competitive environment, but what we *do* know, by exploring what is certain in our uncertain competitive worlds.

Certainty 1: What we call an "organization" is changing. There are many extant definitions of the concept organization. For now, let's characterize an organization as a set of processes, artifacts, customers, and control/governance procedures that exist to accomplish a set of objectives. As Peter Drucker, the doyen of management studies, describes in an *Economist* survey and as many of us continue to experience, the organizational form has some basic rules:

- The corporation is the master, the employee is the servant. Because the corporation owns the means of production without which the employee could not make a living, the employee needs the corporation more than vice versa.

- The great majority of employees work full-time for the corporation. The pay they get for the job is their only income and provides their livelihood.

- The most efficient way to produce anything is to bring together under one management as many as possible of the activities needed to turn out the product.

- Suppliers have market power because they have information about a product or a service that the customer does not and cannot have, and does not need if he can trust the brand. This explains the profitability of brands.

- To any one particular technology, pertains one and only one industry; and conversely, to any one particular industry, pertains one and only one technology. This means that all technology needed to make steel is peculiar to the steel industry; and conversely, that whatever technology is being used to make steel comes out of the steel industry itself. The same applies to the paper industry, to agriculture or to banking and commerce.[6]

This organizational form stems from vertically integrating the people, the processes, and the technology under the same organizational roof to lower the transactional and communications costs of coordinating all the people and the activities needed to deliver products and services to customers.[7] This vertical integration has been very stable for a long time, largely because the transactional and communications costs have been stable, or at least changing gradually and predictably, for a long time. But that time is passing, and quickly, as the influence of new technologies and new models for doing business drive disruptive changes in the cost functions on which vertically integrated firms are based. With dramatic implications. These changes are all known; we list them here to set the stage for our subsequent discussion. They include:

Knowledge as a core means of production. We introduced our notion of tacit knowledge in Chapter Three and explore its role extensively in Chapter Five. In the innovation factory that is the core of organizational evolution, value is created when people share and extend their knowledge. These people—these knowledge workers—provide *capital* to the process as fully as do financial markets or the suppliers of raw materials.

Inherent limits to maximum vertical integration and correspondingly the importance of transactional and coordinating costs. The so-called Coasean *transactional costs* argument states that vertical integration continuously increases as the incremental costs of coordinating people, things, and processes are greater than the value they produce. Two elements continuously challenge the inexorable drive toward larger and larger or more vertically integrated organizations. *First: Knowledge:* As the knowledge needed for any activity becomes more and more specialized, it becomes increasingly expensive and difficult to maintain and control the necessary critical mass of that knowledge. It becomes increasingly difficult, to use our phrases from a later chapter, to *put and keep a lid on the intellectual assets and knowledge.* Furthermore, the shelf life of knowledge, combined with the critical need to continuously refresh knowledge to maintain its relevance and usefulness, compounds the challenge of both keeping knowledge controlled and cost effective for any particular organization. *Second: Communications:* A key rationale for vertical integration centers on minimizing the communications costs of coordinating activities. Yet, as we discussed in Chapter Three, there have been enormous strides in information technology that are driving communications costs downward, and all indications are that the trend will continue. We are all aware of the rapid adoption rates of information technology and correspondingly dramatic drop of marginal usage costs.[8] Internet and e-mail usage have practically eliminated the physical costs of creating communications channels, and with the emergence of common vocabularies facilitated by technology uptake, those communications channels will be filled with actual information. As Peter Drucker puts it, "this has meant that the most productive and most profitable way to organize is to disintegrate."[9]

What we are seeing is the confluence of Metcalfe's Law and Coase's arguments. Metcalfe's Law (named for Robert Metcalfe, the founder of 3Com Corporation and designer of the Ethernet protocol) says that the usefulness of a network is proportional to the square of the number of users (the related, so-called *network effect* says that the value of something on the network increases roughly proportionally to the square of the number of people who can leverage it). In Chapter Two and again in this chapter, we've seen Coase's arguments on transaction costs. We might bill this two-way encounter as *Metcalfe meets Coase: The ubiquitous network provides leverage for driving down transaction costs as the square of the number of transaction partners on the network.*[10] Add to this Moore's Law (named for Gordon Moore, cofounder of Intel) that says that every 18 months processing power doubles while cost remains constant, and we see an exciting three-way billing: *Every 18 months, we double the capacity of a rapidly increasing number of participants to drive down transaction costs as the square of the number of participants.* Don King, the infamous fight promoter would be ecstatic over this three-way billing: The drama alone much less the enormous implications on strategic positioning and revenue opportunities are worthy of any heavyweight bout. The practical upshot is that the stage is set for radical changes in transaction and communications costs that, according to Coase by way of Williamson, irrevocably rocks the foundations of vertical integration.

Drawing again on our earlier comments about *creative destruction* and *the innovator's dilemma,* long-term corporate performance has not, and cannot, match the performance of markets. Why? Because corporations do not adapt to large change as quickly as do markets. Why? Because organizations are designed to produce goods and services for customers. Well-run organizations have a point of view and a direction, and evolve incrementally based on the incrementally shifting needs and adaptations of those customers. There is nothing inherently wrong with this. On the contrary, it's a very good thing for the customers; satisfying customers *is* the basis for organizational effectiveness. Such organizational behaviors simply reflect the design principles and rationale for their existence.

Markets, on the other hand, are designed to respond quickly to large changes and to rapidly deploy resources to exploit the best opportunities ruthlessly—to evolve through exploiting new value. Markets do not have a point of view; they are reactive and opportunistic, the result of a systemic process of creation and destruction that form the basis of evolution. So, as Metcalfe meets Coase, it is no surprise that leaderships' attention turns to the explicit recognition, acknowledgment, and focus on uncertainty. As Metcalfe meets Coase meets Moore, it is no surprise that the organizational rules that "have ruled" organizational behavior so long are ruthlessly being hauled into the light and reexamined.

Certainty 2: Collaborative forms are the next organizational form and the competencies to design and execute them effectively are key leadership criteria. Declining interaction costs, interdependent supply chains, increased complexity of managing transactional costs—all of the things that result from our three-way billing—create a highly dynamic, highly uncertain business climate. As the result of this meeting, there is, as we cannot proclaim loudly enough, a *collaborative imperative*—an imperative of structure, process, talent, leadership—because a *company that collaborates has more dynamic potential than a vertically integrated firm.* Why? Because collaboration is employed specifically to create aggressive responses to the uncertainty of market shifts and injects market governance into the value creation process.

Collaborations are inherently more dynamic than vertically integrated firms. Why? Because their underlying business rationale or context is to respond more aggressively to the *uncertainty* of market shifts and thereby to be more *market-like* than a vertically integrated firm. They are correspondingly more risky as well. Which is why focusing on tactics to make them more likely to succeed becomes so important. This is a continuing theme of this chapter. Understanding the collaborative DNA that drives them is critical to making collaborations more effective. Recognizing that there are different types of collaborations, the forms and underlying bases of which differ, becomes equally critical. And, not to beat the drum of the semantic stack too much, also critical is understanding how walking up and across the semantic stack becomes a central tactic to effectively exploit collaborations and strategically select appropriate collaborative forms and guide their evolution into others.

As we've explored earlier through the Collaborative Landscape, there are different forms of collaboration that evolve, mutate, or die as firms cope with how best to deploy scarce value-creating resources. The Collaborative Landscape initially depicted in Chapter Two suggests a means to characterize these different collaborative types, and the semantic stack identified some of the operational areas where collaborating organizations need to come together. In short, different collaborations exploit different parts of the semantic stack, and depending on the particular collaborative form, there are defined sets of strategic and tactical options both to enhance the effectiveness of and evolve that particular form. Understanding the collaborative DNA that drives collaboration is critical to making collaborations more effective as well as helping you stay ahead of the always running competitive Red Queen.

This chapter explores implications from the perspective of key *elements* of an organization: its people, process, and overall structure. The next chapter explores collaborative implications from the perspectives of how to more effectively identify, celebrate, and use knowledge assets and technology investments. Our structure in this and the next chapters is similar: We'll discuss some observations then identify what we believe to be actionable implications of them.

SOME OBSERVATIONS AND IMPLICATIONS FROM THE FIELD

Starting with the Observations: Emergent Behaviors

How we frame an issue impacts how others understand it; they may not agree with the framing, but at least the discussion has a set of boundaries within which to have a discussion. As we stated in the first chapter, *how* we talk about collaboration, or how we frame collaborative issues, highlights particular issues and downplays others based on *what* we believe the salient points to be about the emerging collaborative imperative and the steps to take advantage of it. This is why we started the book with the quotes about "making sense." Making sense requires more than simply providing a series of anecdotes and stories from the field. Making sense requires exposing the structures, behaviors, or what we keep referring to as the collaborative DNA underlying collaborative dynamics and their differing forms. We continue this exploration of collaborative forms. As before, we use the dynamic characteristics of the Collaborative Landscape and the process of walking up and across the semantic stack to characterize different types of collaborative forms and tactics to increase their effectiveness, starting with observations to frame the issues, and then isolating specific implications and recommended actions to transform *making sense* into *taking action*. It is only the space that is different here: We focus on the organizational implications—on the people, the processes, and organizational structure to both create and exploit the collaborative shifts that are occurring.

Observation 1: Power to the People! The Rise of Free Agency

We hinted at a major shift in organizational behavior earlier as we discussed the role of knowledge and the challenges organizations have of keeping it relevant in a world that requires ever-increasing specialization. Actually, there is a bifurcation happening. As knowledge becomes increasingly specialized and thereby costly to cross-pollinate, much less coordinate across widening pools of expertise, there is an equally critical need that requires knowledge and capabilities to *perform* that coordination. Enter the *conceptualist*—an awkward word for a critical role—a person who can survey the breadth of knowledge and expertise within and across organizations and connect them in new and useful ways. Specialized knowledge is a centrifugal force pulling apart, or less prosaically, crashing through organizational boundaries to seek similar deep pools of dispersed expertise.

We're witnessing a reconsideration of the requisite skills critical for top leadership. It is no longer enough to have been an expert in any particular functional area and to have risen as a result of consistent performance over time. Rather, communication and conceptual capabilities, and the ability to discern broad patterns in both strategic outlines and operational details are the increasingly critical skills of an exceptional leader.[11] The points? First, there are broad implications in terms of the types of educational support and training we provide our employees with commensurate implications on appropriate career paths. Aspirations and support to become a middle manager responsible for coordinating people, processes, and products within organizational boundaries, in general, remains a relic of yesterday's organization. The centrifugal forces of knowledge specialization and conceptual alignment are far too great, demanding a fresh look at career tracks and training within an organization. While a critical topic, this issue is one we highlight but need to explore elsewhere.

It is the second point that is more relevant to our focus at hand: The role and position of knowledge and of the knowledge worker in organizations are having significant implications on organizational structures and processes. Let's take a closer look at this assertion. Work, defined as an organized set of activities to accomplish some task, has always required knowledge, and hence knowledge workers. Fabricators, farmers, sales directors, and investment bankers all require capabilities of planning, organizing, discerning patterns of behavior, and having skills to drive these capabilities into tangible and productive activities. Thus, the many reports we see of *brain, not brawn* as the basis of the knowledge economy and how the percentage of service workers is growing proportionately to those of so-called *laboring* workers are perhaps of interest but misleading. We need to go a bit deeper to understand the characteristics of so-called *knowledge work* as opposed to merely asserting its existence. What characterizes the so-called *knowledge worker* is that the manipulation of symbols is the means of production, or equivalently, that the value produced consists of intellectual property (IP) rather than anything physical. An example of this might be an equity trader who never sees the underlying asset of her trade, but only its *collection* as a set of monetized and *virtual* assets as depicted and codified into spreadsheets. It is this manipulation of *symbols* and underlying executable tools and applications that comprise the domain of the knowledge worker. It is this type of knowledge worker and knowledge that is shifting the rules of organizational behavior.

There are a number of characteristics shifting the nature of work and tearing down their walls to accommodate what Daniel Pink calls the "ingredients of a free agent nation."[12]

The first ingredient is what Pink calls the end of "economic adolescence." A tight compact once existed between an organization and its employees: an employee offered loyalty and, in return, the company offered security. This "loyalty-for-security compact" formed the foundation for organizational structures. These structures could be easily explained by the need to minimize transactions and communications costs and thereby lead to a stable vertically integrated firm. However, IBM in the early 1990s, Boeing in the late 1990s, and increasingly Japanese banks in the early 2000s broke this compact when they began slashing their workforce by tens and hundreds of thousands of workers. A symbolic compact was violated. And the notion of lifetime corporate loyalty was gone.

The second ingredient is "technology." Technology here, to characterize it broadly, performs two roles. One role stems from its transformational capability to codify tacit knowledge into an executable form that can be scaled subsequently to many people. Codifying (or coding) knowledge and ideas into software products and applications is the starkest example of this type of transformational capability. A second role stems from its distribution capability that has an inverse relationship between communications reach and cost: The more bandwidth we have and mechanisms to communicate, the cheaper it becomes to do so. The upshot: Capabilities exist to take the knowledge someone has, codify it into some form (process, software, product), and then sell and disseminate it broadly.

The third ingredient is what Pink refers to as "prosperity." Pink's point is that long-term prosperity and ever-increasing standards of affluence have allowed people to think of work as a way not merely to make money, but to make meaningful choices and commitments regarding the type of work they want to pursue. There are simply more choices that can be made given the range that exists and the financial "bed" in which we find ourselves.

The fourth ingredient is "the shrinking half-life of organizations."[13] This is analogous to the half-life of knowledge that we discuss in Chapter Five. As Pink puts it, "start-up companies can form in a matter of weeks . . . and they can disappear just as quickly. In other words, the half-life of nearly every organization is shrinking." Netscape is a clear example of this ingredient. Formed in 1994, Netscape went public and by 1999, it was subsumed into AOL. "Life span: Four years. Half-life: Two years." As Pink facetiously but appropriately asks, "Was Netscape a company—or was it really a project?"[14] In the same spirit, we pose a Zen-like question: Does the distinction really matter?

A fifth ingredient is our distributed workforce. The tragedy of 9/11 certainly accelerated the trend toward distributing organizational assets—both locations and people—but the trend has been well established for a while. Since 1999, the International Telework Association and Council (ITAC) has conducted an annual survey of the U.S. remote workforce. In 2001, according to the ITAC report, there were "approximately 28 million Americans who are teleworkers work at home, at a telework center or satellite office, work on the road, or some combination."[15] Along with this domestic distributed workforce, there is increased emphasis by technology organizations of many major corporations to perform at least some portion of their technology work overseas, typically using technology companies in India, China, or Russia.[16]

These ingredients paint a picture of our shifting workforce:

- *The fastest growing group in America and every other developed country are knowledge workers.* They now account for a full third of the American workforce, outnumbering factory workers two to one. In approximately 20 years, based on U.S. Bureau of Labor Statistics, they are likely to make up close to two-fifths of the workforce of all rich countries.[17]

■ *The Peter-Out Principle supplants the Peter Principle.* The Peter Principle held that people would rise through the ranks of an organization until they reached their level of incompetence. The Peter-Out Principle holds that people will move up the ranks of an organization until they stop having fun.[18] Because of the economic base in which knowledge workers tend to find themselves, and the inherently distributed pool of deep expertise, talented people tend to walk out of organizations where they are no longer challenged or inspired, often to become free agents or subcontractors.

■ *The nature of loyalty shifts.* Loyalty used to be clearly defined within the boundaries of your working group. This vertical loyalty underlies the organization-employee compact. But think of your own situation: To what degree are you truly loyal to your organization as opposed to your colleagues with whom you work and/or others in other organizations who share your expertise? What is aggressively emerging is a horizontal loyalty to colleagues, alliances, affiliations, associations, friends, and families that can help individuals deepen, expand, and continuously enrich the value that they have—their knowledge.

The crux: a remixing of these ingredients has created a new and more challenging social contract between organizations and employees. Collaborative ventures add complexity by mixing in relationships with other organizations. Combining respective challenging social contracts into any collaborative form creates yet another mixture of uncertainty and potentially a very combustible interaction. Yet there is one thing of which we can be certain: The value of harnessing this knowledge and of figuring out how to do so within collaborative forms will simulate the excitement and agility of the market. Later in this chapter, we discuss specific implications and recommendations of how to manage this emerging social contract, with respect to harnessing knowledge and incentives to effect effective collaborative ventures. For now, we continue our observations.

Observation 2: Process Trumps Applications

What brings down organizational walls? Joshua blowing his horn with the Israelites at Jericho might be one of the first recorded instances, but closer to home, we've already discussed how the Red Queen batters the walls;

with the Red Queen taking organizational form, the characteristics of the changing workforce are shaking the foundations of organizational walls. John Barlow, one of the evangelists of the Internet as a transformative force (and once a drummer for the Grateful Dead), put it beautifully once. "Information wants to be free," he proclaimed, "free of organizational boundaries and any specific attempts to control it."

So, too, does knowledge. Knowledge, in classic economic terms, is nonconsumable (meaning that the more you use it, the more there is to use) and nonrevocable (meaning that once someone has it, it cannot be taken away). Any attempts to control information or knowledge will simply not succeed. The owners of that information and knowledge can walk out the door. The transaction and marginal costs of internalizing and attempting to control all relevant information and knowledge that underlie critical business processes are simply too great. We'll explore the implications of this later. For now, it's enough merely to highlight this particular horn blast shaking organizational walls—the "boundarylessness" of knowledge.

Another blast from the horn comes from the business processes that comprise organizational behavior. Part of this blast draws on lessons of B2B—the business-to-business promise of the past 10 years built on enabling technologies and, especially in recent years, the Internet. Yet another sound blast comes from a reconceptualization of what business processes really are. The function of business processes has never changed; they have always been organized sets of activities to deliver value to customers. However, things get in the way of this crystalline focus of business processes: namely, organizational growth. As we have all witnessed and many of us experience every day, as organizations grow, or mature, their processes mutate away from a relentless focus on delivering customer value to include sets of activities to maintain organizational momentum—keeping the organization alive. The vertically integrated firm requires a great deal of maintenance, and compounded by a business unit focus that subdivides a company into geographical or functional units, nearly as much energy can be spent managing the firm as delivering value to customers. Returning to the customer-focused premise of business processes scrape some of the barnacles off organizational activities. It certainly raises some dramatic implications for organizational design and behaviors. Combined with the enabling Internet technologies, returning to the essence of business processes certainly provides another powerful blast to tumble down organizational walls. We'll extend these observations about both B2B and the return-to-the-process-essence perspectives. Later in this chapter, we isolate specific implications and tactical steps from these observations.

THE B2B OBSERVATIONS   With the benefit of hindsight, we can characterize several generations of B2B activities in the Internet age. The first focused on becoming an online market maker. The business rationale was simple: Set up joint online environments that match up buyers and sellers and collect fees based on the brokering of the parties. Many of us recall the dazzling number of B2B *e-marketplaces* in the mid- to late-1990s. There were more than a thousand of such e-marketplaces ranging from lumber to steel to paper to banking products. The business rationale of this first generation was weak. Large organizations did not need the brokerage role performed by this initial generation; organizations were sufficiently large to garner sufficient attention from suppliers. Small organizations continued to struggle to leverage their multiple connections into sustainable complementary revenue streams. As a result, the first generation of e-marketplaces did poorly, and few survived.

The second generation of B2B e-marketplaces centered on ensuring sufficient liquidity across trading partners. Large companies became the gravitational centers of collaborative online ventures with their current suppliers and competitors. Arguably the most famous, and earliest, of such entities is Covisint, the marketplace founded by General Motors, Ford, and DaimlerChrysler (Big Three) that we discussed in Chapter Two. Dozens of such liquidity-based marketplaces erupted across industries from forest products (ForestExpress) to airlines (Aero Exchange International), to foreign exchange products (Atriax, Fxall, FX Connect). A McKinsey consulting study characterizes this second B2B generation as follows: "For the most part, these marketplaces were initially designed to reduce bid-ask spreads and to bring down transaction costs by matching buyers with suppliers and enabling suppliers to trade with one another—the very kinds of procurement-based benefit that would be expected of an efficient marketplace. Unfortunately, the consortia . . . have generally failed to realize the hopes of their founders."[19]

Two major difficulties bedeviled the first two B2B marketplace generations. Again, back to McKinsey: "For starters, they [did not] focus on improving business processes to unlock additional value, since [they] typically focused on the 'classical' benefits of an efficient marketplace: the ability to clear the market quickly and cheaply and to aggregate the orders of buyers and thus achieve lower prices."[20] Second, these marketplaces were intended to transform the procurement and practices of entire industries. But neither procurement nor sales decisions are made by industries; people within individual companies make them, and they were threatened. For example, in the case of Covisint, the Big Three automakers set out to create an auto parts exchange in a concentrated industry hobbled by mistrust between the buyers and sellers. After a decade of being bludgeoned for price concessions by automakers, suppliers were in no hurry to participate in the Big Three's exchange.[21]

These marketplaces could only provide real economic value to the participants by achieving sufficient volume and scale, which in turn required marketplace participants to fully integrate their systems and buying process with the marketplace and within their respective organizations. They have been slow to do so given the expenditure required and given their concerns that the benefit from trading in the marketplace will not be sufficiently large. Taking it straight back to the principles we outlined in Chapter Two, each participant in such a marketplace forms a collaboration with the marketplace. For that to work, there needs to be value created (in this case, increased access to customers and increased scale), manageable risk (in this case, primarily the cost of integrating and the potential of losing customers to other participants in the marketplace), and sharing of the reward (revenue). If the focus of the marketplace is minimizing spread, it's tough to make the case for the collaboration absent truly massive scale and minimal risk, neither of which has been offered by extant marketplaces.

This leads us back to a central theme of this book: These first two B2B marketplace generations stumbled because of their focus. Merely offering a venue for trading—for transactions—is far from sufficient. What is absolutely critical is to establish a common process underlying that venue. And underlying that common process is the common sharing of information. And underlying that common sharing of information is shared semantics regarding how that sharing will be created, sustained, and evolved over time. We're back to walking up and across the semantic stack. We can use the semantic stack as a tool to assess the type of marketplace being established and its sustainability over time. We can also use it to characterize the emerging third generation of B2B marketplaces.

Back to the McKinsey study: "Indeed . . . the real gains from online B2B commerce will come not from trading but from better access to and the sharing of information. Consortia, stand-alone marketplaces, and perhaps other, as yet undeveloped online structures hold out the promise of facilitating every kind of collaboration between buyers and sellers. Such marketplaces might even help buyers and sellers partially integrate their operations, allowing them to improve their supply chains, to work jointly on product designs, and the like."[22] So this third B2B generation focuses on what was lacking before: Standardization of information, process, applications, and other elements of the stack to thereby create effective means of transacting.

There are a wide variety of marketplaces and forms of collaboration as we've discussed before and will again. Yet, they all share a common feature: Shared semantics at some level of the semantic stack. *Determining what level of the stack is their focus determines the range of agility, transactional focus, and market impact, and hence the viability of the collaboration and the success of the marketplace.* For example, Microsoft's marketplace objective is to create a locked-in economic web. Some of its brilliance stems from creating this web through partnerships and alliances with its independent software vendor and system integration communities. Microsoft's lock-in position stems from these companies standardizing on Microsoft's Windows operating software to create Windows-based software applications and related services. Microsoft's focus is the application and architecture layer of the semantic stack. Its battle is thus to make this layer of the stack the standard and thereby the default for application development and use—this creates enormous sunk value for its collaborators, which Microsoft uses as its "table stakes" for each collaborative transaction. In this case, Microsoft's community is as strong is it is large. The larger the user base is, the stronger the particular community and Microsoft's resultant marketplace power. Codifying and thereby controlling the standards—the language—of the architecture and application layer of the semantic stack is Microsoft's primary objective. Microsoft will, and is beginning, to evolve up the stack, but its core collaborative strategy and community stems from its being the technical platform of choice—in terms of our model, it stems from the rock solid codification of several layers of the semantic stack.

For a different example, Charles Schwab's community of outside financial advisors rests on a different layer of the semantic stack. It seeks not to control any technical platform. Certainly, it has a technical platform—Schwab's OneSource transaction platform. But the power of the community lies in the business process layer of the semantic stack that also entails the information content controlled by those business processes. What draws people to Schwab's marketplace community is access "to the knowledge and expertise . . . [to be derived] . . . ; realizing efficiencies from the network member's sharing of assets; and third, in the case of a service business like Schwab, obtaining privileged access to [Schwab's] own customers."[23] In this case, the marketplace is based on facilitating the exchange of information; the transaction platform is secondary. In terms of the collaboration model, Schwab, like Microsoft, is bringing huge value to its side of the collaboration.

Starkly different models of collaborative community-making emerge from comparing these two companies in terms of their focus and competitive implications. Microsoft and Charles Schwab are obviously extremely different companies. However, rather than seeing what is dissimilar, we suggest understanding what is similar about them. This similarity stems from their respective brilliant strategies (and operational steps) to codify different parts of the semantic stack to build value that flows to any of their collaborators. Yes, they focus on different parts of the stack. Yes, there are extremely different collaboration and competitive implications depending on what part of the stack they codify (as we sketched earlier and focused on in Chapter Two). Yes, their strategic "room to move" is framed by what level of the stack they attack. Yet, the key observation here is that market power and effective collaboration stems from focusing on how to codify some level of the stack, and the processes of doing so.

The generalized observations are:

- The third generation of B2B marketplaces have learned that different models are required for different kinds of transactions and objectives. A marketplace set up to purchase a commodity, for example, might value the liquidity, the transparency, and the price orientation. By contrast, a person making highly specialized purchases might value the customization offered.

- Knowing what kind of marketplace to set up requires a deep understanding of their cost structures (the risk component of the collaboration), a strategic focus on one or more particular layers of the semantic stack (the value component of the collaboration), and crystal clear understanding of the rewards to be gained.

- Understanding that there are strategic implications of what layer to focus on and around which to base your collaborative venture becomes an important a priori consideration of any collaborative venture.

In sum, the B2B battle is, at its essence, a battle over semantics. A key reason the first two B2B marketplace generations stumbled was that their business model focus was based on transactions and brokering relationships. But there was no underlying process or set of shared semantics to enable transactional integrity and leverage, hence the collaboration model broke down somewhere (possibly in multiple places) in the value, risk, and reward dimensions of the collaboration. This is precisely what we're seeing now in the third B2B generation. What does this mean? Namely, that B2B marketplaces will begin to increase their business and competitive viability as processes (at any and all levels of the semantic stack) become the focus of attention, are codified, and are well executed. With what implication? Namely another onslaught on and from within organizational walls with the same result: Breaking them down.

Let's explore this process onslaught from a complementary perspective: the business process.

THE BUSINESS PROCESS   Michael Hammer, a leading management thinker, continues to champion the critical role of business processes as the necessary organizing unit for competitive organizations. As organizational boundaries become increasingly porous and sclerotic, and business structures increasingly become a hindrance to competitive relevance, we have a need and obligation to return to the essence around which organizations are formed: Delivering value to the customer thereby creating shareholder value.

Hammer's most recent book, *The Agenda*, proclaims the need for companies to follow a needed agenda for competitive relevance. This agenda is premised upon focusing on the customer and ensuring the creation of relevant value to the customer through business processes. We borrow Hammer's definition of a business process as "an organized group of related activities that together create a result of value to customers."[24] Any activity that does not directly provide such value needs to be eliminated or outsourced. This is a recurring theme for those of us who endured the reengineering programs of the mid-1980s and 1990s. There are some important different implications now, however, ones enabled by the Internet technologies and extant communications capabilities. So, while many of the arguments remain similar, the reality is that the time is now to capitalize on them.

Business processes, focused on customers, cut across traditional organizational structures. Organizations are commonly structured around functional or geographic lines. Yet, Morgan Stanley's customer base extends globally, as does ABB's, CitiGroup's, Nestlé's, General Electric's, and any number of global companies. Of course, they have customers all over the globe but, more importantly for a discussion on customer-centric process, any one customer might touch any and all parts of their organization anywhere and everywhere across the globe. The very idea of handing off such a customer between business units or geographies, much less presenting a different process to that customer based on an organization's internal structure, is anathema. The customer-centric approach has been the hot business and vendor topic for the past 10 years. It remains one of the highest projected spending priorities for the next several years.[25] The premises of customer relationship management (CRM) are seductively simple: Recognize your customer as one customer across your organization, and provide differential service to that customer based on his or her level of contributing profitability, value, and revenue. The operational reality of realizing these premises is a far cry from the slick demos, the integrated software, and the proclamations to become a customer-centric organization. Sure, there have been successes and lessons to be learned from them. But these lessons are the same as those from taking an overall process perspective as well.

Again, the lesson is the devilishly difficult capability of having a process orientation. Processes cut across regions, across functional units, across the very structure of a vertically integrated firm. They must. The road from raw materials whether hard (iron, steel) or soft (symbolic/pure brain) to customer services is facilitated or enabled across many organizations and technologies. Yet, the actual mechanics of this conversion from materials into customer value is of little if any importance to the customer. What matters is the *use* of the service, not its transformation. So, the easier the transformation, the more transparent its execution, the greater the value that is provided to the customer and derived from the companies involved in engendering that value.

As you might suspect, there is more to the story than just preaching the benefits of a process approach. As we will explore in Chapter Five, the true value of an organization, beyond what is listed on its balance sheet, lies in its intellectual property and intellectual assets. For evidence of this, simply observe the court battles over patents and the emerging trend around companies seeking to harvest and unlock the value of their assets.[26]

Processes form the base of business activities. They are codifications of what people know and how they perform their activities. Processes, then, are instantiations of intellectual property and thus another form of intellectual asset. Business effectiveness is only as good as its processes. As Hammer writes, "flawlessly designed and executed processes are what create superior products, exceptional marketing programs, flawless fulfillment, successful sales efforts, and enviable customer satisfaction. Today a company's processes, even more than its short-lived products, define its identity and shape its opportunities for growth and diversification."[27]

So, what does this mean? It means that again we have another horn blast heralding a threat to organizational boundaries. No doubt, partitioning a business unit structure (into functional and/or geographical units) provides means of ensuring control of manageable units. But by so doing, we destroy the power of the company as an integrated whole.[28] Someone's customer is another person's supplier who is, in turn another person's customer, and on and on the recursive business relationships go. From a customer's perspective, what is important is the delivery of some service or product that is of value. Yet, complexity, inefficiency, and unnecessary costs are added to that service or product when the process for delivering that value travels through multiple, rigid organizational boundaries, often with their own unique way of conducting business. Much as information wants to be free, processes will be free as well, free of tight organizational cossets. And over time, the opportunistic market will deliver plenty of hungry efficient competitors to the niche left open by your inefficient processes. The Red Queen runs, and she runs relentlessly.

Collaborations are accelerating this time line. Marketplaces and collaborative ventures exploit inefficiencies; they attack margin opportunities, wringing out inefficiencies and thereby creating new value, then moving on. Much process inefficiency exists based on how organizations are designed and run. Modifying existing processes much less creating new processes to support identified market opportunities is often difficult—requiring careful negotiations regarding role clarity, metrics, and just plain turf. Add these complexities on top of a nascent market idea and the cost and therefore the risk of supporting anything new goes up and thereby becomes difficult as well as a challenge to the status quo. This is a blueprint for a roadblock to innovation. Again, we can use the Coase model of assessing the transactions and coordination costs to get a snapshot of the economic viability of the degree to which a company is willing to take on the additional risk of new ventures. Bad business processes increase the internal cost of innovation, which suggests that market approaches to innovation become attractive. Enter collaboration—to minimize the risk and to maximize the agility to respond to the specific opportunity. A collaboration can be designed around a new and particular value proposition with a new set of processes to support them. This gives them a degree of process engineering flexibility to be designed from the perspective of the customer. The Red Queen always runs and the road she runs on is made of business processes. Our traditional organizational structure cannot stop the dismantling of its walls.

So far, we've presented the logic of how processes will crumble organizational walls, but more than logic is at play here. Many organizations have already begun creating cross-organizational processes or, at least, begun the process of creating a process-based organization. Enterprise resource planning (ERP) systems have been a Trojan Horse for creating a more process-oriented focus for years.

ERP systems focus on creating a system of record and consistent processes for financial, human resource, and accounting activities. The ERP business need was clear: Create more streamlined and consistent processes across our activities that add cost to our operation but little if any value to customers. The financial need was equally clear: Reduce the spending on coordinating these nonvalue-added activities. While the implementations tend to be costly (in the tens if not hundreds of millions of dollars), benefits have included both expenditure reductions in back-office or administrative activities as well as, more importantly for our case, a needed breaking down of the walls internally into a consistent set of ERP-driven processes. As the administrative processes become standardized internally, organizations often experience a collective epiphany, realizing that standardized processes can bring increased value on the customer-facing and supplier-facing side. Major ERP vendors, such as Oracle, SAP, PeopleSoft, and increasingly Siebel, are heralding the benefits of the next ERP wave. ERP II recognizes that a customer order triggers a set of activities that end when payment is booked and a customer receives what was ordered. So, a question emerges: What really is the difference between the initial ERP focus (on finance) and the CRM focus on selling and servicing to the customer? Financing, selling, and service are part of the same process; so, too, should be the applications underlying that process. Hence the refocusing of the ERP vendors into a new competitive space, and hence yet another pressure to break through any particular organizational wall.

Next we'll explore even more pressures and emerging dynamics of cross-organizational processes and resulting collaborative forms. We'll spend more time drilling into one of the most aggressive process-oriented trends—that of outsourcing and managed services. For now, however, let's review where we've been so we can go forward.

We've explained the logic of how business processes, especially when combined with a customer-centric focus—put pressure on our traditional organizational forms. We've explored how that pressure leads to collaborative ventures as well as how different collaborative types exploit different types of processes to make them effective. We've argued that *the emerging battleground is over business semantics—critical to create the standardized processes essential to drive effective cross-organizational and collaborative ventures*. While it is difficult to create such codified processes, what is becoming easier is knowing where and how to manipulate that battlefield.

As more and more companies take a process perspective, recognizing and acknowledging that the processes they create are inherently cross-organizational, a network effect will kick in: the more people who build on and participate in codified processes, the more who will build on and participate in those codified processes. We've seen that tautology before: It is the basis of the network effect—or, if you prefer, *positive economies* or the *virtuous circle*. Whatever the term used, the choice remains the same: Move toward a process focus or die. The Red Queen always runs. The question is: Where are you in the race? Before answering that question, let's further explore an extension to the process issue—one of great immediacy to many—the issue of outsourcing and managed services.

Collaborative Options Supporting Core and Noncore Processes

THE OFFSHORE DEVELOPMENT MODEL   Many organizations experimented with changing business models and technologies over the past several years. The crashing of the economy put a quick end to many of these experiments and drove organizations to confront some difficult questions such as: What are we really good at? What are our core strengths? How do we take advantage of them? Answers to these questions have led to an aggressive focus on which activities contribute to shareholder value and which do not. The former comprises *core* activities—those that contributed directly to shareholder value. The latter comprises *context* or, as Geoffrey Moore calls them, "hygiene" activities—activities that need to be performed but do not directly contribute to shareholder value.[29] This tightening of focus is not new; nor is the continual reassessment of which activities contribute to shareholder value and which do not. Such reassessment is part of effective management 101. However, there has been tremendous, almost frenetic, focus on what to do with hygiene activities, with outsourcing and managed services seemingly the answer du jour. We'll briefly explore what's pushing the accelerator pedal around outsourcing and describe some its implications for collaborative activities over the next couple of years.

Goldman Sachs has flatly stated that outsourcing and the offshore development model are two of the most important trends for the IT services sector and large clients.[30] These two activities, outsourcing and offshore development, are complementary: They both involve partitioning business activities and performing them outside of specific organizational walls.[31] There are few large firms that are not pursuing either outsourcing or offshore development. The business imperative for them both is compelling: *The reduction of operating and/or capital expenditures.* While there have been and will continue to be concerns about the security of offshore and outsourcing activities to India and Southeast Asia, the economic possibilities continue to outweigh the current political risks. Goldman Sachs estimates that the offshore industry has grown approximately 40 percent to 50 percent year-after-year the past several years and is projected to maintain a more than respectable 20 percent to 30 percent year-after-year growth the next several years. This growth rate will increase as security concerns abate and/or the economic downturn flattens with a return to large project expenditures from the telecommunications, financial services, and high technology industries.

A wide range of application development, from administrative through mission-critical applications, is being considered for offshore development. The economic pricing disparity between onshore and offshore development is too great and the quality disparity too small to not consider it. As we would expect given what we have seen in this book, effective use of offshore development requires shared processes and communication standards, but, as we noted in Chapter Three, the IT industry is fairly well progressed in codifying standards and processes for how to manage the cross-pond and different cultural expectations of on- and offshore software implementation (even if most organizations still face the challenge of implementing those standards and processes). Many offshore development activities are performed as classic fee-for-service arrangements, much as any organization would contract with any service provider, such as a systems integrator or business advisory firm, but increasingly, there are collaborative arrangements being established on the basis of locking in and committing to sharing both the value and collaborative risk.

It is instructive to explore the business strategies and supporting collaborative arrangements of some large outsourcing firms as windows into subsequent offshore partnering models. Some of the largest offshore development firms are Indian, including Tata Consulting Services, InfoSys, and Wipro. Their value proposition to major organizations lies in their low cost but highly skilled application of development resources, coupled to a robust and rigorous software development process rooted in industry standards and best practices.

Beginning in 1987, the Software Engineering Institute (SEI) of Carnegie Mellon University had the task of creating and promulgating a model for assessing and expressing the maturity of a software organization. First released in 1989, the Capability Maturity Model for Software (CMM) is based on an industry-recognized set of best practices for software development. The CMM defines five levels of maturity, with CMM Level 5 representing a highly mature organization. A CMM Level 5 organization executes software process in what SEI terms "optimizing" fashion—that is, they have a repeatable, managed process for which they collect statistics on effectiveness, and use those statistics to improve the process.

The top offshore firms have deeply codified development processes that are assessed at CMM Level 5. This has two benefits. First, many of the organizations using offshore firms do not have a mature software process, but recognize the value of a good process, so the offshore firm adds value to the transaction simply by having such a process and making it available. Second, the CMM rating provides mitigation (or at least the appearance of mitigation) of the substantial risks involved in creating software, including the risk of cost overruns, missed schedules, and incorrect functionality. One of the reasons the Indian offshore development model has been so effective is its commitment to the CMM. Such standards facilitate communications and clarify expectations. They are critical to fostering shared communications, guiding effective actions and managing distributed risk. Such is the first part of the Indian offshore model.

The second part deals with their business extension model. A low-cost, high-quality development option for regional and global corporations is an important piece to the offshore development model, but only the first step. A second important step is to gain positioning for higher value and higher margin development business. This is just beginning. It is no surprise that while more and more global corporations are attempting to reduce their application development costs by relying on lower cost talent, the providers of the lower cost talent are leveraging that same low cost talent to move up the services chain to provide higher margin capabilities. As a result, we are currently witnessing, and can expect to see continuing, partnerships between offshore and onshore service providers as they recognize the mutual value they bring to providing services to regional and global organizations, providing anyshore services for solution development. The onshore providers bring project management skills, industry expertise, and client relationship; the offshore providers bring a low-rate base but highly skilled development talents. Together, that is a powerful collaborative venture. The Global Straight Through Processing Association (GSTPA) was provided services through a teaming arrangement of BearingPoint and Tata Consulting Services who brought precisely the mix of skill sets listed above. The effectiveness of this teaming arrangement for GSTPA led to similar teaming efforts that, in turn, have led to a collaborative structure between the two organizations. So much for the premise.

As in any competitively collaborative situation, the Red Queen runs; and she runs relentlessly. The competitive base always shifts; what was once tacit knowledge becomes codified and what is today's advantage becomes tomorrow's commodity service. Much as the Tata Consulting Services (TCS) of the world have eaten away at the margins and taken significant business away from the more traditional system integrators, they are finding their margins being eaten away by competitors in China, Indonesia, Mexico, Pakistan, Russia, and other places. Following the established pattern, the TCSs of the world recognize that they need to continue to push up the value and margins of their service offering, and that is what they are doing. The collaborative arrangements between offshore companies and onshore providers like the BearingPoint/TCS collaboration for GSTPA are time-bound, relevant only insofar as mutual opportunities of value creation exist, mutual reward is produced, and respective risk is managed. Taking the case of a BearingPoint collaborating with TCS, there is a large, reasonably stable market for teams that can provide full service from concept through launch and operation. Therefore, it should not be surprising that, as we write this, TCS is building organic capabilities to move up the chain, while BearingPoint is building organic capabilities to provide low-cost, high-quality programming services down the chain (if this is surprising, go back to Chapter One, and start over!). These collaborations are great examples of the temporal reality of Jericho Zone collaborations. In Jericho Zone collaborations, the dynamic toward the other areas of the Collaborative Landscape is intense and the pressures to cannibalize respective positions are great. The Red Queen runs; and she runs relentlessly. There's no point in fighting her. Rather, like BearingPoint and TCS in this example, run with her and make other people's lives interesting.

MANAGED SERVICES: PUTTING THE PRESSURE ON OR TAKING IT OFF?   The last several years have witnessed plummeting communications costs, the widespread standardization of technical interfaces, an aggressively widening gap between the cost of service providers globally, and a relentless focus on how to shed operational costs to boost margins. One result has been an almost giddy rise in attention paid to offloading operational processes via managed services and IT outsourcing. The arguments *are* compelling: Global access to vendors, reduced technology costs, significant operating cost differentials, moving capital expenditures off books, increased use of English as the global business language, and so on. Paralleling these operational drivers, strategic considerations have pushed companies to at least consider seriously the offloading of some of their business processes. The managed services business provides a means for companies to maintain a laser focus on core competencies, while reaping the benefits of outsourcing.

The extension of many of the traditional outsourcing firms, such as EDS and CSC, into the once clearly distinguished system integration space, of the systems integrators, such as Accenture, CGEY, and BearingPoint, into the managed services space, or of hardware and software vendors such as IBM and CompaqHP into both spaces merely shows the frenetically shifting competitive space around managed services offerings.

What drives the economics of managed services? Simply stated: Standardized economies driven by standardized business processes and technology to support them. This is why we saw the first wave of outsourcing around nondifferentiating operating processes such as administrative functions, card processing, contract manufacturing, call center activities, fulfillment, logistics management, and IT maintenance. The focus here was on leveraging economies of scale. Yet, an intriguing question is: Scale of what?

The first phase, until the middle to late 1990s, focused on pooling nondifferentiated service offerings. The excitement around application service providers (ASPs) was based on hosting similar software and application capabilities. The business justification was based on removing these operational processes from a company's books at a dramatically reduced cost because of the economies of scale the ASP could provide. But immediately, the flavor of managed services started to shift giving rise to its second, and current phase, from the late 1990s through early 2001.

Customization undermines economies of scale. The ASP business model was in essence a one-size-fits-all model, and the demand for customization spelled trouble for the ASP marketplace in the late 1990s. The demand came from two directions. The first came from the side of the service providers: to win business in the still early but widely competitive marketplace, managed service providers offered more and more services merely to differentiate themselves and thereby to win business. From the side of the buyer, increasing concerns were raised about the integrity and access to their data. On top of these Janus-faced pressures, the measurable success and reduced cost of such arrangements accelerated movements to outsource even more business operations. These pressures on managed services providers were great, resulting in two significant implications. First, customization pressures cut deeply into their already razor-thin margins. The result: Many providers were forced out of business, which fueled a frenzy of consolidation activity among outsourcing and managed services players. Second, the very basis of the managed services offerings shifted.

Phase one managed services offerings were based on economies of scale—on nondifferentiated offerings. Phase two offerings started to pick up more of the core business processes that supported increasing differentiation and operational customizations. From the late 1990s through today, major managed services are offered around such critical, but well understood processes such as mortgage processing, financial and human resource functions, and some core banking processes. As this applications shift occurred, so too did the skill-base required of the managed services provider. Economies of *skill* became necessary to complement the economies of *scale*. Knowledge of the business processes to be managed became as important as knowledge of the host platforms. This is why the focus of today has moved more to managed services, rather than merely the outsourcing of applications. This shift has had significant implications on who are best positioned competitively to offer those services. It is no surprise that the major managed services providers combine large-scale hardware and traditional outsourcing facilities with systems integration and business consulting capabilities. IBM began this shift over 10 years ago as a hardware and software company into the services domain. EDS, in 2002, announced a major reorganization accelerating their global focus around industry-specific knowledge and consulting services to complement their huge installed base of outsourced and managed services offerings. Unisys has been undergoing a powerful but quiet transformation into this extended managed services/BPO/management consulting space. Accenture is migrating their business model heavily around managed services with service extensions. This shift explains why so many systems integrators are moving aggressively into the managed services space: to build on their considerable business expertise thereby leveraging themselves into the managed services business.

This trend will only accelerate. We will see increasingly specialized managed services offerings around increasingly focused business processes. Human resource and finance functions remain relatively standardized across companies. Of course there are differing requirements and intensive security procedures needed to manage their production and access, but there is enough regularity that economies of scale are achievable. What differs in the third managed services phase is the focus on business processes that tip the scale from economies of scale toward economies of skill. Increasingly, attention is shifting to what are known as vertical BPOs—or, industry-specific business process operations. Examples might be real-estate management services, credit risk management, global logistics and procurement, or financial advisory services. Managing these processes requires more business acumen and industry-specific experience than managing those of IT outsourcing (phase one) or functional processes, such as finance or human resources (phase two). For these different phases and process focuses, the margins are different, although, again, only for a while.

As more and more of the routine operational processes become automated, codified, and standardized, they become easier and cheaper to outsource. This puts pressure on the managed service providers to drive more volume to get greater economies as the margins of these commoditized offerings shrink. Hence, competitive pressures on the managed services to continually seek higher margins in the more customized and domain-specific processes—those areas and processes that are still early in the codification process. Thus, the managed services story of shifting from managing *economies of scale* to those of *economies of skill* with corresponding shifts of who the competitive players are finds itself reflected, again, in the story of walking up and across the semantic stack as the Red Queen continues to run. And on and on we go.

What observations do we take away from this brief walk through managed services? At the broadest level, managed services creates yet additional pressures for the breakdown of traditional organizational walls. Managed services have become merely another operational option for companies. This option involves establishing collaborative ventures to host, to manage, to maintain, and to upgrade ever increasingly critical elements of a company. The objectives? To take capital costs off the balance sheet, reduce operating expenses, and refocus scarce managerial talent and capital on what is core to the business.

Yet, a competitive irony and a caution emerge from this headlong rush toward managed services. First, the irony: Handing off operational processes to collaborative managed services partners accelerates the competitive dynamic in any industry. As managed service businesses focus on more business domain processes, they become more industry savvy and the blurring between operational support and value-added industry knowledge becomes more prevalent. Higher margins result from less codified activities. As managed service providers move more to exploit economies of skill as much as economies of scale, they have the potential to challenge their customers in their own businesses. New business opportunities will result as managed services organizations leverage the knowledge and information acquired from their portfolio of business services. For example, providers of financial call center services could go into the business of financial advisory services; a pure-play credit card processor could create an information-based direct-marketing business and challenge the role of any in-house marketing department; a logistics provider that provides visibility into warehouse and transportation networks could become a freight-forwarder consolidator. And all of these shifts are happening. Thus, short term, the expediency of operating costs requires serious consideration of collaborative managed services opportunities. Longer term implications, however, warrant serious consideration regarding potential competitive impacts.

This irony forms a common thread throughout this book and any collaborative venture. We have said before that collaborations are inherently risky. These examples put a very real face on that statement. A collaboration is created to innovate or to exploit a high-margin opportunity, and its effectiveness is driven by how well the resulting shared value is balanced by the management of distributed risk. A major risk is that when you collaborate, you are putting some portion of your core value into the hands of your collaboration partner, which puts your partner in the position of being able to compete with you. But that's okay, because you are not standing still, and by the time your partner matures into a threat, the market has moved on. The rise of the major managed services firms results from recognizing the opportunities extant in exploiting both economies of scale and of skills. This bundling of both scale and skill economies puts pressure on the types of contracts and relationships established between the managed service providers and their customers as increasingly domain-specific business processes become managed by the outsourcers. The dynamic driving this is clear: Walking up and across the semantic stack as not only the network and applications become standardized, but the underlying semantics of how to model, automate, and support *business processes* become more prevalent:

- *The observation.* Organizational walls are coming down and managed services accelerate the pressures to bring them down—first by function and now by domain-rich, business-specific processes.

- *The scenario.* An increasing array of collaborative ventures will emerge as managed services providers begin to become differentiated not by their scale, but by their domain or industry-specific capabilities—their domain skills.

- *The implication.* There will be significant structural realignments to support these collaborative ventures—a topic of our next section.

Observation 3: Organizational Hollowing

Organizations aren't going away any time soon. Much as the claim of the paperless office has been met with ever more reams of paper at the office photocopier, proclamations of the demise of the vertically integrated firm are also premature. Yet, their form will not remain the same. There is, as business schools teach, an inexorable maturation process of industry structure. The Hirschorn Index, a measure of industry concentration, indicates a market efficient correlation between market size and organizational structure. Other business-laden terms and analytics could be provided as well to explain the dynamics and structure of any evolving marketplace. But more simply, the observation is that natural industry evolution leads to the establishment of organizational whales, dolphins, and minnows—very large organizations, moderate sized ones, and very small ones. Relevant size is determined by the degree to which transactions and coordination costs are internalized. What is particularly intriguing right now is that the organizational size trends tend toward whales and minnows: The dolphins are being decimated.

Thomas Malone and Robert Laubacher, in a *Harvard Business Review* article, argued that "when it is cheaper to conduct transactions internally, within the bounds of a corporation, organizations grow larger, but when it is cheaper to conduct them externally, with independent entities in the open market, organizations stay small or shrink."[32] As communications and coordination costs fall, the ease of collaborating tends to make it possible to engage with many small businesses. As Ronald Coase adds, "and the existence of many small businesses enables some firms to get bigger. But the middle-sized organizations will have to leap to one side of the divide or the other, lest they slip into the abyss as the fault line widens."[33]

We described earlier in this chapter the changing nature of the workforce and its juggernaut-like impact shaking organizational walls. One implication of this, along with some of the other wall-breaking forces we've described, is the emergence of a variety of new business organizations, as much project as structurally based. The model of the movie business— where people, production houses, and finance companies come together to produce a movie and then disperse only to come together in some other configuration with other parties for subsequent movies—is as likely a characterization of emerging organizational styles as not.

We will continue to see the natural evolution into three or four mammoth-sized organizations as any industry matures. Yet, the core tenets of the bigger-is-best as the preeminent path to competitive success are being questioned. Owning the largest market share, integrating vertically to capture incremental value, controlling key channels, and driving economies of scale are no longer the only strategic roads to long-term effectiveness, at least not in uncertain times. A McKinsey study recently pointed out that this bigger-is-best bias is not necessarily successful if success is measured in terms of creating shareholder value. This study noted that while the Fortune 100 companies, ranked by revenue, generated over half of the revenues in their sample, they generated only 6 percent of the shareholder value creation. "By comparison, companies too small to make the Fortune 500 generated only 10 percent of the revenues, but two-thirds of the shareholder value. In other words, small companies created more than 65 times as much shareholder value relative to their size."[34] Without doubt, much of this disparity stemmed from the halcyon days of the eBusiness bubble. Nevertheless, the observations and lessons to be drawn are directionally correct if not accurately precise. And the lesson? *Plummeting interaction costs driven down by ever-emerging computing and communications technologies and the increasingly codified set of behaviors easing cross-organizational behaviors, make it possible for companies to specialize as never before and capitalize on fast-moving and high-margin collaborations.*

Stepping back, we've made some observations about pressures on our organizational walls—from the perspective of our workforce, business processes, and organizational structure. The next section builds on these observations and identifies resulting implications to engender effective collaborations.

Some Implications of What This Means to You

Implication 1: It's about Process—and the Battle over Semantics

Process can be both a noun and a verb. As a noun, it refers to the business processes that make up our organizational activities. As a verb, it refers to a set of actions to accomplish an objective. For our purposes, it refers to the process—the steps, the activities—of walking up and across the semantic stack. There are two specific implications of this combined noun and verb process characterization.

FIRST IMPLICATION: VIEW YOUR BUSINESS FROM A PROCESS NOT AN ORGANIZATIONAL PERSPECTIVE   Business processes inherently cut across organizations. Processes are sets of activities that result in some value for customers. From a customer's perspective, the fact that one company's supply chain is another company's demand chain is irrelevant to his or her needs, expectations, and fulfillment. Customers only care about organizational walls in a negative sense: the displeasure they experience when they bump up against one. Consequently, organizing around processes naturally puts pressure on how the majority of organizations are structured. This chapter has observed pressures on organizational walls and commensurate challenges to the vertically integrated organizational structure. Internet technologies are often cited as key reasons for the plummeting communications and coordination costs that make internalizing these costs less important than before. Many examples exist that point out the agility and increased performance of companies collaborating around processes and across organizational boundaries.

But the Internet technologies are merely one of the enablers. What we've seen again and again is that the issue is not any particular technology or sets of standards, but the existence and energy toward creating such codified behaviors along the layers in the semantic stack. Agility stems from shared mental models: Great friends, great marriages, and great partnerships rest on knowing what the others will do without explicitly saying it. They, analogously, finish each other's sentences. How? By sharing models of how to act or, rephrasing this point using our framework, by codifying tacit, unstructured, information, knowledge, and technology into sets of executable, standardized processes—by walking up and across the semantic stack.

Thus, the battle over business process is a battle over semantics. Thirty years ago, and as we discussed in Chapter Three, there was no Internet. There were only competing network connectivity protocols and one national telecommunications monopoly that dictated how phone calls would be made, not data and applications passed. Codifying the Internet protocols (IP) into a set of network connectivity and communications standards launched the Internet transformation—the results of which we are merely beginning to experience. This codification was, at its essence, a process of building common grammar tools thereby getting people to talk and understand the same language for data transmission. With what result? Enabling technology and competitive energy to begin focusing on the next layer up the semantic stack: architectural platforms and applications.

On and on we walk up and across the semantic stack—with commensurate shifts in organizational structure and competitive pressures. Standardizing on TCP/IP as the network standard contributed directly to a major disruption of most of the large computer vendors (except Sun, who had bet on TCP/IP). The existence of a standard protocol outside their walls drove them to break through the wall or become irrelevant. Cisco emerged as the new market leader around this layer of the semantic stack. The brilliance of Cisco's business model lay in recognizing that its competitive power depended upon continuously extending the design of the network, rather than manufacturing, distributing, or building out the networks. It recognized that the battlefield of owning what was in the ground, while important, was one that would, over time, become commoditized and face fast-shrinking margins. The high-margin battlefield was in identifying, harvesting, and codifying new ways of exploiting and designing the network. The strategic challenge would center on acquiring the tacit design knowledge that would, over time, be built or codified into subsequent evolutions of network connectivity applications. As we saw before, as any particular stack becomes codified, not only does the nature of competition shift (in terms of who the competitors are and the bases of their competition), but also the lines between the stacks begin to blur. So, again, using Cisco as an example, Cisco remains one of the leaders of network design. Even so, however, Cisco has been forced to move up and compete into the architectural and applications part of the semantic stack. Why? Because absent some disruptive technology in the connectivity part of the stack, gaining larger margins depends on moving up the stack building on the marketplace standards established on a lower part of the stack.

Now the battlefield has shifted aggressively to focus on business processes. Tremendous energy is being spent on figuring out how to create a process-oriented organization. Much of this energy rests on attempts, from different directions, to create common languages, methods, and tools to create standards for processes—a critical precondition for creating a process-oriented organization. Six Sigma, a current hot focus, is one burst of energy creating standardized methods of identifying, controlling, and optimizing business processes. Business process monitoring (BPM) tools are another source of focus. The return-to-basics campaign of many organizations is yet another focus, paralleling the relentless focus on cost rationalizations and cutting. Building on industry-specific data and process models, and the increasing use of standardized methods of representing, modeling, and coding business processes into software components are yet others. Here's a suggestion: Pull out your list of tools, hot consulting topics, and projects and ask a simple question: What do many of these have in common? Here's a suggested answer: Many of these activities attempt to put order to, shape to, and a common basis for communicating then executing common processes with implications of how to do so across organizational walls.

Summing Up   The first implication here is the critical need to view your business from a process as well as an organizational perspective. Collaborations are created to create value propositions that inherently cannot be effectively or quickly exploited from within any one organization: The risks are too great; the coordination and transactional costs too high. Why is that? Because collaborations are built around processes that are, by their very nature, different from the existing organizational process. What are the lessons for how to take advantage of this situation? First, recognize the criticality of processes and the central role they perform in designing effective collaborative ventures; and second, recognize that the competitive battlefield is really over semantics, about walking up and across the semantic stack.

Second Implication: Build Your Semantics and Your Interfaces into Them   Forrester Research, an industry analysis firm, summarizes the changing role of processes. They label this shift, "process trumps apps." Within this awkward term lies an elegant characterization of the shift. "Linking together the apps that make up the value chain . . . [a] process is a lot like stringing beads on a necklace. One bead—or one app—is noteworthy, but it's not until they all are connected that the necklace—or business process—becomes valuable."[35] No doubt many of the beads can be and are being forged through many of the efforts listed earlier. But how might we accelerate creating a valuable string of beads? Where and how would we start to build our semantics—the needed fuel for the acceleration? Answers to these questions are suggested in this section.

Business processes are made up of activities hooked together to serve some purpose. There are two parts of this sentence that we need to take apart to answer the questions just listed. First, let's focus on *activities*. Activities are actions we perform to do something. People create activities. Activities create outputs. Over time, these activities and their outputs may become codified into software, tools, methods, training materials, or commonly accepted ways of doing things. What is critical, here, is that their origin lies in people. This may be obvious. But it may also be so obvious that it often becomes hidden or ignored, so we need to highlight it once again.

In the beginning, intones the Old Testament, was the "Word." Among other things, the Word begat speech which begat shared actions which begat common rules of behavior which begat community forming, and on and on the begattings continue. Analogously, in the beginning of business processes was the "Person." And the Person, from knowledge and experience, begat specific ways of doing activities that begat shared ways of conducting businesses, and on and on. Processes, then, are no more than the codification of the tacit knowledge—that resides in a person of knowledge and experience—into common ways of conducting business. Why was this biblical excursion needed? To emphasize the similarity in role and source performed by words and business processes.

Processes begin with people and the knowledge these people accumulate through experience over time. Processes are the embodiment of this accumulated knowledge. Harvesting this knowledge and expressing it in a way that is reusable, across companies, and across collaborations is arguably the most important determinant of processes and, not surprisingly, collaborative success. Making this knowledge meaningful and shared is the focus of codifying semantics. *Saying that the battlefield is over semantics means that the battlefield is over making sense of the business rules and the knowledge inherent in any instantiated business process.*

The second part of the sentence to explore is the phrase *hooked together.* Business processes are composed of islands of knowledge hooked together to create activities of value. This hooking together can in general occur across functional areas and, as we've pointed out again and again, should be able to cross organizations. Here's the challenge: Often, these islands, because they exist in different functional areas of different organizations, or were created at different times and almost certainly from the tacit knowledge in the heads of different people, mean different things and/or are housed in different applications and systems. Which means that stringing them together like pearls on a string is not trivial. Just take a simple process like opening a customer account: At the simplest level, this process involves targeting a customer, acquiring or signing up a customer, integrating the customer data into systems of record (or establishing the account), profiling the customer for service and cross-selling opportunities, and communicating back that the account has been established. More detailed steps exist behind each of these high-level activities. Many of these high-level steps, much less the more detailed ones, require different data from different systems supported by different parts of an organization or organizations, with differing pressures, time lines, operating procedures, metrics, and governance guidance. In one major global financial services organization, there are no fewer than nine internal systems, each a system of record for client account data within some unit of the organization, each with its own rules for administration, mapping clients to accounts, and so on; as long as a business process stays within the domain of one of these nine systems, there is no ambiguity, but as soon as it crosses boundaries, it is time to get out the data thesaurus.

This is something many of us contend with daily. Data exists in different systems within an organization. Having a consistent data model within an organization is rare; having a consistent one across organizations is even rarer. The same goes with characterization of even what type of data *should* be consistent, much less the data model or process to support it. What *is* a customer? Is it an account? A phone number? A social security number? A link to nine systems worth of data? What is an account? What is a customer profile? Who and how should we communicate with a customer? How often? How do you characterize a supplier? What is the core element of a business process? How do you even model a business process?

And on and on into the labyrinth of process elements, data structures, and organizational boundaries—that is as complex as human thought itself (which is not surprising since humans constructed these organizational processes before the distinction between tacit and codified even made sense to talk about). Tying together our morass of data or process elements into something that is consistent and useful is a challenge—if not impossible, then at least expensive and time consuming. Middleware, enterprise application integration (EAI), and ERP suites that purport to enable consistent business processes drawing on disparate data sources, elements, and applications can help provide connectivity between the applications and databases within and across organizations, but do not help resolve the real semantic differences that exist among those systems and databases and the businesses that they support.

Yet, hooking together process elements is precisely what we do every day. That's what business processes do, but we do so on a small scale in ways unique to our specific organization. Multiply these activities by the dozens if not hundreds of processes a company has and multiply that number by the number of companies there are, and it's no wonder that the complexity of process integration and functional silos leaves systems integrators and consulting firms with enormous revenue targets and business executives with migraines.

So, what do we do and how do we do it?

1. Recognize that processes are composed of these meaningful units that need to be hooked together—across functional areas and organizational walls.

2. Recognize that these units are *meaningful* and can be valuable in and of themselves. Identifying, valuing, and potentially harvesting them becomes a critical focus for leadership to realize incremental value of the assets they already possess. These assets comprise the real value of our organizations. In Chapter Five, we explore the increasing recognition of these assets and steps many are taking to monetize and leverage them more aggressively. They are also the raw materials for creating effective collaborative ventures.

3. Building on the first two points, take the lessons from system integration that we discussed in Chapter Three: Create abstractions of these meaningful units that admit different instantiations for different organizations, and set about the task of getting agreement on the abstraction—that is, codify the meaningful units and their underlying processes.

These three points are critical to help you walk up and down the semantic stack. Building abstractions of and interfaces into disparate data, and applications, and networks is key to codifying them and making them executable and thereby scalable. Middleware, EAI, ERP, and related technologies are focused on creating interfaces. Other SI tools, such as eXtensible Markup Language (XML), XML schemas, and metadata tools and repositories are focused on creating abstractions. Yet, again, building these interfaces is costly. In Chapter Six, we discuss the emerging battles to create such technical and architectural (semantic) standards and the implications on organizations of these battles. We also provide scenarios in terms of how and where this battleground will shift over the next couple of years; the battlefield over applications and architectural standards is fairly clearly defined, even if the armistice remains years away.

The battlefield over business process standards, however, is not clearly defined. Yet the challenge and the next tactical steps are clear: Build the abstractions of the processes and the data, and interfaces into these processes—into the domain or industry relevant knowledge—that get the codification process started. This is what we mean by *identify the process, celebrate the semantics, and build the interfaces.* To date, building the interfaces has been difficult and expensive—even within the technical part of the stack where things are relatively well defined. What hope is there for doing the same within the business process part of the stack—where things are inherently, messier, diffuse, fragmented, and more dependent on tacit knowledge?

Hope springs from clarity and clarity from lessons learned. Clarity we have from a perspective of the dynamic of walking up and across the semantic stack as an explanatory tool for competitive and collaborative activities drawn from the lessons learned from system integration. And lessons we have from using that tool and culling relevant operational implications of previous and current attempts to walk up and across the stack provided in this chapter.

Hope also rests on pragmatic understanding of how to use the lessons and refocus efforts to take advantage of the new understanding we hopefully are providing. It rests, then—we'll say it again—on creating useful abstractions of the business process and its data, and of using those abstractions to build interfaces into process elements from which agreement, in the form of standards, will emerge, collaborations form, and competitive positioning shift. An emerging technology also offers a simple yet elegant tool to accelerate the building of these interfaces. It is a technology that is also blurring both the conceptual and pragmatic distinction between the application and business process of the semantic stack. We'll explore this technology and recommend specific steps to direct it toward harnessing some of the key assets in your company—your business processes.

WEB SERVICES: LET A THOUSAND INTERFACES BLOOM   Web services, as Ted Schadler of Forrester Research puts it, "is a bad name for a very good idea."[36] The idea is simple: Add functionality to the Internet that lets applications discover and interact with one another in an industry-standard way. This will encourage the creation of thousands and thousands of interfaces into data, applications, and devices—all of which can be connected to create business processes across organizations and functional areas. Web services, as we discussed in some detail in Chapter Three, defines a mechanism for exchanging information (XML), a protocol for applications to communicate (Simple Object Access Protocol or SOAP), a way to describe the inputs and outputs for a service (Web Services Description Language or WSDL, so you can figure out what a service does without having to read a manual or contact the developer), a place to stash the WSDL descriptions (Universal Description, Discovery, and Integration or UDDI) and a way to reference things on the Internet so you have names to use for everything (Universal Resource Indicator, or URI). These technologies define nothing more than the way that you plug into Web services—for example, Ethernet jacks, electrical outlets, software modules, business applications. Ted Schadler continues, "what you plug into the interface is up to you: lamp, radio, or washing machine;" finance information, banking transaction reports, or credit risk assessments. The content, the device, and the application you access is immaterial to Web service standards (though very relevant to the Web services that you create or use).

Conceptually, think of Web services as an Internet analog to EAI: Where EAI software is used to provide connectivity standards among a set of applications that use the same EAI software, Web services provides connectivity *across* organizations through the ubiquitous Internet and IP protocols. So, Web services *equal* Internet (not enterprise) middleware. Its as simple as that—with profound effects. Figure 4.1 depicts how Web services sit on top of well-codified Internet protocols.

Business processes inherently extend across organizational walls and functional areas. Web services define a way to encapsulate "stuff" that can be delivered across Internet protocols and understood by any application on the Internet. Web services can thereby deliver this stuff easily across organizational walls and functional areas. This is why exploiting Web services becomes so important and how Web services will in turn be in the frontlines of the battle of codifying business processes. As Schadler continues, "the truth about Web services is that companies and individuals will use Internet middleware to unlock vast stores of data and to link and relate unconnected apps, services, devices, and even actuators. The impact will be bottom-up, cumulative, and ultimately pervasive as developers use simple tools to build new software networks. SOAP, and WSDL

FIGURE 4.1   WEB SERVICES: CODIFYING APPLICATION INTERACTION

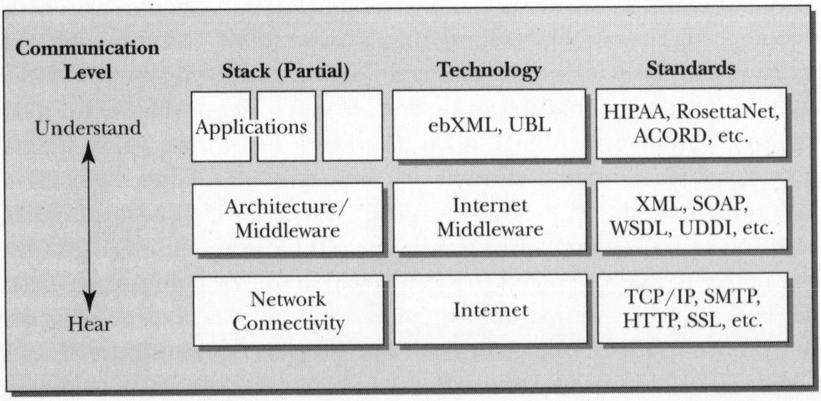

Communication Level	Stack (Partial)	Technology	Standards
Understand	Applications	ebXML, UBL	HIPAA, RosettaNet, ACORD, etc.
	Architecture/ Middleware	Internet Middleware	XML, SOAP, WSDL, UDDI, etc.
Hear	Network Connectivity	Internet	TCP/IP, SMTP, HTTP, SSL, etc.

will make applications available to any other application, any place and anytime."[37]

This is fine as far as it goes. Given a tool set like Web services, the battle will ultimately turn on the ability to create business process abstractions that are meaningful to reasonably sized subsets of the Internet population, and get widespread agreement to use those abstractions. There is hope in this regard, as XML, the *lingua franca* of Web services, has served as a rallying point for creating and disseminating a variety of industry-specific vocabularies, including among others the Research Information Exchange Markup Language (RIXML) for investment and financial research, Security Assertion Markup Language (SAML) for exchanging authorization and authentication information, and eBusiness Markup Language (ebXML) to enable global use of electronic business information. XML-based shared vocabularies and the ubiquitous nature of an Internet-based programming resource opens the door to codification. Think about this a minute. Unlike EAI, traditional middleware, and ERP, which traps integration methods inside proprietary networks, Web services messages travel over the Internet (or private intranet or partner extranet). This means that any application, data, or business process element enabled for Web services can be accessed by *any* other authorized Web service—regardless of its location. The resulting pressures on organizational walls will be great; they'll just keep tumbling down.

The classic virtuous circle will result from the increasing use of Web services. Again, back to Schadler, "the cumulative effect of adding hundreds of SOAP interfaces that publish information to which millions of SOAP clients can subscribe is dramatic. The combination of simple interface tools, untapped value, and existing Internet wiring will lead firms and individuals to create new software networks that raise employee productivity, streamline trading relationships, empower consumers, and control the physical world."[38] The enthusiasm here is palpable, if a little over the top. Web services have a way to go before they change the world as we know it, but their elegant design principles coupled with the brute force of ubiquitous availability will definitely lead to significant implications:

1. Standards and simple tools will continue to drive connection costs toward zero. Once built, any application can tap the interface and thus be pulled, called, and used by anyone using a standard message set.

2. The impact on system integrators who tend to focus on unlocking the value *within* organizational walls will be tremendous as interface skill-sets shift and the costs of large-scale integration shrink since

interface design becomes the focus of cross-enterprise integration. System integrators will have to retool themselves to accommodate the shifting skill-requirements as integration becomes a function of Web services assembly and aggregation as much as intracompany integration.

3. The competitive requirements to unleash data stores from locked-in CRM or ERP systems will force these software vendors to SOAP-enable their applications thereby creating a fluidity of data unlike anything we've so far experienced. So-called UDDI yellow pages or Web services directories are being created where firms go to find and start using published Web services.

4. The business model underlying Web services will accelerate momentum toward managed services businesses and those aggressively in position to take advantage of them now, and will shift organizations from thinking in terms of engineering to thinking in terms of consuming services. Web services will change the economics for the software industry. Shifts will occur from licensing of software to subscriptions for web services as well as revenue sharing of them. Why? Because Web services are encapsulated elements of value (data, business processes, analytics) available to anyone who calls them. These services could result from the combination of multiple elements from differing companies. This will require Web service-based billing software to break apart components of a service to thereby assign revenue to the contributing parties. This shift away from bundled to service-based software has significant impacts on how companies engage with their software and service providers. It will also have implications on how companies design and fund their services-based architectures, as we discuss in Chapter Six.

5. More and more applications, devices, and sensors will become part of the Web service network. The classic network tautology fits here again: As more corporate applications are exposed through Web services, more Web services' consumers will be built and hence more will be used. In addition, more and more devices will be hooked up to receive and accommodate these services thereby creating even more demand for yet more Web services. Around and around we go.

What does all this mean, from a collaborative perspective? Simply that we're beginning to codify business processes; we are beginning to move across the semantic stack from tacit to more standardized knowledge. We described earlier some of the efforts at creating a common language to express business processes. Web services are a key tool in operationalizing that expression. The boundaries between the application and business process stack are blurring. Such blurring is an inevitable part of walking up and across the semantic stack. As the lower level of the stack becomes codified, the nature of competition shifts and the layer of the stack adjacent becomes a key battlefield. Why? Because the more codified the layer is, the lower the margin. This is why Web services are potentially such a disruptive technology: It offers tools to harvest and extend the rich tacit knowledge embedded inside organizational data and processes; it offers an entry-point into the high-margin domain of industry-specific business processes and underlying knowledge. As more and more services are created, and as its supporting business directories expand, it is likely that domain-specific directories will be established. Therefore, those who excel in managing business processes and understand the business value of those processes will be well positioned to use Web services to further harvest the value of those processes.

Further implications include the following:

- *Web services will accelerate collaborations.* Directories or listings of Web services will expand geometrically. They are easy and cost effective to create. As more are created, firms will go online and automatically engage new partners in real-time to exploit—and to partner to exploit—these services.

- *Organizational bifurcations accelerate.* The transaction and coordination costs will continue to go down thereby accelerating the division between the industry whales and minnows. The value ports enabled by Web services means that firms will not have to build new capabilities. Instead, they can plug into external services thereby, again, fueling more energy toward collaborative ventures and continuing to build their expertise. The pressure will be on the organizational dolphins who face a classic organizational problem of being too small for the big things but too big for the small ones.

- *New business models emerge.* We've already described how Web services will accelerate the managed services business. We've also described some implications on service providers (systems integrators and consulting firms) and challenges to existing software pricing models. Yet, an emerging opportunity also arises. The existence of thousands and thousands of Web services raises a conundrum of how to combine them (much less find them) in a way that is pragmatically and rapidly useful. It is one thing to know that there exists thousands of possible services from which to draw. The UDDI and yellow page directories are repositories to house and communicate what SOAP enabled services exist. But this is very different from being able to discern which ones are most applicable and having done that, how to assemble them quickly for use. The result: New business offerings and transaction services will emerge to perform those roles. For example, Avantrust, a new business spun-off by AIG, the insurance giant, and co-developed by Unisys Corporation and BearingPoint, was established in 2001 to provide new risk products and services for Internet transactions. It is a short step to extend these risk products to underwrite the liability and guarantee provisions of networked Web services. Some of the B2B software vendors, like BEA and CapeClear, are working to develop Web service assembly tools. Some emerging vendors are starting to design Web service billing capabilities to appropriately partition and allocate value to the Web service providers. Even some of the software gorillas, like Siebel Systems, Oracle, and SAP, have begun to unbundle their application suites into Web services accessible components. Companies with premier business process or manufacturing knowledge, like Procter & Gamble, General Electric, and even those systems integrators with deep industry knowledge, are likely to create and brand domain specific UDDI repositories. They thus will begin to generate complementary revenue sources from their deep knowledge as well as accelerate collaborations with others to further drive this trend.

■ Distinctions between managed services, software vendors, and systems integrators continue to blur.

As a result, two strategic activities to reposition yourself as a key collaborative partner within the next few years are: First, identifying what types of domain knowledge to extract and abstract, and what parts of your business processes to expose through Web services; and, second, creating a domain-specific UDDI directory to establish brand presence, derive complementary revenue, and serve as a foundation for collaborative ventures. Collaborative forms differ based on business objectives and focus. More importantly, for our purposes, much of their differences stems from what layer of the semantic stack they use as the foundation for the collaboration. Microsoft's networked model is based, as we've seen earlier, on creating *the* technical platform for use and thereby precluding the use of any other technical platform or standard for creating business applications. They attacked and well codified the architectural/platform layer of the stack. Charles Schwab, in striking contrast, created a collaborative community on top of its OneSource application environment. Schwab's objective was to create an environment for sharing and distributing financial information, not locking in people around technical tools or platforms. Both collaborative models work. Yet, both have very different implications on the types of collaboration engendered and resulting competition. Both also differ in terms of what kinds of processes, and Web services, to prioritize.

Understanding that such distinctions have strategic implications should help you prioritize where and how to begin exploiting Web services. Having said this, however, what is most important is merely to begin creating the abstractions and writing interfaces for your business processes. At the beginning of this section, we used a phrase, "let a thousand interfaces bloom." That is entirely appropriate now. One approach is to build dozens or hundreds of interfaces into your business and functional processes while keeping a strategic perspective on what your business processes are and how to begin to leverage their underlying value more aggressively—from both process and *Last Mile* perspectives. At the very least, you will have mobilized these resources inside your organization and possibly will have taken the initial steps toward an entirely new business. As Ted Schadler points out, while a single Web service is about as interesting as a phone with nobody to call, the network effect of thousands—then millions—of interfaces will be as great as the phone system. Web services will affect every member of the executive team:

- For the CEO, Web services are about *strategy*. Lock in customers with better product and service links; reach new markets by assembling new applications, such as private label services for your channel.

- For the COO, Web services are about *productivity*. Build role-based portals that put information in the hands of employees; improve time-to-market by linking partners into development processes; outsource noncore business services.

- For the CFO, Web services are about *cost replacement*. Cut transaction costs with automated direct procurement; reduce customer service spend with self-service; replace admin staff with self-service interfaces.

- For the CIO, Web services are about *control*. Transform IT functions into technology services; protect against security leaks by governing access to the registry of SOAP interfaces and flow of SOAP messages.

- For the CMO, Web services are about *influence*. Put the corporate brand on SOAP interfaces.[39]

Web services certainly are not manna from heaven. In fact, Web services are one of the emerging technologies whose impact will not be systematically felt for a couple of years. But it is a further pressure on the organizational walls as well as a key accelerator to the process view that acts as a battering ram on those organizational walls.

Implication 2: It's about Carbon Entities: The Battle for People

Digital efficiency does not equate to organizational effectiveness. Automating all processes does not lead to well-run companies. These are competitive myths, touted by consultants and pundits but disastrous in practice. Why are these myths rather than realities? For a simple reason: Processes are nothing but codified sets of activities based on how people perform work. Processes are therefore instantiations of tacit knowledge. At its core, the process battles are ones of ever-continuing attempts to codify as much of that tacit knowledge into reusable and repeatable processes as possible; the competitive battles are ones of ever-continuing attempts to compete around those processes; and the collaborative battles remain ones of ever-continuing attempts to take advantage of new business opportunities—tacit knowledge—in a way that balances mutual value with distributed risk. All of these depend on people—what they know and how they do what they do. So, an underlying issue is: How *do* we capitalize on this knowledge and keep people engaged and challenged?

Earlier in this chapter, we explored how changing dynamics of our workforce are breaking down organizational walls. In our previous social contract of work, the organization offered the individual job security and in return, received organizational loyalty. But changing workforce dynamics have altered the type of loyalty that exists. We're radically shifting from vertical to horizontal loyalty. Vertical loyalty stemmed from being fully committed and tied into your organization and organizational chain of command. Increasingly, however, loyalty is not to the company, but to teams and workgroups, to colleagues and ex-colleagues, to professions and industries, to clients and customers, and to family and friends. Harnessing this horizontal loyalty has several profound implications. These implications all require a mind-set shift in terms of how we understand, then harness, the power of tacit knowledge. We'll list three of these mind-set shifts.

1. *Attempts to control knowledge and people simply won't work.* Pink talks about the Peter-Out Principle where people rise to the level to which they no longer have fun.[40] Once they rise to this level, they will simply take their knowledge and leave. Thus, the risk of intellectual property leakage is a critical and real concern. Collaborations, as we have said again and again, are Janus-faced. They are inherently risky yet offer great opportunities. Being built on exploiting new business propositions and processes yet to be codified, they are inherently based on identifying and exploiting tacit knowledge that cannot be controlled nor yet cost-effectively coordinated or exploited by either of the collaborative parties—hence the business need and rationale for collaboration. Thus, they are inherently dynamic and can be great testing grounds of how not to control but to support, adapt, and encourage tacit knowledge in a distributed environment—all critical tactics underlying this mind-set shift to encourage how we work with our colleagues.

2. *Horizontal loyalty involves having multiple relationships.* Job security is built on those relationships and the value a person can bring to them. Rather than the vertical or linear relationship, horizontal loyalty is diffuse and much more network-based than linearly based. Consequently, understanding how people informally work rather than how their roles are formally defined requires understanding with whom and how they interact—for example, understanding their networks of interactions. Connections and networks form around particular people, particular processes, and particular knowledge. Understanding how to identify and measure how networked and distributed work gets conducted is key to being able to harness its underlying knowledge effectively. Collaborations are effective to the degree that the underlying processes are coordinated. As we have seen, these processes are built on tacit knowledge.

3. *Consequently, "keeping a lid" on collaborative knowledge requires understanding the networked aspects of the work and of the people performing that work.* Gradually, some companies are beginning to understand how to identify, support, and measure the informal networks and collaborative connections that underlie distributed work processes. Becoming

familiar with and then using some of these techniques will be important tools for any effective collaborative venture.[41]

It's easy to say that people are an organization's key asset. We hear the phrase time and time again. We all know that the role people play and how well they do so fundamentally determines the viability of any collaborative venture. Defining the business proposition, assessing the balance between shared gain and distributed risk, ensuring the execution discipline, and the measurement and disbursement of the resultant gains/losses are all functions of underlying business processes and the people who drive them. Consequently, the shibboleth of "power to the people" is good, but not enough. Drilling down to understand the dynamics of the tacit knowledge people possess—of its half-life, of how to feed, nurture, sustain, expand, retain, and distribute it—becomes critical to exploit it effectively in any collaboration. It is because of the criticality of this issue that we devote the next chapter to this topic and explore it, from a number of additional perspectives.

Implication 3: It's about Leadership: The Battle over Core Competencies

We've already stated that collaboration is about process. We've also stated that collaboration is about people. Now we're saying that it's about leadership. Which is it? Much of our argument is based on building a new vocabulary to make sense of collaborative ventures and thereby to see and take advantage of their opportunities more effectively. We're trying to change how we understand collaborations and their underlying drivers and resulting opportunities. Furthermore, we're attempting to provide different perspectives or vantage points into collaborative ventures. From these vantage points, the issues *are* completely framed by what we are looking at—the process or the people perspective. So, each of these perspectives does warrant the usage of being *about* them. Clearly, leadership is an equally important vantage point, required to enable these other perspectives to be viable, so along with collaboration being about process and about people, collaboration is crucially all about leadership. We discuss two specific implications from a leadership perspective.

First: Collaboration is not a thing separate from business or IT strategy, nor some thing isolated from operating considerations and decisions. Instead, collaborations, as we argued in Chapter Two, are an inherent part of any strategic or operational consideration—they are certainly already ubiquitous throughout operational activities. Preferred provider relationships, master service agreements, procurement marketplaces, and outsourcing arrangements are all different collaborative forms central to the operational execution of many companies. The head of strategic procurement at UBS Warburg, one of the world's leading investment banks, described the ubiquity of different collaborations throughout UBS Warburg as the establishment of multiple mini-markets throughout the firm.[42] The proliferation of collaborative activity, and the different forms these activities take, opens up a huge strategic need to understand the different forms, business rationales, and means to drive them consistently and aggressively.

Different collaborations have different characteristics and take different forms. These forms differ in terms of the degree to which they focus on core business processes—the intimacy—and the designed longevity of the collaboration—the dynamism. Collaborations range in duration from short, project-based activities to multiyear contractual arrangements. Each is appropriate, for different purposes. Yet, the dynamics underlying all these forms are similar: The Red Queen runs, continuously putting pressure on margins which, in turn, are determined by the resultant competitive battle on the underlying basis of the collaboration. Clearly understanding what holds together the collaboration is key; clearly, knowing what layer of the semantic stack is the currency enabling the collaboration is key; clearly, recognizing that the type of collaboration and skills to sustain it will differ depending on what semantic layer holds together the collaboration is key; and so too is the recognition that the type of competition will shift as you continue to walk up and across the semantic stack—as the tacit knowledge at the edge of innovation becomes increasingly codified.

The insight to be gained from delineating the type of collaboration and the underlying mechanisms of holding it together is as clean as is its strategic impact profound. If you can easily plug into and out of collaborations, then you have significantly lowered your cost of doing so and thereby broadened your competitive arsenal and agility to respond. Shared semantics—at whatever level—make people more agile. Less needs to be said, less energy expended on attempting to understand what is intended and more on simply getting the job done. This is the simple premise and explanatory principle of the Collaborative Landscape and the semantic stack.

Second, embedding collaborative considerations into your everyday decision-making process requires you to nurture and sustain a new set of skills, and requires a consistent process to assess the type of collaboration appropriate to the strategic opportunity. There are two types of assessments to make: one, identifying the layer(s) of the semantic stack that are involved, and two, assessing the overall readiness to undertake the collaboration. Thus far, we have spent much time discussing the former. In the paragraphs that follow, we'll suggest how to perform the latter. Figure 4.2 shows a Collaborative Readiness Assessment tool. The factors underlying this tool are the ones we've discussed again and again: leadership, process, technology, and people.

This tool can be used to evaluate your company's readiness for a collaborative venture. The scale from 0–5 rates each factor associated with each assessment category:

0 = Haven't considered the issue

1 = Thought about the issue and people have been assigned to develop a plan

2 = Plan is in place, but no action has been taken

3 = Plan is in place and progress is being made on the plan

4 = The plan is operational

5 = Work is complete and the criteria are met

FIGURE 4.2 COLLABORATIVE READINESS ASSESSMENT TOOL

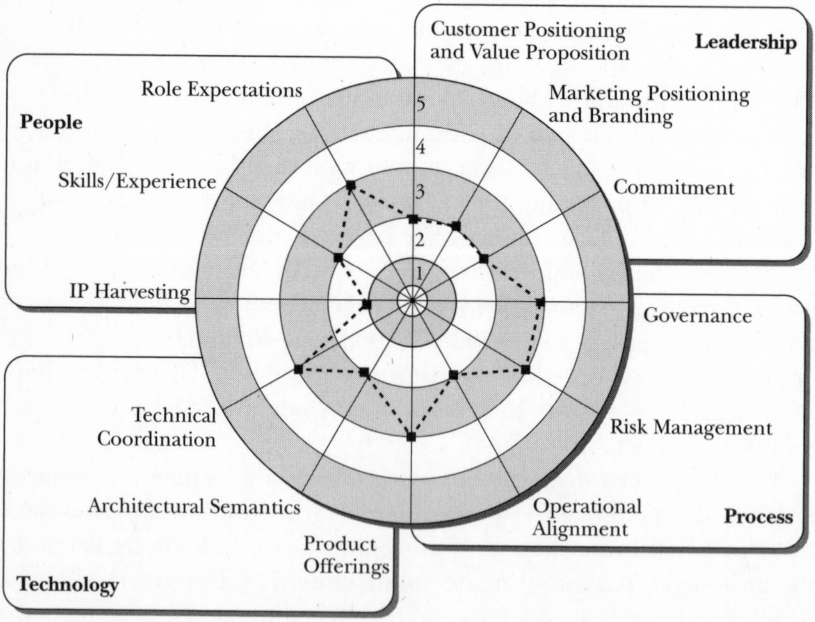

Each of the factors can be scored, the sum of which helps assess your degree of readiness to engage. Comparing the scores of each assessment category provides a quick snapshot of where the effort is being and needs to be spent. Refinements of this assessment tool and its supporting analysis can be made—for example, the factors can be weighted depending on the level of risk or mutual gain to be expected, the amount of core assets being contributed and/or the specific role the company is expected to play.[43] However, at a minimum, a relative balance among these assessment categories is necessary to help minimize the risk and maximize the effectiveness of the collaboration.

Being ready for any collaboration is obviously important. This is where the readiness assessment tool comes in handy. But the real importance, from a leadership perspective, is to be able to identify the type and focus for the collaboration. What becomes particularly critical from a leadership perspective is being able to answer the following questions:

- What is the value proposition of the collaboration—the value to be created?

- How will we share in the reward?

- What are the risks, and how will we manage them?

- What part of the semantic stack will be the organizing principle for the collaboration?

- What is our process for walking up and across the semantic stack, that is, how will we codify the knowledge used in the collaboration?

- What is the migration path of the collaboration—for example, where does it go as the underlying knowledge becomes codified?

- What are the disruptive impacts on the collaborative venture that need to be anticipated prior to its establishment?

- How do we build in a collaborative mind-set and execution discipline throughout the organization—to make it part of the everyday decision making process and an integral part of the company's competitive arsenal?

Again, and as we've stated before, the capability to plug into and out of collaborations quickly lowers the cost of doing so and thereby broadens your competitive arsenal and agility to respond. From a strategic perspective, then, defining the value ports or the codified interfaces into collaborative ventures—and into the different layers of the semantic stack—becomes a critical focus, core competence, and key strategic need for a collaborative focused organization.

SUMMARY: COLLABORATIVE UBIQUITY

Picture a building; say, an office building. Now, ask yourself: What is this building? More than likely, your response will be: A building is a structure that contains people and processes performing some work. This is a start. We might add a few more particulars referring to the foundation and framing; the power system; the communication system; plumbing and heating; doorways and windows; the partitioning into commercial, residential, and mechanical spaces—typical elements of a solid, functional building. Now imagine that we transport this building to a city where extremes in the weather make it difficult (or unpleasant) for people to spend a lot of time outdoors—a city like Minneapolis, Minnesota. Downtown Minneapolis has adapted to its extreme winters by creating a system of elevated walkways, tunnels, and underground common spaces that connect the buildings downtown, so that a pedestrian can get pretty much anywhere without having to go outside. Our building, relocated to Minneapolis, will be the same building, but will sprout some walkways and connect to some tunnels in order to serve its function in its changed environment. The building has a standalone role—an office building—and it also collaborates with the other buildings in an important role as part of the downtown pedestrian transport system. This changes the building's function and its range of possibilities of who enters and participates in it. But it's still basically the same building. That is analogous to what is happening to organizations today.

The organization as we know it is changing significantly. These changes are redefining its function, its role, and its range of competitive possibilities. The organizational adage of bigger is better no longer holds the undisputed title for competitive dominance. The drive to vertically integrate processes and functions to support business objectives has shifted—dramatically. Communications and coordination costs have dropped drastically and the cost equation regarding whether to control or coordinate transactional and coordination costs has shifted. With these shifts, there has been a change in how companies interact. Organizational walls are coming down; collaborative business models are increasingly common. This chapter explored some of the pressures and implications of those pressures on organizational walls. What we're left with is yet more perspective on why collaborations are becoming an integral part of our organizational fabric.

Collaborations are ubiquitous. They take multiple forms and these forms will continue to multiply as they mutate and respond to changing technology and business opportunities. There is no doubt that the roles and structures of organizations have changed. There is equally no doubt that we are just now walking on to an enormous playing field of collaborative venturing, a field of tremendous challenge and opportunity.

We have attempted to paint a Collaborative Landscape, identifying some patterns of different types of collaborations and suggesting some of their underlying dynamics. In this chapter, we focused on collaborations from the vantage of point of an organization: its people, its processes, and its leadership. In the next chapter, we drill into the role and implications of a company's workforce and its people—and more specifically, how a key challenge for effective collaborations stems from the capabilities to identify, harness, and leverage the knowledge that is brought to bear not only for the collaboration but back to the collaborative parties who established the collaboration.

CHAPTER HIGHLIGHTS

The Issue

Breaking down organizational walls has significant implications on the people, the business processes, and the leadership styles of an organization. What are the key implications of instilling collaborations as organizational core competencies?

The Insight

Collaboration, by design and intent, cuts across organizational walls requiring significant agility and shifts to how we understand, support, and nurture leadership and business process capabilities.

What part of the semantic stack serves as the focal point for the collaboration is less important than that the process of codifying tacit knowledge becomes the critical operational challenge and need for sustained collaborative success. Paraphrasing the advice given to

(continued)

Dustin Hoffman in the classic movie, *The Graduate,* "Semantics, it's all about semantics," and the process of identifying, exploiting, and leveraging the semantics of business processes, leadership, and workforce activities.

The Phrases

Collaborative ubiquity; business semantics.

The Implications

Building collaborations as core capabilities has significant implications on our organizational design and leadership challenges, particularly around the semantics of business processes, the battle for people/talent, and instilling collaborative skills as core competencies.

The other fundamental implication is the unmitigated, absolute, and critical need to make collaboration a core organizational and leadership skill.

CHAPTER FIVE

Business Knowledge: Celebrating the Edge and the Crux of Collaboration

Collaborative ventures are inherently risky, and dynamic, from both the perspectives of how they are structured (the internal view) and how they fit within their competitive environment (the external view). Let's explain this working backward—starting from the external view.

Collaborative ventures exist within a market environment that, by its very nature, continually shift the competitive environment of those ventures. The irony here is that the very nature of the competitive marketplace demands the existence of collaborative ventures yet challenges the stability of any particular collaborative structure. This is a key observation of Chapter Four. Within this irony lies a significant risk.

The risk derives less from the nature of collaboration itself than from the continual shifts of business dynamics, disruptive technologies, and changing business models—what Foster and Kaplan characterize as "Creative Destruction."[1] The corresponding challenge stems from the critical need to manage the "creative tension" between capitalizing on specific business opportunities while cannibalizing organizational assets in a manner that ensures that those opportunities remain relevant and competitively viable. Acknowledging, then managing, this *creative tension* is not an option; it is a competitive necessity. Not managing this tension, or managing it poorly or, worse yet, not acknowledging it as a strategic requirement—entails a significant risk of falling behind competitively. The *Red Queen effect,* as it was called in earlier chapters, characterizes the inescapable competitive dynamic whereby companies are forced to run faster and faster merely to keep their relative competitive position. Their relative competitive position *will* change, for the worse, if the tensions between the *here-and-now* and *what-must-we-have-for-tomorrow* are not managed, and managed at the highest level and aggressively. The insightful book, *The Innovators Dilemma,* demonstrates the visceral risk for even the most innovative and market-leading companies when this creative tension is not effectively managed.[2] Companies must figure out how to break the running gait of the Red Queen.

In previous chapters, we defined the *Collaborative Landscape* as a way to characterize collaborative relationships. We further characterized it as a dynamic environment where collaborative ventures inexorably push or mature away from the Jericho Zone as high-margin processes, products, and services become increasingly codified and commoditized and thereby require changes in the types of collaborative ventures to support them and organizational implications to sustain them. The bottom line: There is no rest for the savvy organization. The challenge and resulting opportunity is to continually surf the dynamic wave within the Jericho Zone. This inherent dynamic restlessness is the reality of our business environment, with the Red Queen its prime mover.

We face complementary issues extending this argument to *any* specific collaborative venture: How to reconcile the market dynamics each participating company within a collaborative venture faces with those of the particular collaboration, which itself faces its own set of Red Queen pressures and dynamics. To what degree should the collaborative venture take precedence over the exigencies and pressures faced by its supporting organizations? How do we reconcile these, very possibly, competing pressures? How do we untangle them? Or, at a minimum, how do we even start to untangle them? As we discussed earlier, Jericho Zone collaborations entail higher margins, yet greater risk in terms of assessing their market viability. Why? Because these collaborations focus on the creation of new value propositions and business opportunities.

Collaborations are the pooling of assets and capabilities from different participants, and, as we have seen, they entail risk. In this chapter, we continue to explore aspects of inherent collaborative risks and suggestions on how to manage them. We focus on the people side of the collaboration—on the intellectual assets involved in the establishment and execution of collaborations and on the criticality of managing them tightly to ensure that they are used effectively within the collaboration, and that they are harvested back to participating companies. Yet, risk tends to correlate directly with opportunities. As we've pointed out throughout the book, the types of value propositions and underlying margins differ depending on the types of collaborative ventures established— or in what areas of the collaborative landscape you find yourself. Jericho Zone margins tend to be higher because the battle here is over innovation—of untested value propositions. The value propositions are untested in the sense of pushing the competitive edges, of collaborating over tacit knowledge to innovate through the three-arrow picture, hence the margins, hence the risk, hence the high-value potential, and arguably most importantly, hence the competitive opportunity to outrun the marketplace Red Queen.

This chapter builds on the organizational implications of the previous chapter. It explores the opportunities, risks, and implications of collaborative ventures from the perspective of the *key assets* critical to make any collaborative venture effective—its people. We continue to primarily emphasize the dynamics of the Jericho Zone collaborative ventures for a simple reason: The very nature of Jericho Zone collaborations makes their dynamic and people issues more extreme, and therefore more explicit in terms of lessons to draw on. There is also an inherent dynamic from Jericho Zone collaborations into other forms as they evolve which, again, helps us cull out particular lessons. The dynamic is straightforward: There is and will continue to be an inexorable dynamic from high-margin/low-volume to low-margin/high-volume processes as tacit knowledge/ideas become codified and enabling processes and technologies turn them into commodities. This is the Red Queen argument. In this chapter, we focus on the process, the risks, and the implications of how to harness the tacit—the high-margin—knowledge as it migrates toward the more codified, and leveraged, knowledge. Therefore, focusing on the people implications within the Jericho Zone provides a perspective on how to support the highest margin efforts at the competitive edge.

This chapter makes and explores the implications of the following key arguments:

- The battle over tacit knowledge is critical to achieve competitive positioning.

- The value of this tacit knowledge lives at the edge of an organization as well as of any collaborative venture.

- There are inherent risks in the potential leakage of intellectual property (IP) that must be managed within collaborative ventures to protect your assets.

The bottom line of this discussion is the criticality of making collaboration a key managerial and organizational set of skills within your organization. This overly simplistic summary results in vital but challenging implications regarding how to harness and harvest the tacit knowledge within collaborative ventures.

Much of this chapter discusses the mechanics of how to balance the risks and accelerate the exploitation of collaborative ventures from the perspective of what provides them much of their energy, namely, the tacit knowledge in the heads of the people creating the value. While exploring these mechanics, we identify some lessons, highlight specific implications, and suggest how to address each of these points. As we do so, we suggest some alternative approaches to help manage the distributed risk inherent in collaborative ventures.

THE KNOWLEDGE MODEL

Figure 5.1 shows the framework of a collaborative venture in a slightly more abstract view than we used in Chapter Three. As we've discussed earlier, collaborative ventures are designed to create incremental value beyond a single organization's core capabilities. The reasons for this are straightforward, especially in light of the back-to-basics discussion earlier in the book: *As organizations understand and focus on what they do best, they increasingly recognize the power in mobilizing the core strengths of other organizations to innovate in response to uncertainty—that is, to exploit high-margin opportunities kicked up by the Red Queen as she runs through the landscape.* Such a powerful collaborative venture is, to use a common phrase, more than the sum of its parts. This *moreness* rests on a simple calculation: The marginal value (of the value-bundle) to be created must be greater than the incremental costs of creating it. This statement is simply the application of the arguments made by Coase and Williamson that we discussed in Chapter Two—determining the degree of integrating functions into your organization based on the transactional and communications costs of doing so—applied to organizations in uncertain times. If the costs outweigh the

FIGURE 5.1   A COLLABORATIVE VENTURE

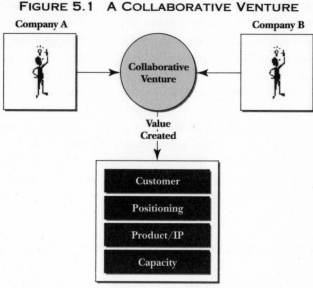

marginal benefit of the value created or the projected revenue potential of the opportunity, then the pragmatic response is, don't do it. Instead, seek partnerships or some form of collaborative venture to realize the potential value that cannot be derived from internalizing the activities yourself. Driving down the costs of innovation—through operating in the Jericho Zone—opens up the field of opportunities that you can pursue.

Extending this obvious point slightly with respect to Figure 5.1, company A and company B each provide capabilities or skills into the collaborative venture that result in the creation of new value for the collaboration. This new value generates shared rewards to companies A and B, typically in the form of revenue created as the value created is rewarded in the marketplace. A and B also expect incrementally to harvest back their share of created value in the form of new knowledge, skills, or capabilities. As we stated before, the value of collaborative ventures stems from enhancing and/or accelerating customer access, market positioning, product/IP, and/or organizational capacity and scale. The relative importance of these four business objectives differs venture by venture. Which of these business objectives—these value-bundle components—takes precedence has significant implications in terms of how the collaboration is set up, executed, and measured.[3] This is no straightforward task. What is straightforward, however, is a general equation for evaluating any particular venture. Again, we simply need to ensure that the value created from the collaborative venture is greater than incremental value that could be created by going it alone from the contributing companies. Or is it really that simple?

Let's add a wrinkle. All collaborative ventures entail transactional set up costs. From these costs, the venture creates incremental value, but many also suffer what we refer to as *leakage*—additional costs in the form of productivity decay, loss of intellectual property, shifting employee loyalties, and so on. So, actually, the evaluation of cost and benefit in a collaboration requires an additional, critical, consideration. If *Value (A)* is the amount of value company A brings to the collaboration, *Value (B)* is the amount of value company B brings to the collaboration, and *Value (collaborative venture)* is the value created in the collaboration, then the collaborative venture only makes sense if:

Value (A) + Value (B) > Value (collaborative venture) + Leakage

Leakage includes things like transactional costs, intellectual property theft or reduction in value over time, customer theft or loss due to brand confusion and most of the risk elements we discussed in Chapter Three. The critical issue is to include the impact of inevitable leakage when evaluating a collaborative venture. Carrying forward the spirit of the Jericho Zone: Given that we need to collaborate effectively and efficiently to cope with the Red Queen, our challenge is to figure out how to control this leakage, converting it from a collaborative loss into a collaborative value. Figuring this out requires understanding the sources and types of leakage and how to manage them.

In Figure 5.2, each company is contributing to, and benefiting from, the collaboration as represented by the two-headed arrows connecting them to the collaborative venture. Their contribution is that part of their core value that they are making available to the venture, often embodied in tacit knowledge via the people involved in the venture. Their benefit— the shared reward in our formulation of a collaborative venture—is the business benefit that accrues from the new value created in the collaborative venture, typically related to revenue. The collaboration also creates innovation—new value—depicted as a value-bundle that emerges from the collaborative venture. This new value is the focus of the discussion on leakage.

Collaborations are intended to offer an environment from which to harvest back to the contributing companies some of the value created, depicted by the solid arrows from the value-bundle back to the contributing

FIGURE 5.2 "LEAKAGE" AT THE EDGE OF INNOVATION

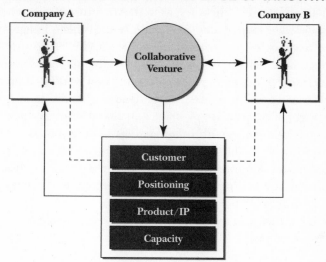

companies. For example, Avanade, a joint venture between Microsoft Corporation and Accenture, was designed for several reasons, not the least of which was to get assets off of Accenture's balance sheet and into a separate venture where the economies were more amenable for lower cost development work based on using Microsoft platform and software technologies. One of the economic drivers for this particular venture was margin pressure on system integration development rates. Other strategic objectives of the joint venture included:

- Obtaining customer lock-in through providing dedicated teams experienced in using Microsoft technologies
- Assisting Microsoft in becoming more effectively positioned in the larger enterprise space (through building on Accenture's strong client base)
- Enhancing intellectual property and product expertise through a close alignment between the two firms
- Increasing both companys' organizational capacity and scale around Microsoft technologies

In addition, both Microsoft and Accenture expect to transfer benefits of this collaboration back into their respective organizations. For

Accenture, this includes, as mentioned earlier, taking expensive assets off of their balance sheet. It includes, as well, Accenture being able to leverage the knowledge created and to pull additional systems integration work back into Accenture—in terms of the value-bundle, Accenture harvests IP and customers. For Microsoft, the value of the harvest is based on obtaining a clearer understanding of how to sell and position their software and services in a new client base. These lessons will additionally be leveraged throughout Microsofts product and marketing groups as well as through its relationships with other systems integration partners far removed from any Avanade- or Accenture-influenced activities. In terms of the value-bundle, Microsoft harvests IP and positioning. These are examples of some direct organizational benefits that are both expected and appropriate from collaboration.

With the benefits come some risks. Figure 5.2 shows three channels for leakage of value:

1. Leakage of the value of companies A and B into the venture due to the simple existence of a new entity (the collaborative venture) in their marketplace

2. Leakage of IP in the harvesting of the new value created—inevitably, some of A's IP will leak to B, and vice versa, through the channel created by the new value-bundle

3. Leakage of IP into the people involved in the collaboration

The first channel we discussed in some detail in Chapter Three. This is the business risk that results from simply implementing the collaborative venture. In terms of the value-bundle, there may be value leakage that affects the customer base—in the form of weakening relationships, challenges, or threats. For example, customers might become confused about how to think about the capabilities offered by the venture versus the capabilities of the contributing companies. We saw such confusion and dissatisfaction in some of the early eBusiness ventures as customers became confused over the specific value propositions of particular ventures, punishing not only the venture (Wingspan, for example), but the companies involved (BankOne). As we discussed in Chapter Three, this sort of leakage is worse when the target of the collaborative venture is close to your core, and, at least in uncertain times, the sweet spot for collaboration is in creating those things that are sufficiently far from your core such that you cannot respond quickly.

The second channel deals with the flow of technology or core intellectual property that becomes part of the collaborative venture and thus available to your collaborative partner. As a participant in the collaboration, you contribute value—for example, you expose intellectual property in creating the product of the collaboration, you use your customer base as the target market for the product of the collaboration, and so on. At each step of the way, your partner in the collaboration—quite possibly a past, present, or future competitor—is learning your IP, meeting your customers, and so on. Some amount of this sort of leakage is going to occur because the nature of collaboration. As we discussed in Chapter Three, the better you can codify the behaviors/values part of the semantic stack, the better you can control this leakage.

Yet another key risk for IP deals with the half-life of any technology or core intellectual asset that becomes part of a collaborative venture. As mentioned often, collaborative ventures are inherently risky. With intellectual property—highly skilled assets and talents, the raw materials of competitive virility—it is no surprise that the exploitation of relevant intellectual property poses one of collaborations more significant risks. As we've argued again and again, it is precisely the domain of intellectual property—and tacit knowledge—that is *the* dynamic engine of collaborative movement and effectiveness in the Jericho Zone, yet it is also the zone of, arguably, the highest leakage potential because of the very nature of the IP underlying much of the Jericho Zone collaborations.

The leakage types we just discussed constitute a real risk to collaborative effectiveness. They threaten the market viability of the venture thus requiring, at a minimum, continual monitoring of not only the business objectives but the half-life of their viability and leakage into the marketplace. Yet again, ironically, it is the very nature of the risks—the knowledge to be exploited—that provides the maximum value, and very reason, for the collaborative venture.

Another leakage channel has even more potential impact with respect to the ventures long-term success. As we've argued a number of times, collaborations exist to create incremental value, some of which is intended to be harvested back to the organizations involved. Some of this harvesting back is part of the shared value part of the collaborative relationship; some is part of the shared reward part of the collaborative relationship; but some of it is true leakage of value—lost value to one, the other, or both of the organizations participating in the collaborative relationship. We refer to this leakage as the *direct individual leakage benefits,* the dotted line labeled 3 in Figure 5.2. It comprises the IP created in the collaboration that is captured only as tacit knowledge in the heads of those people working together as part of the collaborative venture. We'll take a closer look at this leakage process and spend some time exploring its dynamic and its implications.

Leakage from the perspective of the organization is knowledge accretion from the perspective of the individual involved. Collaborative ventures are built on business propositions and the creation of value. They are established and operated by people. No matter the degree of codified or executable processes or software, the actual implementations are driven and delivered by people.[4] We all know this. We all experience this. Every day. The people who work for you are well aware of the classic organizational survival skill: Knowledge is power. Increasingly, they also recognize the potency, fungibility, and leverage of the tacit knowledge that they possess. This results in a potent risk formula for any collaborative venture. Here's a resulting challenge from this risk formula: Given the intrinsic premise that any effective collaboration would only be based on a sufficiently attractive business proposition, how do you manage the inexorable collaborative leakage that does and will continue to result? *Stated slightly differently, an inherent collaborative dynamic is to create new value and harvest back capabilities while minimizing leakage or to figure out how to harness that leakage so that it becomes part of the ongoing value of both the collaborative venture and the ongoing harvesting process of the contributing companies.* With that mouthful said, we're left with a key collaborative challenge: to recognize and respond to this inherent dynamic. How do we do it?

Years ago, there was a Welch's grape jelly television commercial describing the story of why Welch's grape jelly was so much more flavorful than its competitors. It showed the open pot that its competitors used to cook their jelly, allowing steam and flavor to escape. How, asked the narrator, does Welch's keep the flavor in and thereby enrich the flavor of the grapes? In the final scene of the television commercial, this question is answered: A pot of Welch's grape jelly is shown cooking—with the lid on. But not just any lid; this special lid had a crucial flavor return loop on top, returning the steam, and flavor, to the cooking jelly. That's all there was to it! And that's the challenge for the designers of collaborative ventures—fashioning that special lid with the value return loop on it; that is, figuring out how to leverage the intellectual flavors back to the participating companies.

Creating such a lid is a challenge. Collaborations are based on the creation of new value, arguably at high margin. As we've explained throughout this book, high-margin value stems from its being largely tacit; it is not sufficiently codified to allow it to be scaled, processed, and delivered automatically or simply by many. Tacit knowledge intrinsically is difficult to scale. By definition, tacit knowledge is not codified knowledge. The knowledge—the collective expertise and kinetic experiences—lies in the heads of the participants. There is, thus, a critical human dependency for collaborative ventures, particular those in the Jericho Zone. Intellectual property is both created and absorbed by the people most intimately engaged in the innovation of a collaborative venture. These people are directly in line to realize benefits of the lessons learned and experiences derived. This is why we characterized this collaborative intellectual property issue as a double-edged sword: To a participating organization, leakage is the loss to the organization that results from not internalizing lessons and capabilities (lessons and capabilities that are probably still tacit and thus difficult to capture) yet to the participant, it is *knowledge accretion* and hence an increase in their potential value, both to the organization that employs them today, and to potential employers. Thus, the challenge we see depicted in Figure 5.2 is how, following the humorous but appropriate example of the Welch's television ad, to keep a lid on the newly created intellectual property. We respond to this challenge from different perspectives in the rest of this chapter.

SOME OBSERVATIONS AND IMPLICATIONS FROM THE FIELD

Starting with the Observations: Intellectual Property

Let's step back and extract some lessons from the stylized framework we have outlined. We start with three observations, followed by three complementary implications. Each of these observations and implications deals with the intellectual property challenge of collaborative ventures. However, responses to the challenge need to be placed within the context of the shifting dynamic of collaborative ventures. Thus, the rest of this chapter begins to weave together the arguments of the previous as well as anticipate some of the arguments of the next chapter to help make the implications and recommended actions more understandable and useful.

Observation 1: The Battle over Tacit Knowledge Is a Battle over the Creation and Leverage of High-Margin Value

Knowledge and intellectual property are key to creating effective collaborative ventures. That knowledge is critical to support, nurture, and exploit is neither in question nor novel. Much has been published on this topic explaining knowledge as an underlying driver of our so-called information or knowledge economies.[5] What is novel is delineating knowledge's dynamic role in being, first, the key ingredient in establishing an effective collaborative venture and, second, the key engine inexorably making what is today a highly tacit and high-margin business tomorrow's codified set of processes. Let's take each of these in turn.

There is a temporal dynamic to collaborative ventures. Jericho Zone collaborations start out being based on identifying new business propositions and requiring highly skilled, high-value knowledge to create the innovation necessary to exploit them. These propositions, as do most, focus on taking advantage of some sort of market inefficiencies, value being derived from either eliminating or taking some type of arbitrage position among them. The earlier in the life cycle of a market opportunity, the greater are the inefficiencies, the higher are the barriers to entry, and the higher are the potential margins. Over time, the value propositions and methods to take advantage of them become more routine and codified—a result of fast follower behaviors or market imitators, rapid acceptance of effective practices or processes, or the increasing adoption of new technologies that arbitrage away the inefficiencies of the offerings and make the barriers to entry easier to scale. At the crux of this dynamic is the shifting role of what underlies the value propositions—tacit behaviors and knowledge.

More specifically, we've argued that the real crux lies in the shifting of these behaviors and knowledge from being tacit to becoming more codified. What becomes codified becomes more scalable and executable as we walk across the semantic stack and move from tacit knowledge to executable processes. The result? An ongoing movement from the Jericho Zone to some other form of collaborative venture, over time, as the economics of the value proposition shifts. Figure 5.3 depicts this perpetual machine migration of high-value/margins collaborative forms to other forms.

That there is a dynamic pushing from high-margin, high-value to lower margin business processes is not new. Rather, our exploration of this dynamic is a complementary story to those within *creative destruction* and *the innovator's dilemma* we discussed earlier.[6] What is new is providing a complementary explanation of *how* this dynamic occurs, not *that* it happens. This dynamic results from walking up and across the semantic stack. Walking up the stack continually pushes into the once-privileged domain of people-to-people interactions, creating mechanisms of more interchangeable interaction and requiring people to continually think of new

FIGURE 5.3 HOW COLLABORATIVE VENTURES CHANGE OVER TIME

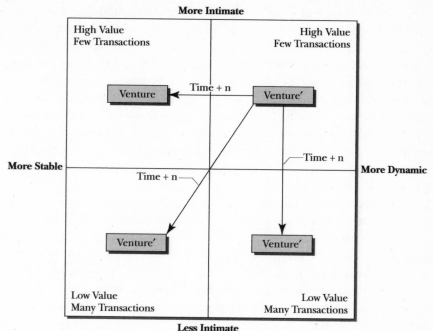

ways to differentiate product and service offerings and delivery mechanisms to deliver them. Walking across the stack is the mechanism of codifying tacit knowledge into more usable, more scalable, more executable processes.[7]

As collaborative ventures become more mature, the inherent dynamic of walking up and across the stack changes the value propositions of the particular venture. The relative position of the venture begins to move out of the Jericho Zone as the economics of the venture shifts—the result of walking up and across the stack—the point of Figure 5.3. To clarify, there is not a necessary impact on the specific value proposition of the venture; the value proposition around enhancing customers or market position, increasing product or capacity scale does not necessarily change. What does change is the degree to which the operations of the venture become increasingly codified, hence changing the economic proposition and as a result, the amount of competition and the relative placement of the venture within the collaborative zone.

This is intuitively reasonable; think of the American West, where the adventurers gave way to the cattlemen who gave way to the settlers who gave way to towns and cities—the same patch of ground, but the world moved around it. Think also of stock exchanges, where the one-on-one partnership deals for financing that took place in eighteenth-century Dutch coffeehouses codified into the capital markets that we have today. Thus, another way of thinking about this movement of a venture within the Collaborative Landscape is that the entire landscape is always in motion up and to the right. Even though the proposition of your venture doesn't change, the landscape moves past it. Which is yet another way of saying that the Red Queen doesn't have anything personally against your company or your collaborative ventures—she just runs up and to the right, dragging the business environment along with her.

The Red Queen never stops running. Which is why understanding the mechanics of how tacit knowledge and high-margin propositions become codified becomes so important. Again, we're arguing that irrespective of the particular form of your particular collaborative venture, knowing the dynamics of how those ventures change over time—how you walk up and across the semantic stack—helps you more effectively anticipate the inevitable evolution of your venture as well as anticipate and manage some of the risks of doing so. This is what we meant by the battle over tacit knowledge—the first implication of the framework presented in this chapter.

Observation 2: Value Is at the Edge

We have discussed numerous times in this book the notion of walking up and across the semantic stack. The stack, which we introduced in Chapter Three, goes from familiar technology things, like connectivity, at the bottom, through to very abstract and human things, like behaviors as you move up. To walk up the stack means to explicitly recognize and embrace the impact of the humanity involved in connecting two organizations. Left-to-right the stack moves from tacit, meaning understood only by way of substantial shared context among the people trying to understand it, to executable, meaning so thoroughly specified that computers can meaningfully exchange and operate on the information. Therefore, to walk across the stack on a given layer means to codify the information relevant to that layer.

In other words, if you are walking up and across the semantic stack, you are codifying more and more complex human behaviors. When we introduced the semantic stack in Chapter Three, we were introducing the mechanics of creating and operating collaborative ventures. We argued that codifying some of the more complex behaviors would help us lower the friction, and thus the cost and time in setting up and tearing down collaborations. By analogy with system integration, we introduced the notion of a *value port* where the mechanics of creating a collaborative interaction are sufficiently codified that setting one up to pursue a particular opportunity becomes simple, quick, and efficient.

Note, however, that we have never said anything about codifying the innovation process itself, and for an important reason: Innovation is a uniquely human activity, and in its essence depends on humans working together with other humans.

In fact, most of what we have dealt with in this book is the framing around collaboration—around how to recognize when it is appropriate, how to streamline the setup, and how to tear it down, how the structure might evolve over time—so that we could make these processes easier and mechanical so that the humans involved in the collaboration can concentrate less on the mechanics of the collaboration and more on that uniquely human enterprise of *innovation*. We want the valuable human assets thinking and interacting to create new ideas, new approaches, and new avenues. The setup and operational details add no value; they are important, because without them, the collaborative venture won't exist and can't work. But, ultimately, we want to make this supporting stuff automatic and mechanical, so that the humans—the stars of this particular show—can get on with the innovation and the value creation.

Our recurring mantra in this book is: *There are many different types of collaborations. But they all share common objectives regarding why to undertake them, an inherent dynamic in their evolution over time, and that there exists pragmatic steps of how to enhance their effectiveness based on understanding and exploiting their underlying dynamic.* The *why* constitutes the value proposition underlying collaborations—not a particular collaborative opportunity, but collaborations in general, to provide a framework that makes it easier to recognize the patterns and structure of what makes a good candidate for collaboration.

To recap briefly from our discussion in Chapter Two, organizations establish collaborations to create value that we've expressed in terms of:

- Increasing customer access
- Increasing capacity/scale
- Enhancing market positioning/branding
- Increasing their product/IP portfolio

Which of these elements dominate the consideration depends on the opportunity and the organizations involved. The *how*, or mechanics or collaborative DNA to make collaborations more effective are equally straightforward. They are to:

- Create and share value created
- Manage distributed risk
- Share the reward

These elements encompass the strategic fit of collaboration, help you decide when collaboration is appropriate, and help you create value ports in your organization so that you have the tools and capabilities to set up collaborative ventures to exploit these opportunities quickly and efficiently. That leaves the hard part: innovation.

Humans in your organization, working with the collaborative framework, can identify opportunities and determine whether collaboration is a good approach. Then humans, working at the edge of your organization—wearing your company badge, carrying your company's business card, but working in another organization, the collaborative venture, that is really separate from your organization—do that thing that only humans can do: They think and innovate, and from their efforts, they create a new business proposition. This is where the value of the collaborative venture is created: *at the edge of the organization,* by people holding enormous amounts of tacit knowledge, applying that knowledge in novel ways to address a business opportunity.

Observation 3: Managing Knowledge Is Inherently Risky

Managing knowledge in a collaborative environment is even more risky. There are simply more opportunities, and risks, for leakage. Remember, what is leakage for participating companies is knowledge accretion for the individuals involved. Consequently, a key challenge is to figure out how to manage this knowledge effectively—how, to refer back to the Welch's lid example from their television commercial, to keep a lid on it. A major means to keep a lid on it is to drive the process of walking up and across the semantic stack—for example, figuring out how to codify as much of the knowledge created as possible, and as quickly as possible. The tacit knowledge created in effective collaborative ventures will, over time, become increasingly standardized, or codified into a routine set of business processes, updated applications, and shared set of norms and values guiding the venture. This process of moving from the tacit to the codified is just that: a process. It is an ongoing set of actions that is only as effective as the attention people pay to it. This process is an effective way to think about knowledge management and needs to be a key focus of knowledge management.

Knowledge management, then, is not something you buy; nor is it a set of technologies and applications into which to dump your documents and rules of engagement to extract them. Sure, these could be enablers of an effective management process. But let's go a bit further to explain the underlying DNA elements of knowledge management. Knowledge management, from our perspective, is not a noun, not a *thing*, but a verb—*a process*. Knowledge management is the process of guiding and managing the migration of tacit knowledge into codified, executable behaviors. It is the process of walking up and across the semantic stack, both for the framework of the collaborative venture, and for the intellectual property that gets created. The first of these is mere "hygiene" for implementing strategy in uncertain times, necessary for being able to collaborate in the Jericho Zone. The second of these is needed to maximize your sharing in the value and in the reward; if you know that some leakage is going to occur, then it makes sense to figure out how to claim value from it.

Putting the lid on the collaborative venture, in terms of managing intellectual property leakage, requires (1) understanding the process, (2) acknowledging its importance, and (3) addressing it. Putting a lid on intellectual property leakage reduces the risk of that leakage and keeps the flavor in the collaborative venture.

The next section draws on these three requirements and suggests specific implications and examples to keep the lid on.

Some Implications and What This Means to You

The observations we've drawn are not new. Nor were they intended to be so. The value we're offering here is an alternative perspective—of viewing a common set of materials, information, and common knowledge differently—to challenge your thoughts on and thereby increase the effectiveness of your collaborative ventures. One key objective of this book is to get you to think differently about collaborative ventures. A second key objective is to provide suggestions about what to do with those new thoughts. This section describes a set of tangible implications of the

observations we've identified and provides examples of collaborative organizations and their attempts to address the observations we've discussed.

Implication 1: Celebrate the Edges and Aggressively Exploit Tacit Knowledge

Market leadership results from being among the best at some type of
value discipline—operational excellence, superior customer service, aggressively innovative, or creative, just plain large-scale reach and capacity, or some combination of this set. Being among the best requires having
some edge over your competitors—being ahead of the indefatigable Red
Queen. Having this edge means possessing and exploiting knowledge and
its enabling processes more effectively than your competitors. Yet, like
everything else, this advantage doesn't last. Over time, as technology
changes, processes become codified, best practices get copied, and knowledge gets transferred; what was once a competitive advantage becomes
table stakes—something you need merely to play in the game. For example, online and discount brokerage transactions were effective differentiators for Charles Schwab, Inc. during the mid-1990s, but by the late
1990s, they were commodity offerings, and competitively necessary for
any brokerage house merely to play the competitive game. Differentiating
among the once Big Five consulting houses over the last couple of years
has become more difficult; distinguishing themselves as having large-
scale systems' integration capabilities and being client focused have become nonstarters as mergers among them continue apace, collecting more
and more common capabilities. Even Nike, one of the world's most cele-
brated and well-branded companies, aggressively and continuously attempts to differentiate its brand, recognizing that its market blazing path
will soon be covered by its competitors upon the release of any new
footwear technology or even branding and market positioning activity.[8]

The Red Queen is ever present. She requires staying at the edge to
remain competitively viable. The *innovator's dilemma* convincingly demonstrates how becoming too wedded to a once competitively innovative and
profound way of doing business, by its very success, leads to organizational
resistance to change and hence competitive atrophy.[9] Technologies
change. Business models evolve. Today's competitive advantage becomes
tomorrow's commoditized stance.

Staying ahead of the Red Queen requires celebrating the edges—the
edge of technologies, the edge of business models—the edges of knowledge.
By its very nature, the edge is unknown by most. As such, it remains tacit—

not yet a competitive standard much less codified, and therefore inherently not scalable. Celebrating the edges means seeking the higher margin areas. Exploiting the tacit means staking the ground of the highest potential competitive advantage. The implication is that it becomes critical to figure out how to institutionalize the tacit knowledge and thereby minimize the risk while maximizing the harvesting back of intellectual property leakage of collaborative ventures.

At Unisys Corporation, for example, we have market evangelists whose responsibilities include staying abreast of industry and technology trends. They talk with our key clients about those trends and how clients might take advantage of those trends. Cisco Systems has had their Internet Services Business Group (ISBG) group—market evangelists with respect to emerging networking technologies and their range of possible impacts on yet-to-be determined business practices. Microsoft Corporation has recently defined a new evangelist role in their aggressive stance toward becoming more relevant to the larger enterprise marketplace. Their objective is to serve as dialogue partners discussing and clarifying business issues, then using Microsoft technologies to help redress those issues. Many other companies have similar evangelist roles whose responsibilities are to stay ahead of the curve. Staying ahead of the curve—irrespective of your particular core competencies or value discipline—is critical. Institutionalizing, supporting, and celebrating the roles and people who create your tacit knowledge is as strategically wise as it is pragmatically critical.

The role of the market evangelist is not a simple one. Nor is it a role easily boxed within traditional metrics of operational expenses and revenue generation. Yet, neither is it a role that can be ignored. The evangelist's job involves figuring out how to manage the creative tension between the operational realities of *what* and *how* you conduct business today and how to help you prepare for emerging competitive opportunities 12 to 36 months out. Their job, in short, is staying ahead of the Red Queen—exploring what is still new—and tacit—and figuring out how to make it operationally viable. This leads us to the second implication.

Implication 2: Aggressively Migrate Tacit into Codified Knowledge— Manage Your Semantic Stack

Being able to scale rests on getting more people to do the same thing in similar ways—the more similar, the more standardized; the more standardized, the more executable. Network economies and network effects are based on this simple basis: The more people who use your system, your platform, your applications, your processes, your fill-in-the-blank, the more people will use it. Why? Because they have little economic choice not to do so; the transactional costs of *not* using it are too great. The tautological nature of this strategy is precisely what makes it so powerful. The more people (are forced to) use something, the more they tend to use it in an ever-virtuous cycle of use and reuse. This is the classic competitive lock-in strategy. The underlying premises of this strategy are straightforward:

- Control the platform and you force your competitors, and induce your customers, to use it.
- Establish high barriers to challenge the predominance of the platform.
- Add value-added services on top of the lock-in platform to further expand your market dominance.[10]

Simple. Powerful. Elegant. Microsoft's antitrust trial centered on how Microsoft attempted to lock customers and competitors into their software and services given their overwhelming market dominance. The AOL/Time Warner merger in 2001 was premised on creating an environment of content and entertainment synergy—or more aptly labeled their customer lock-in and competitor lock-out strategy.[11] CitiGroup's recent wholesale financial services vision for becoming the global dial-tone and liquidity engine for global payment transactions is fully cognizant and aimed at enabling global customer and competitor lock-in. The power of a McKinsey Consulting firm, or other premier strategy consulting houses, resulted from their explicit efforts at creating the strategic language to use when discussing, analyzing, and implementing strategic efforts. McKinsey's S-curves, Boston Consulting Group's Pigs and Cows strategic boxes, even the Gartner Group's Magic Quadrants are all demonstrably successful attempts at creating the language that organizations use to communicate with one another with respect to strategic efforts. On and on this game has and will continue to be played.

And it is a very serious game; the game of customer lock-in where the underlying objective is to create the environment in which competitors and customers will interact, and interact in a manner that is consistent, common, and understandable—a game with high barriers to entry and even higher transaction costs of not interacting within that environment. We often characterize the mechanisms of creating such a consistent, common, and understandable environment, as *grammar tools*. Why? Because at their essence, what we are all striving to do is create environments that make sense to and are used by our customers. Grammar tools are no more than mechanisms to allow us to communicate simply, consistently, understandably. Positioning such mechanisms as grammar tools also helps us understand how customer lock-in strategies can be accelerated and, later, tacit knowledge codified.

Figure 5.4 depicts the phases of this classic customer lock-in strategy that, not coincidentally, are the same as the maturity phases for an effective collaborative venture.

Our particular insight regarding this discussion lies not in the existence of such customer lock-in strategies. Nor even our claim that effective collaborative ventures need to pursue similar strategic directions. Again, our objective is not to suggest that such a strategy is critical, but to explain *how* it occurs and perspectives on effectively using such a strategy to increase the effectiveness of your collaborative ventures. *And the underlying explanation of the how lies in walking up and across the semantic stack.*

As we've seen over and over again, tacit knowledge has potentially high value and high margins. Yet it is not scalable. It resides in a few heads and is subject to multiple interpretations, hence fragmented uses and possible conflicting standards. Tacit knowledge, then, by design and structure has inherent scaling limits. Only through codifying that knowledge into a set of processes, protocols, platforms, and connectivity standards can the power of scaling kick in with remarkable implications on

FIGURE 5.4   THE DYNAMIC OF COLLABORATIVE VENTURES

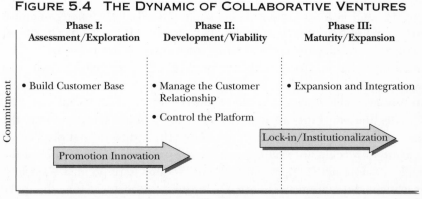

the competitive environment. If you can codify knowledge faster and more efficiently than your competition, your advantages in scale become a competitive advantage. As we saw in Chapter Three, this tacit-codified-market-transformation process well characterized the 1960s and 1970s with respect to network connectivity, the 1980s and throughout the 1990s with respect to standard technical architectures and platforms, and well characterizes today's battlefield of application standards, programming models and business processes. Not until Internet protocols (IP) were clearly codified into a set of executable global standards could we witness the rise of the Cisco Systems and other (once) network dominant enterprises nor could we have a reliable network environment enabling the plug-and-play of IP-enabled devices thereby moving the battlefield to other sources. The network battlefield shifted. Rather than battling over which protocols would underlie global connectivity and lock-in the network environment, competitors jousted over what architectural platforms, what applications, and how to accelerate the speed of those protocols. Thus, what was once a high-value, high-margin business—defining the IP standards—again driven relentlessly by the Red Queen, became a commoditized, highly scalable, codified business shifting the competitive battleground.

The Global Straight Through Processing Association (GSTPA) provides another example. We introduced the GSTPA in Chapter Two. Recall that the objective of the GSTPA is to create an automated clearing and settlement utility to automate foreign exchange clearing and settlements of global trades. The participants, all aggressive mutual competitors, came together to create this utility in response to what are known as the T + 1 requirements. This regulatory requirement mandates that global financial trades must be settled one day after the trade (hence the label T(rade) + 1). The T + 1 requirements, moving as quickly as possible to real-time settlements—or T + 0—are wringing out transactional inefficiencies in global trade and settlement activities. Financial institutions make much of their money as a result of marketplace and processing inefficiencies. In fact, exploiting inefficiencies—whether monetary floats, financial arbitrage, and asymmetrical knowledge that are the basis for providing financial and fiduciary advice—are key revenue sources for investment banking: The greater the capability to identify and exploit these inefficiencies, the greater the potential margins and competitive differentiation. Consequently, any regulatory requirement that wrings inefficiencies out of the system causes alert competitors to reconsider how to respond. T + 1 is such a mandated requirement. Hence, the business rationale for something like GSTPA. There simply are no economically justified reasons for financial institutions to underwrite or attempt to build their own straight-through settlement systems. The margins are disappearing out of such global transactions; so too are corresponding grounds for competitive differentiation.

GSTPA was created to remove financial settlement and clearing process inefficiencies. The battleground has shifted. Exploiting the inefficiencies of global trades and settlements was once a high-value, high-margin business. It was followed relentlessly by the Red Queen and is becoming a commoditized, highly scalable, codified business. Again, the tacit knowledge, embedded in the differing methods and processes of financial institutions handling global trade settlement and clearing, was codified into an executable platform and set of processes shifting the competitive battleground.[12]

Simple. Powerful. Elegant. The Red Queen continues to run. Relentlessly. What is today tacit becomes increasingly codified and, over time, executable. Today's differentiation becomes tomorrow's commodity offering. How does this happen? It happens as people walk up and across the semantic stack. Irrespective of industry or of company core competency, the dynamic remains the same: The Red Queen continues to run. As she runs, the nature of competition shifts. And it shifts as tacit knowledge becomes increasingly codified and scalable. As the platform for customer lock-in becomes settled, attention must shift elsewhere. Yet, herein lies the *innovator's dilemma*—of relying too much on what it was that made your organization great, and thereby setting the stage for falling behind relative to your competitors as the competitive battleground shifts. Even the collaborative ventures in the Jericho Zone shift as the basis for their competitive position changes. So, the second implication of this chapter is the criticality of both anticipating the need for and actually driving efforts to walk up and across the semantic stack. So . . . put on your walking shoes!

However, there are significant implications of walking up the stack, namely, the innovator's dilemma implication: How do you celebrate and extend your core strengths while recognizing that marketplace dynamics are shifting requiring you to reposition differently to stay ahead competitively? This leads us to a third implication, one based on the recognition of and underlying what we've called the collaborative necessity.

Implication 3: Make Collaboration a Core Competency

Many organizations have experimented with differing business models and technologies over the last several years. But the crashing of the economy put a quick end to many of these experiments and forced organizations to confront some difficult questions, such as:

- What are we really good at?
- What are our core strengths?
- How do we take advantage of them?

In response to these questions, we have seen an aggressive refocusing on core values, core assets, and core strengths with two significant implications: (1) Stronger competitors who have a better sense of who they are and what they do; and (2) more collaboration, based on the recognition that it makes sense to partner with others around *their* core strengths to thereby enhance mutual competitive positions—an increasingly necessary core competency.

Given the dynamic environment of the Red Queen, we know that change is one of the only constants in our business environment, and that we must innovate to survive. We know things are changing, but we cannot predict how things will change, so we are faced with uncertainty and, as we saw in Chapter Two, collaboration is a necessary strategic tool for innovating in uncertain times. Thus, collaboration is an inherent part of conducting business, whether you are improving the way you perform your current business, or changing the business that you are in. Collaborative skills need to become part of the strategic arsenal for competitive leadership. Frances Cairncross, management editor of the *Economist,* describes the underlying managerial skills and technology shifts that create the potential for more effective collaboration.[13] As she writes, these include the reality that:

- New technologies are driving down the cost and speeding up the rate of processing, transmitting, and storing information . . . and that the falling price of a new technology is one of the main forces that persuade people to adopt it.

- The innumerable applications of the Internet make the changes it brings more pervasive and varied than any that have gone before.

- The Internet makes markets of all kinds work better because it increases access to information . . . and reduce[s] one of the main costs of doing business.

- The Internet speeds up the dissemination and adoption of new techniques.[14]

These conditions are driving commensurate shifts in managerial capabilities and company-to-company partnerships, both to take advantage of the underlying technology shifts and to get ahead of their inevitable consequences toward more visibility, rapid communications, and streamlined operations—for example, more collaboration.

Cisco Systems has been considered one of the poster children for the emergent model of collaborative business partnerships. Cisco's insight was that the high-margin work of network connectivity devices and technologies is in their design and architecture; manufacturing, production, and distribution, while profitable, have different scale and margin economies. Following this logic, it makes pragmatic and strategic sense to establish organizational relationships to explicitly support the different economies. This is what Cisco System has been doing for the past 10 years, and Ciscos shareholders, overall, have realized the value from its rule-breaking insight, at least during the late 1990s.

Cisco has established partnership agreements and outsourcing relationships to handle its production, manufacturing, and distribution while the design and architecture work remains internal to Cisco. Nike has pursued a similar strategy, again focusing on the high margin and tacit-rich areas of design while leaving production to its network of production and distribution partners and a similar bifurcation. Viewed from another perspective, the insight and focus of Cisco, Nike, and increasingly many others is to operate in the Jericho Zone, efficiently and effectively acquiring companies that are on the technology edge—that will help these companies maintain their position in the high-margin business they desire, and collaborating with partners to help them maintain their position in the lower margin high volume business. What is instructive about the Cisco case, and bears emphasis here, is that Cisco, through 2001, stayed ahead of the Red Queen by its world class ability to operate in the Jericho Zone, creating new relationships with other companies at a truly impressive rate, but not all of the relationships Cisco makes are intended to create cutting edge innovation. Some are allowing Cisco to maintain its focus and expertise in its core technologies, but others, such as Cisco's supply chain partnerships, play a supporting role.

Cisco's acquisition and partnership model, the IP marketplace for mixed-signal chip designs that we discussed in Chapter Two, Charles Schwab's move into the higher valued advice space discussed in Chapter Four, and Avanade's joint venture discussed earlier in this chapter are all examples of a trend—from many industries—of companies recognizing the importance of their knowledge assets, and of the importance of collaboration as a tool to exploit them. We call this trend the *last mile*.

The last mile is a term from the telecommunications industry. In its original usage, it referred to the most difficult part of providing ubiquitous phone service—getting a wire into everyone's house. In traditional analog phone service, your telephone is connected via a pair of copper wires to a telephone switch in the central office (CO). The phone company lays large feeder cables—containing thousands of pairs of wire and thus capable of servicing the needs of thousands of households—that run from the CO out in various directions. These cables typically run along established rights of way such as railroad tracks, pipelines, and so on, and so are fairly easy to put in. The CO and the feeders account for a huge percentage of the capital involved in providing phone service to your house, but none of that investment is of any value unless a pair of copper wires is run that last mile between the nearest feeder cable and your house.

The last mile problem has to do with how labor intensive, expensive, and time consuming it is to connect up to every single consumer who desires service. In the days of the telephone company monopoly, long distance rates were used to subsidize the last mile costs needed for providing local telephone service. Companies like MCI were able to compete with the incumbent AT&T on long distance service where the connectivity is restricted to connecting up relatively few telephone switches with one another, but nobody was in a position to compete over the last mile. In fact, to this day the only industry other than the phone company to actually address the last mile effectively is cable television.

As a business metaphor, the last mile is the gap you must close with your customers to actually deliver value and thus receive the rewards. As an analogy, it characterizes an emerging trend of organizations recognizing the critical role and value of their knowledge assets but unsure of how to most effectively take advantage of them—particularly if they are not part of the core organizational focus/competency. There are actually two parts of the last mile relevant to our discussion.

The first part deals with making sure that the business objectives you lay out for any project—say a collaborative venture—get realized, and are realized in such a manner that you can replicate both the process of how the project was executed (extracting what worked, and learning from lessons that did not work) as well as the capabilities and skills that were developed as a result of the project. This is the *knowledge transfer* part of the last mile—ensuring that the skills developed and deployed can be reused by your teams for similar types of activities requiring similar types of capabilities, skills, and functionality. This part of the last mile ties a nice, tight bow on a project, helping to ensure that you received as much benefit from it as possible.

The second part deals with *harvesting intellectual property* from your projects, and focuses on finding other things that can be done with the capabilities, skills, and functionality developed in the project. All organizations have intellectual property—ranging from soft skills (such as project management, or deep knowledge of specific business processes) to harder assets (such as software applications, financial models, or workflow algorithms). The full range of intellectual property, often developed in specific projects, potentially has market(able) value outside of any of the projects in which they were developed or enhanced. These pieces of intellectual property—or assets—can potentially be reused internally or packaged up and sold externally into the marketplace. This harvesting process—from identifying to harvesting to assessing to packaging to selling—is one that many organizations are grappling with as they recognize that they possess assets that have value not only to other parts of their organization, but also to their clients, their suppliers, and perhaps even to their competitors. This recognition is leading to efforts to harvest and exploit organizational assets—or intellectual property—in order to accelerate the returns of investments made to create those assets.

However, some of these assets developed are outside the core focus and competency of the particular firm. This is where the lessons of Cisco become highly relevant again. Cisco's core focus has been on infrastructure design, architecture, and network connectivity. This is their sweet spot, the focus that drives their acquisition, collaboration, and strategic focus. The last mile indicates that many organizations are recognizing the potential value of their assets. The question is how to most effectively take advantage of these assets while not cannibalizing the core business. Yet, this is precisely the *innovator's dilemma* discussed earlier. A degree of cannibalizing is critical to remain in the competitive race. The challenge is how to do so in a manner that manages your risk while optimizing the value of the assets you have. And this, again, provides the driver for collaborative ventures. Let's look at another example of a global firm not walking, but running, the last mile.

Procter & Gamble (P&G) is one of the world's largest consumer products companies and boasts one of the world's most recognized brands. P&G well recognizes the power and criticality of their intellectual capital to keep them ahead competitively of both market positioning and operations. They continue to invest hundreds of millions of dollars a year to improve their manufacturing effectiveness in a marketplace furiously focused on driving down operating costs. One rich area to attack to reduce costs is that of machine reliability and new machinery installations. P&G has spent significant time and resources attacking this target-rich cost environment.

Over the past decade, P&G has worked closely with Los Alamos Laboratories in an effort to reduce the time and increase the effectiveness of new machinery implementations. Los Alamos helped P&G design the algorithms to optimize machines throughout, assess inventory optimization, and develop data architectures critical to support the multivariate analysis comprising complex and global operations. Building on these algorithms, P&G has developed a set of reliability engineering tools, methodologies, software, and training to minimize production line downtime and optimize machinery use during production maintenance and during the introduction of new machinery into existing production lines. More specifically, they have developed and implemented manufacturing process tools; machinery setup tools; an overall manufacturing strategy and analysis; a set of software to guide, implement, and optimize machinery implementations; and a set of post-implementation data analysis and ongoing supply chain improvements. Over the past 10 years, P&G has deployed this collaborative set of software, assessment tools, methodologies, and training in well over 100 of its manufacturing plants worldwide. From these deployments, P&G has realized well over $1 billion in savings from improved system reliability, a 30 percent to 40 percent improvement in equipment reliability, a 60 percent to 70 percent benefit from faster startups of new equipment and a more robust and reliable supply chain to meet consumer demands and promotion variability. Bottom line: P&G has avoided capital investment while increasing capacity—a core objective of the strategic initiative.[15]

Along the way, P&G realized that the intellectual assets they have created—the algorithms, the software, the methodologies, the training—are powerful in and of themselves. These are key assets that have been tried and tested with phenomenal results, assets that could be leveraged into the marketplace. With that recognition, P&G established a collaborative relationship to combine the hard assets of P&G with the industry knowledge and supply chain expertise of a consulting firm—BearingPoint—to take these capabilities to market. Why didn't P&G take these assets to market themselves given their obvious potential impact? Applying these assets internally is a competitive requirement and fiduciary responsibility for P&G. It is also a core capability and corporate credo to continuously reengineering and aggressively attack supply chain and machine production costs. However, the very process of packaging the assets, defining a marketplace for them, crafting the value proposition, refining the deployment methodologies, allocating teams to support them, and other elements necessary to forge beyond their core area of competence (and control), was not in line with the focus of P&G. Yet, the assets they had developed were demonstrably viable and valuable. Hence, the opportunity and the collaborative partnership, where BearingPoint provides the customers, positioning, and scale, and P&G provides the product.

Deutsche Bank has recently built a collaborative venture around a new interface technology within its asset management practice, one that minimizes bandwidth usage while downloading applications.[16] Merrill Lynch frequently seeks to establish creative ventures to leverage assets developed in its core business, assets that could be monetized or perform some revenue-creation function to offset their costs.[17] Chevron/Texaco has begun aggressively seeking how to leverage some of its data analytics expertise derived from upstream oil exploration into other companies. In fact, a whole industry exists to identify and increasingly to broker appropriate relationships—from collaborative ventures to acquisitions, and so on, across industries and across geographies. Companies are beginning not to walk but to jog the last mile. These aerobic activities stem from increasingly critical competitive realities and organizational recognitions that:

1. Many companies have tremendous assets that have been developed and implemented within their organization and that can be exploited more broadly.

2. Exploiting these assets usually requires the addition of core capabilities not possessed by the organization (Deutsche Bank, Chevron/Texaco) that created the asset, thereby requiring partners to assist them in doing so.

3. The opportunity costs of merely selling the assets to another firm (and thereby losing perceived ongoing value of the particular assets) or the risks of attempting to go it alone (the transactional costs and potential risk of losing organizational focus) further suggests alternate collaborative ventures.

4. The window of commercial opportunity for many of these assets is relatively short: They are relevant for a particular amount of time, but given the dramatic democratization and global dissemination of information, technology, and just plain copycat communications, there

is a need to move quickly, which, as we saw in Chapter Two, implies collaborating with a partner who already has the missing pieces.

The Red Queen runs on and on. She is as relevant for professional services companies as she is for everyone else.

The Gartner Group has defined an emerging collaborative model of professional services companies such as systems integrators and consulting firms. They believe, as do we, that no one systems integrator or consulting firm can be all things to any particular client organization. The demands that client organizations place on consulting firms have changed. No longer do client organizations merely want smart people to come in and figure out how to assist them. They demand, require, and need people who know their business and can add value, rapidly and tangibly. Consequently, the days of the chest-beating consulting firm proclaiming that they can do it all are over. As Shakespeare might have written: "Fungibility be damned. 'Tis the time of proven relevance . . . the Red Queen is upon you!" Instead, service providers, much like any commercial organization, must figure out what their core strengths and differentiators are and figure out how to collaborate with others to demonstrate their competitive relevance to their clients.

We are witnessing more and more collaboration among service providers in their bidding and delivery of client work. Gartner claims that by 2005, well over 40 percent of service provider revenue will be derived from other service providers through providing services with and through each other to their clients. The U.S. Customs Service's modernization effort is a case in point. The U.S. Customs has begun an aggressive initiative to transform itself, driven by a fundamentally new vision of global customs and the needs of increased global visibility, service, and security. This transformation has an initial budget allocation of over $1 billion, most of which will go for professional services. There is no single service provider that could reliability deliver the services—from concept to launch—of such a globally massive project without assistance. Consequently, U.S. Customs required a set of solution providers to partner, design, and develop the set of initiatives necessary to undertake the transformation. IBM, BearingPoint, Computer Sciences Corporation (CSC), and Sandler & Travis have partnered—in a relationship very similar to that characterized by Gartner as *solutions aggregator*—to support the U.S. Customs Service in their aggressive transformation. This is but one of many types of such project-bound collaborations, and many more are coming.

Figure 5.5 depicts what Gartner calls their *Solutions Aggregator Model*, in which multiple service providers collaborate effectively deliver a large-scale project.[18] Table 5.1 depicts some of the roles and value propositions of parties within this model.

Again, the drive for this solutions aggregation model is the need to exploit what each firm does best—their knowledge, often tacit, the challenge to which is how to integrate, how to scale, how to codify their relevant and high-valued knowledge to make it useful to many and more valuable both to their collaborative venture and their respective organizations.[19]

We've seen that a key collaborative challenge is putting the "lid on." But, how *do* you do so in collaborative ventures that are inherently leaky? Next are some pragmatic and straightforward recommendations to start answering these questions. We've already discussed the need to learn how to walk up and across the semantic stack, and about how what passes as knowledge management needs to shift to become more of a process—a walking stick to use up and across the stack. There are other implications as well. We next discuss one implication regarding what we call the *death of the proprietary methodology*.[20]

FIGURE 5.5 SOLUTIONS AGGREGATOR MODEL

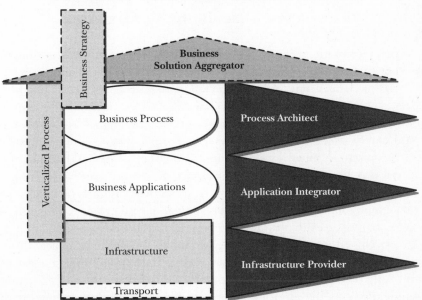

Source: The New Services Roles (Gartner Group, 2002).

TABLE 5.1   ROLES OF THE SOLUTIONS AGGREGATOR PARTIES

SERVICE PROVIDER ROLE	ROLE	VALUE
Business solution aggregator	Retains the relationship with client organization and all strategic business partners	Assumes risk Measurable business value Partner management Validate business strategy
Process architect	Defines unique solutions for specific business process within specific vertical sectors	Process innovation and best practice Link IT to business strategy
Application integrator	Builds, integrates and optimizes applications from components for the specific business process	Modularity Agility in applications development
Infrastructure provider	Optimizes the environment to host the application, for highest performance	Continuous available, secure infrastructure

THE COLLABORATIVE DELIVERY FRAMEWORK

Proprietary methodologies are dead. There, we've said it. It is time to push the wheelbarrow throughout our organizations and chant the memorable line from Monty Python's *Holy Grail* regarding our respective proprietary methodologies: Bring out your dead! As we argued earlier and as our clients tell us on a daily basis, no service provider or software company can be *all things to all people*. Service providers and competing software companies must work together. The client is king. What must be served is delivering value to the customer. By dint of argument (from a logic point of view) and of reality (from a client organization point of view), it no longer makes sense to presume to have a proprietary methodology that assumes that it (1) can cover all capabilities and (2) can prescriptively enumerate everything we need to do to execute those capabilities The *Open Source Movement,* which sprang up in the mid-1980s and fully reflects the Internet's potential of rapid and democratic communications, is the appropriate model for ongoing and collaborative methodologies.

The Open Source Movement is possibly best known by one of its products, Linux. Initially created by Linus Torvalds, Linux has subsequently been extended, morphed, modified, and powerfully enhanced by thousands of developers the world over. Individual programmers developed the Linux code and commented on each other's ideas in an iterative cycle of development, commentary, revision, and enhancement.[21] This peer-to-peer process is a powerful model of effective collaborative behaviors. Pulling us back to the discussion of methodologies, the peer-to-peer collaborative model forces companies to reevaluate the design and use of their once differentiated and proprietary methodologies and their use of them. What is needed is less a set of proprietary methodologies than a collaborative delivery framework. An example follows.

A collaborative delivery framework (CDF) is just that: a framework that identifies, aligns and coordinates among various best practices, tools, approaches, and once-proprietary methodologies to solve a set of business initiatives. CDF reflects the collaborative principles we've described throughout this book, and it is based on the recognition that companies will—by necessity and thus by choice—be working collaboratively on initiatives and that no single company, no matter their expertise or attitude, is able to work alone. It is also based on the reality that a key issue we all face is the lack of time to manage our disparate projects and that doing so requires as much time attempting to make sense of what it is we have to do and how to do so as actually executing on the projects. Making sense of what we need to do—building a common vocabulary such that people on a project can communicate consistently, and hence, execute effectively—is both a challenge and a requirement for us all. This is why earlier in the chapter we characterized perspectives, frameworks, and models as grammar tools to help us make sense of what it is we need to do. These challenges and requirements exist within our own companies. Now, we compound these challenges and requirements by adding in working with other companies and clients as well. This creates a real specter of the tower of Babel with different people, different service providers, different software vendors each with their own, proprietary methodologies—all speaking different languages or possibly, and even more confusing, using the same words but with different meanings. A real mess. A real time drain. And a reality we all face.

What is needed to reconcile this potential mess is to develop and use a pragmatic framework. Or even more importantly, to select, align, and use what is most relevant for your particular business needs. Again, this is where and how CDF provides an effective example. At its simplest, CDF is a tool that can help you clearly define:

- The scope of strategic initiatives, and interdependencies among them
- The overall approach and communications methods across collaborative and different parties
- The ownership of activities and interdependencies among vendor and client teams
- The execution model to align, extract, and use different best practices from multiple parties, including the entrance and exit criteria necessary to ensure effective lock-in and consistency among differing contributing assets from multiple parties

CDF can thereby help you manage your risk of scope definition, approach definition, multivendor management, and program management. Figure 5.6 depicts this high-level CDF structure.

Along the top of the framework are distinct project or program stages—from strategy to production. Along the side of the framework, disciplines depict major groupings of work requiring similar skills and knowledge. These two dimensions create a sufficiently neutral and generic environment into which project activities, skills, and embedded tools, approaches, and methodologies can be poured. Figure 5.7 depicts the CDF work grid that fleshes out the high-level structure.

The CDF work grid depicts the highest level framework objects, or processes, of a life-cycle model that is sufficient to execute any project that purports to create a solution to something—conceptually from concept to launch. Each object within the work grid comprises a set of expected entrance conditions, inputs, processes, activities, tasks, tools, guidance, artifacts, deliverables, and templates as well as expected exit conditions. These objects, following the principles of object-oriented design, form the top of a class hierarchy from which other, more specific, objects can be derived for specific purposes. For example, Solution Construction & Integration means something different for a software development project, the installation and customization of an off-the-shelf product, or creation of a military weapons system, so each of these applications of CDF would derive specific Solution Construction & Integration processes, activities, and tasks from the base Solution Construction & Integration object. Processes, activities, and tasks thus derived give the

FIGURE 5.6 THE COLLABORATIVE DELIVERY FRAMEWORK

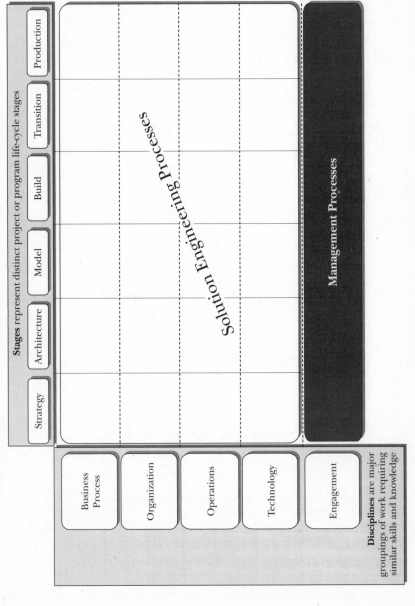

Stages represent distinct project or program life-cycle stages

Strategy | Architecture | Model | Build | Transition | Production

Solution Engineering Processes

Management Processes

Business Process

Organization

Operations

Technology

Engagement

Disciplines are major groupings of work requiring similar skills and knowledge

FIGURE 5.7 CDF WORK GRID: MAJOR PROCESSES

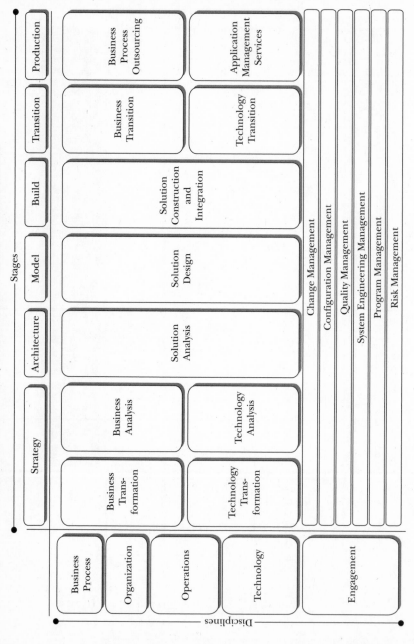

FIGURE 5.8 CDF WORKGRID FOR COMMUNICATING RESPONSIBILITIES AMONG COLLABORATIVE PARTNERS

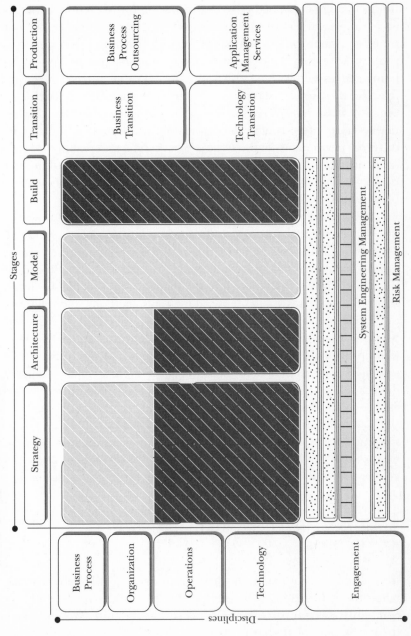

people who are expert in the particular type of project a chance to customize them as necessary, but they also inherit from the base object those things that are common between all Solution Construction & Integration activities regardless of specific project. CDF thus becomes the common set of grammar tools to communicate and hence position what types of projects are being done and what tools, vendors, and methodologies are being addressed by whom and where, for all projects in all fields and domains of the professional service providers business, *even though it does not prescribe specific rules for execution.* Specific projects and methodologies and, maybe more interesting in the context of this discussion, the activities of different participants in the same project can be mapped to the work grid to identify how they fit together. Thus, CDF is also a tool to use to communicate what is being done and how. Figure 5.8 shows how such an overlay within the CDF work grid might occur.

The shaded areas depict the project scope, in this case a project that will deliver strategy through to the build (creation) of a solution. There are four organizations participating in the delivery, and the areas of the project that each is taking are indicated by the particular shading in the different activities. A drill-down into the shaded areas provide the default set of project templates, plans, deliverables, tools, methods, and relevant parts of various methodologies appropriate to the project, but each participant is free to use whatever methodology they might have in performing their work, provided they can satisfy the requirements of the relevant CDF objects. The result: a rapid and simple means to build a common language to discern relevant assets and methodologies for a particular project to quickly enable collaborative delivery.

The collaborative delivery framework is one tangible means to begin moving toward building collaborative core competency. Many other means exist. The key issue is less to enumerate a set of tangible tools to engender collaborations than to recognize the criticality of doing so.

SUMMARY: INTELLECTUAL PROPERTY AT THE EDGE

In this chapter, we made few distinctions among different types of collaborations. Instead, we focused primarily on the dynamics of how the competitive bases of collaborations shift over time. We characterized these dynamics as similar to the relentless running of the Red Queen as the competitive basis for any particular collaborative venture shifts over time requiring organizations to keep shifting merely to keep their relative competitive position. What was once high-margin, differentiated value becomes codified and scalable. This led to our discussion of one of the key mechanics underlying these shifts. Technologies are major disruptive drivers of competitive shifts—changing the nature of production economies, of communication methods, of information dissemination—as are corresponding changes in business models. Many have written about these aspects of shifting competitive fields. Our focus complements their explanations. In fact, we could stretch the bounds of credulity by suggesting that our focus underlies the cogent arguments of technology and business model disruptions. How so?

Words are merely the manifestation of thought—of tacit knowledge. The use of words, and their codification into languages were rooted in the need of people to express themselves with a broader group of people—to realize scale and enhance group/collaborative behaviors. Not just words and not just languages, but ways of sharing their meaning became important. Such means require the codification into languages or other codified methods for meaningful communications. Codification, enabling shared expression, is precisely what is necessary to engender and extend both technology and business model disruptions; they must be expressed before they can be executed. Their *tacitness*—their inspiration—must be codified to be scaled, and scaled to be used, and used to be effective.

We explored how tacit knowledge becomes the basis for innovation at the edge of Jericho Zone collaborations and the criticality of figuring out how to keep a lid on that bubbling knowledge to minimize collaborative venture leakage and maximize harvesting that knowledge back into participating companies. We also discussed walking up and across the semantic stack as a key means to begin the codifying, capturing, and scaling the tacit knowledge and the knowledge accretion that results from collaborative ventures.

The Collaborative Landscape shifts; what was once of high value and high margin becomes commoditized with lowered barriers to entry. Much as the Collaborative Landscape shifts, so must our appreciation of the mechanics and the reasons for those shifts. So must our expertise with respect to taking advantage of them. Our recommended bottom-line: *There is an unmitigated, absolute, and critical need to make collaboration a core organizational and leadership skill.*

This section of the book focused on organizational implications of collaborative dynamics. Chapter Four described implications on business processes and the aggressive marketplace competition toward creating shared business process semantics. Managed services, outsourcing, and Web services were described as tools both to accommodate and accelerate the collapsing of organizational walls. They were also characterized as tools to help build consistent business semantics critical for collaborative success.

This chapter explored some of the people implications of collaboration, including intellectual property leakage. Individuals on the edge become the shock-troops of collaborative ventures with the resulting need to keep the lid on the knowledge secreted (from the collaborative venture) and accreted (to the individuals involved). Focusing on the processes to manage this accretion of tacit into codified knowledge becomes a critical requirement of effective collaborations.

Collaborations result from efforts to exploit specific market opportunities—or market inefficiencies in the sense that a high margin exists for some specific opportunity. The high margins result from the barriers or, in classic economic terms, asymmetries of information, knowledge, or capabilities that exist to exploit that opportunity. Over time, however, as the opportunity becomes demonstrably successful, the high margins will be squeezed as the processes, the technologies, the capabilities, the information—in short, the knowledge underlying all of these—becomes more codified and hence more available, reusable, and scalable. *Thus, the very process of codifying knowledge is at the crux of sharing the value and sharing the reward of collaborative activities.* What knowledge and what part of the semantic stack serves as the focal point for the collaboration for our point, right now, is less important than that the process of codifying tacit knowledge becomes the critical operational challenge and need for sustained collaborative success. It's all about semantics and the process of identifying, exploiting, and scaling tacit knowledge.

Chapter Six extends our focus of the semantic stack and its critical role. We provide a framework to characterize relevant and emerging collaborative technologies around the concept of architectural semantics. By so doing, we provide some tools and identify operational implications of how to exploit this emerging architectural approach both to respond to and to drive business collaborations.

CHAPTER HIGHLIGHTS

The Issue

To say that people are an organization's key asset is fine, but not nearly enough. Drilling down to understand the dynamics of the tacit knowledge people possess—of its half-life, of how to feed, nurture, sustain, expand, retain, and distribute it—becomes critical to exploit it effectively in any collaboration. What are these dynamics and how do we leverage them to create effective collaborations? How do we manage the inherent tension and risk of intellectual property leakage (from any participating organizations perspective) and intellectual accretion (to the individual involved) that inevitably results, from any collaboration (for the organization)?

The Insight

Collaborations result from efforts to exploit specific market opportunities—market inefficiencies resulting in high-margin business opportunity. These high margins result from the barriers or, in classic economic terms, asymmetries of information, knowledge, or capabilities that exist to exploit that opportunity. Over time, however, as the opportunity becomes demonstrably successful, the high margins will be squeezed as the processes, the technologies, the capabilities, the information—in short, the knowledge underlying all of these—becomes more codified and hence more available, reusable, and scalable. Thus, the very process of codifying knowledge is at the crux of sharing the value and sharing the reward of collaborative activities.

What is important is the notion that knowledge in a domain can, should, and will inexorably move toward greater levels of codification with significant implications on issues such as with whom to collaborate, how to do so, and consequences on the nature of competition as that codification occurs—as you walk up and across the semantic stack.

The Phrases

Tacit knowledge; knowledge is at the edges; IP leakage.

The Implications

The battle over tacit knowledge is critical to win with respect to competitive positioning; the value of this tacit knowledge lives at the edge of an organization as well as of any collaborative venture.

CHAPTER SIX

Technology at the Collaborative Edge

I n Chapters Two and Three, we introduced collaboration as a strategic tool for use in uncertain times and introduced two frameworks
for discussing collaboration: the Collaborative Landscape and the semantic stack. In Chapter Three, we drew heavily on analogies with the
software industry, especially the field of system integration, to derive
some principles of what it takes to operate in the Jericho Zone: codification of the knowledge, process, and technology within your organization to create *value ports,* places where your organization can easily
connect with other organizations to form collaborations to drive innovation. Then in Chapters Four and Five, we explored collaborative enablers from the perspective of the organization and the people in it,
paying particular attention to business processes, governance, the role
of people who innovate at the edge of the organization, and critically,
the importance of the tacit knowledge that gets created in the innovation
process, leakage of that knowledge, and the importance of controlling
that leakage.

Underlying it all is technology. Recognizing the underlying patterns
of technology as a driver of change helps to make sense of some of the
operational aspects of collaborative opportunities; and systematically making sense of collaborative opportunities gives us some guidance to making
sense of the type, the role, and the nature of technologies underlying

different collaborative forms. It requires, as well, making sense of the technology dynamic on which collaboration rests, along with much of your traditional business.

The role of technology as a juggernaut on organizational walls is unquestioned. We've explored in some detail Metcalfe's Law and its impact on business processes. Recall that Metcalfe's Law says that the usefulness of a network is proportional to the square of the number of users. We have extended its application to collaboration, especially as we have discussed walking across the semantic stack, where codifying the intellectual property at any one layer of the stack becomes more useful as the number of people who agree on the codification increases, eventually forming communities of people with a shared vocabulary who have, in effect, created value ports in that layer of the semantic stack.

In this chapter, we build on the collaborative DNA lessons from earlier chapters and explore their implications on architectural design and business/technology governance. One of the key challenges for effective collaborations, as we have said time and time again, is the construction and use of a shared vocabulary or semantic base that reconciles different understandings, expectations, and processes. Given the vital role of technology to enable effective collaborations, aggressively exploiting what we call *architectural semantics* becomes critical to support the agility and scale needed across multiple collaborative ventures.

As a society and as business organizations, we are profoundly affected by the way technology has enabled semantic understanding. Technology has given us the ability to quickly operationalize semantic understanding, aside from merely enormously increasing the sheer quantity of communication with which we are deluged. Much of the message of Chapter Three was that technology has profoundly influenced the codification of large amounts of knowledge across large populations. The challenge for technology groups in organizations wishing to operate in the Jericho Zone is to mobilize this unique power of technology to help other layers in the semantic stack along the path from tacit toward greater codification, hence executable and scalable knowledge.

Given that our organizations need to walk up and across the semantic stack, there are profound implications on both collaborative ventures and those organizations building collaborations as core capabilities. We explore those implications through identifying some of the trends that are increasing the reach of technology into the more human layers of the stack and pushing those layers to the right. We also explore what impact a requirement to operate in the Jericho Zone has on your technology strategy. Specifically, we explore the following:

- The semantic stack as a model for evaluating the actual and potential impact of technologies within an enterprise on collaboration
- Some of the larger technology trends that have the potential to affect codification in the higher, more human, layers of the semantic stack
- The technology impact of supporting the Jericho Zone and the resulting move from syntax oriented architecture toward *semantic architecture*
- The special goals of architecting for collaboration, the unique knowledge, skills, and tools required, and some resulting Jericho-specific roles such as the *collaborative architect*

This chapter provides a framework for characterizing relevant technologies around the concept of technology architecture informed by collaborative imperatives. We explore the push-me/pull-me tensions at the heart of technology/business investments in emerging technologies, showing that the business goals of efficient, effective collaboration drive key architectural goals of enhancing the semantic understanding of an organization. We describe *architectural semantics* as the resulting focal point for guiding technology strategy, innovation, implementation, and leveraging organizational IT assets within the emerging models of business collaboration to create business value. Grounding this chapter around architectural semantics provides a simple but effective means to cut through the tremendous amount of technology noise around collaborative opportunities.

Some of this exploration is a challenge—this book is not targeted specifically to a technology audience, but, as in Chapters Two and Three, we need to get our hands dirty technically to uncover some important topics. For those places where we gloss over details to get to the business essence of a point of technology, we offer our apologies to the technologists. Conversely, in those places where we dig into a technology topic and get some bits under our fingernails, we also proffer apologies to the business reader. But we believe that beyond respective discomfort lies shared appreciation for that discomfort—our goal is to identify specific operational implications for more effective collaborations.

SOME OBSERVATIONS AND IMPLICATIONS FROM THE FIELD

Starting with the Observations: Semantic Architecture

This is not a technology book, therefore, we will not base this chapter on our observations about the state of technology. We do not look for technology to drive strategy; nor do we believe that enumeration of technologies and technical possibilities, while possibly interesting, has any lasting relevance. Consequently, this chapter takes a different path. Rather, we look at how the target collaborative interactions that we have discussed in the preceding chapters—interactions that a business may be required or expected to support in the next few years—drive the relationship of technology to business. From these observations, we derive some specific implications on your business' technology and on the technology organizations that create it and support it. To start with, very simply, a company uses technology to run its day-to-day operations, and a company uses technology to support its people in the innovation process. In both of these cases, the technology organization views the business as a customer—a very close, strategic customer that it treats like a partner, but still, a customer that makes demands that drive the approach of the technology organization. Much as companies have changed their relationship with their customers, as we discussed somewhat in the context of Customer Relationship Management in Chapter Three, the information technology (IT) department is changing its relationship with the business.

One of the key challenges for effective collaborations, as we have said repeatedly, is the construction and use of a shared vocabulary or semantic base. Given the vital role of technology to enable effective collaboration, aggressively exploiting architectural semantics becomes critical to supporting the agility and scale needed across multiple collaborative ventures. The implications on an organization's overall approach to its relationship with the business—its focus, architectural approach, and implementation approach—leads to specific decisions, behaviors, and practices.

Observation 1: The Technology Dynamic—Walking up and across the Semantic Stack

In Chapter Three, we introduced the semantic stack as a way of representing the domains in which organizations need to have a common vocabulary to collaborate. As we have seen, there is an organizational view of the stack, and a people view of the stack, so it should come as no surprise that there is also a technological view to each layer of the semantic stack. Like the organization, technology is not a contributor to innovation itself. People, and only people, innovate. But technology is a vital player in enabling the collaboration. The lower layers of the stack have been the focus of a great deal of technology and, as a result, the very way we think of the layer is shaped by the technology used to support it. Other layers—especially the upper, more human layers—have a more subtle or indirect relationship to technology in its current state. In the next few pages, we walk through the semantic stack layer by layer and identify some of the underlying technologies. We extend the analogy between system integration and collaboration that we developed in Chapter Three to show how disciplines, practices, and methods born out of necessity in the technology space can be applied to business elements in the various domains of the semantic stack. We then discuss the technology families that can be applied to increase the level of codification of the domain. We also show where and how higher degrees of semantic codification increase not only internal, but also interenterprise capability.

Connectivity Layer: Standards Helping People Connect

As we saw in Chapter Three, some parts of the semantic stack have been driven into highly codified states and are fully executable. In terms of technology, the success of the technology standards bodies (e.g., the IETF, introduced in Chapter Three) in the lower parts of the semantic stack has created an environment where software and hardware vendors can create products in a virtually transparent market. Ubiquitous connectivity based on the Internet Protocol (IP) is a clear example as connectivity via an IP-based network is essentially a universal prerequisite to modern business. This highly codified knowledge is consequently embedded into most commercial technology by most commercial vendors.

From the perspective of the semantic stack, the connectivity domain connotes communication, so semantically this is the layer of connectivity among people, using technologies such as e-mail, Web-based collaboration software such as Webex[1] or NetMeeting,[2] collaboration software such as SharePoint™,[3] and instant messaging (IM). As we saw in Chapter Three, the power of a ubiquitous Internet has made IP the definitive connectivity medium, and has defined the semantics by which we refer to network connectivity. This has been reinforced by widespread business acceptance of the standard, and thus Metcalfe's Law has taken hold.

As also discussed in Chapter Three, there are numerous standards—such as MIME, HTML, HTTP—that have been universally accepted largely because of IP's universal acceptance. Each of these provides functionality across a range of software products from various vendors. In collaborative relationships between people, the need to communicate is key, and so the observation in this layer of the stack is that collaboration will be served by pervasive, standards-based technologies for the exchange of information both within your organization and with other organizations. The open exchange of information creates concerns about the security of your company's intellectual property, computing resources, and information—concerns that are valid, but that should not be addressed using means that sacrifice information flow.

Architecture and Platform Layer

Semantic understanding through patterns is a comfortable, familiar concept from our everyday life. From a computer technology perspective, architecture refers to the description of components and the way those components interact with one another. Architecture creates an abstraction of some set of human, business, or technology capabilities that allows us to think about and manipulate those capabilities, revealing patterns of interactions and allowing analysis. To think about the architecture layer in terms of the semantic stack, we should think about the business entities or capabilities that are involved in innovation, and the interactions between them. The interesting technology in this part of the stack will be technologies that help to codify those entities and their interactions.

Large organizations are actively using the concepts of architecture to help them think about diverse aspects of the business, such as their overall business structure and operation, their organization, business process, personnel career paths, and skills distribution. For example, an organizational architecture view might examine organizational units in terms of the business value they steward and create, and the way the units interact with one another. Abstracting the details of the people involved, departments, former company affiliation, and so on, it is possible to analyze these components and interactions and explore improvements.

In this context, technology has had a codifying effect in that technology architecture, following the motivations that we discussed in some detail in Chapter Three, has worked out techniques and practices for characterizing components. Such characterization allows architects to partition complex sets of capabilities in ways that are demonstrably ideal—at least in some limited sense of the word—and to encapsulate those capabilities to form components that have ideal—again in some limited sense of the word—interactions. The practical upshot of this sort of architectural approach can be seen in numerous examples of companies encapsulating, and then exposing, discrete pieces of their business functionality in a way that they can create new sources of revenue from what were once internal business processes. In Chapter Five, we discussed companies, like Procter & Gamble, that have discovered valuable assets within their day-to-day operations and created collaborative relationships to commercialize those assets. The process of taking an internal asset, creating the boundaries around it that allow it to be used within the organization that created it and also in other organizations, requires *identification, partitioning,* and *encapsulation.* In so doing, the asset itself is codified, and, critically, *so is that part of the organization that needs to interact with it.*

The technology overlay on this is that the technology architecture needs to enable an architectural approach for the nontechnology aspects of your business. This includes technologies that enable identification, partitioning, and encapsulation. For example, we have found in our day-to-day interactions with clients that tools and methodologies created for internal use are rarely finished to the quality expected of a commercial product. Therefore, when companies choose to externalize assets that were formerly internal assets, they usually have work to do to bring them up to commercial standards.

The Internet has been responsible for exposing many internal corporate assets to the outside world. A simple illustration of this point involves a company that wants to make it possible for customers to access statements via the Web. The company has its customer data stored in some back-office system that has been used for years. That system was designed to support the business process that existed before the Internet, where it was necessary to provide online support only for callers during normal business hours. Operationally it requires frequent scheduled offline time outside of normal business hours—typically for operational tasks such as accepting batch loads of data from some other system. Adding an Internet presence for customers means that the back-office system needs to be up and available all of the time, requiring an engineering effort to enhance the capabilities of the existing systems or to replace the system altogether. This sort of requirement has driven major rearchitecture efforts throughout organizations that have chosen to do business online. As a result, there has emerged a common *pattern* of how to partition and share the resulting processing load through the creation of specialized functions, which has aided semantic understanding. There has not been a singular market adoption of a standard product, but rather the market's agreement on a common set of patterns, or abstractions—such as the thin-client approach to creating application software.

Thus, the technology observation for the architecture and platform domain is that disciplines that have been used for technology architectures have been demonstrably extensible to provide tools and insight for describing and improving nontechnology business entities. The patterns revealed provide insight to technologies that can be applied to the business to extend codification in this layer of the stack. Going back to the three architectural concepts we identified earlier, codification of the architectural aspects of the business includes identification, partitioning, and encapsulation:

- *Identification* of the business entities and the capabilities that they provide can be codified through the rationalization of the sources and semantics of the data used throughout the corporation. Many companies have entire organizations whose task it is to reconcile the meaning of the data used within the company. For example, we discussed one major company where there are nine distinct usages of data identified as customer—each unique, and each embedded in legacy computer systems that are here to stay and are not amenable to modification. By cataloging such ambiguous data and describing that data in such a way that the ambiguity can be managed, an organization creates a data abstraction that codifies the data being used in various parts of the company, thus helping the identification task. Such "data about data" goes by the name *metadata,* and repositories of metadata are concrete ways in which technology aids codification.

- *Partitioning* the identified entities into components that can be treated architecturally and *encapsulation* of those components is facilitated by technologies that help to make explicit the implicit characteristics and behaviors of business entities. Thus, technologies that support the identification and externalization of business rules and workflow, as we discussed in Chapter Three, can play a huge role in codifying this layer of the stack. Further, technologies that support a component's ability to describe what it does and to communicate with other components about which it might know little or nothing can enable the interaction between components that make the partitioning and encapsulation useful. This is the role of other technologies that we examined in Chapter Three, such as the WSDL and UDDI used in Web services to provide known repositories of component descriptions, and the business-specific vocabularies of XML that provide for loosely coupled communication among components.

Our technical observations show us that the technology dynamic in the semantic stack is pretty much the same as the dynamic that we saw when we examined organizations and people. The drive to codify higher and higher layers of the stack is one of the key characteristics of the Red Queen. She runs, and she runs relentlessly. Your technology provides part of the equipment to help you run along with her.

Application Layer: Patterns and Best Practices

Recall from Chapter Three that *applications* as we use it in the semantic stack could just as easily be termed *service,* or *capability,* or *functionality.* Applications are the things that provide chunks of useful capability, possibly through people, possibly by way of a computer program. In architectural terms, applications are the components that interact. So, the architecture domain is about identifying, partitioning, and encapsulating functionality into services or applications. What are the lessons that technology teaches about the application layer, and how does technology help us keep up with the pressure to walk across this layer of the stack?

Architectural principles applied to the business will likely result in the identification of a set of business components that fit a reasonably typical pattern. Consequently, the components themselves tend to have certain common features that should make it reasonably straightforward to understand what they do, what they need in terms of support services to do it, and how to work with them. In terms of the business components that we have been discussing, this means that a good partitioning of business entities results in very little duplication of effort, identification of shared and common services, and a lot of interaction between entities to accomplish business goals.

This is exactly what we see as corporations reorganize to accommodate the inclusion of a new entity after a merger or acquisition, or to increase internal efficiencies. It has become common practice, for example, to create shared services for such functions as human resources, payroll, benefits, finance. Functions that are not part of the corporation's core value and innovation engine, but are crucial for support of its operation. Corporations carefully craft interfaces among the operational business units and these shared services to make sure that the services provide precisely the service needed for the business. So, for example, the PeopleSoft[4] implementation for a large financial institution required extensive configuration to handle in a common service the disparate compensation needs of senior equities traders and the customer service representatives on the hotline. The success of companies that provide systems targeted to providing such shared services—companies like SAP

214 THE JERICHO PRINCIPLE

and PeopleSoft—is evidence of the prevalence of partitioning and encapsulation at this layer, and to the degree of codification in the definition of some of these shared services. If the services—the applications—of organizations are identified, partitioned, and encapsulated according to architectural principles with a defined set of capabilities and interfaces to each of these services, then we have the beginnings of an environment that understands how to support collaboration. Returning to the system integration analogy of collaboration used in Chapter Three, the conditions for effective collaboration were the ability to find something that does what you need it to do, and to understand how to interact with it. The architected organization provides those conditions.

It is reasonable to assume that over time companies will create components that provide more and more tightly focused functionality, with different means of implementing the needed functionality—some of them might be provided by internal organizations, some outsourced, some provided through collaborative partners, and some provided through marketplaces. In fact, as component definitions get better, the boundaries of the organization will become less well defined, and the distinction between providing a capability in-house or from outside will become less important. If the capability in question is the ability to innovate to take advantage of a particular opportunity, this is the *Jericho Zone*. The technology observation, then, is that operating in the Jericho Zone will require the methods and practices to define the architected organization, the tools with which to express the functionality of the components and the means to interact with them, the interfaces, agreements (in the case of outsourcing), and the infrastructure needed to run them.

Defining the architected organization, and having a language in which to express and communicate the definition, puts us in the domain of modeling and design. Over the years, there have been many approaches to modeling and design, but it appears that the clearly preferred approach is object-oriented design, with the design expressed in the Unified Modeling Language (UML).[5] We will not go into any detail regarding object-oriented modeling and design other than to say it is a means to express the essential details of something you want to describe in a way that is independent of the specific way that something might be implemented, and that allows you to express and use the design at different levels of interconnected detail. Object-oriented design is a discipline that must be learned, and UML is a language in which we strive to be fluent. Why? For a simple reason: The reward for the effort of learning is access to a vocabulary that is shared by a very large population across all industries globally.

Hopefully by this point in the book, you accept that the codification represented by such a shared vocabulary over such a large population has high value. Another very nice thing about UML is that the highest level description of a component is done using something called a *Use Case,* which is easily learned and used by people with no technology background, thus serving as a good common language point between business people and software engineers.

The tools for expressing the functionality of the components and how to interact with them include UML, which provides for robust definition of interfaces and interactions among components, tools that support the modeling of business process, and tools for expressing business rules. These last two sets of tools are generally provided as design-time tools to create a model, and an execution-time environment to interpret the model and actually execute the process. In the case of business rules, the execution component is a rules engine. In the case of business process, the execution component is a workflow engine. As far as defining the data to be passed across the interfaces, XML provides the vocabulary that, like UML, is understood by a large population of humans, as well as an equally large, if not larger, number of applications.

The infrastructure needed to support an architected organization with many interacting components needs to support ubiquitous connectivity via a common network (read IP), and will have numerous applications that implement specific partitioned component functionality working together to provide complex business functionality. The technology term for this is *N-tier application architecture,* meaning multiple (*N*) interacting components where the relationship between components determined by the business problem to be solved rather than by some fixed hierarchical structure. *N*-tier architectures are characterized by components that interact via some common communications mechanism using some common interface mechanism (where communication moves the bits intelligently between the components, and interface specifies the format and content of the bits being moved). In *N*-tier architectures, the communications mechanism is often in the form of a function-rich "bus" such as the messaging bus provided by products such as Tibco,[6] Vitria,[7] or Neon,[8] or as a function-rich environment such as .NET, COM, or J2EE.

In the application layer of the stack, the services-based partitioning of functionality that has driven leading edge distributed software development over the past few years enables a similar partitioning of business functionality. As discussed here, supported by technology and process born of technology, the resultant codification of business functionality can be distributed widely through a variety of relationships, including collaborative relationships in the Jericho Zone.

Business Process Layer: A Common Need to Understand Variation

Business process is the new frontier for operational excellence, business agility, and efficiency.[9] Across industries, companies are focusing on *business processes* and their best practices. Many organizations are very interested in understanding how they compare to companies that they consider benchmark companies, and even more interested to know what they can do to create flexible scalable process—and the associated operational capability—to cope with the Red Queen and her continually changing business environment.

We have discussed business process modeling, workflow, and business rules elsewhere in this chapter and in this book. We discussed the drive to externalize the business rules and the workflow of the business process to make explicit the embedded, often tacit, rules and flows that are key to the outcome of the business process. We then discussed how externalizing rules and workflow is a crucial first step in codification because it provides the common ground needed so that companies can compare themselves with others like them, or with industry benchmark organizations. As a result, best practices can be identified that guide organizations toward some degree of commonality in the way they break work down, and in the steps and sequencing of the work. Everyone tries to emulate best practices; as a result, the business rules and workflows tend to start looking similar from company to company.

Along with the technology we've discussed for modeling, rules, and workflow, which help with defining and enabling business process, there is additional work needed to create an actual operational capability, that is trained and focused humans. Technology has a major role to play in communicating change and in training people to execute in a changing, highly flexible environment. Thus, technologies to support distributed training— so-called e-learning technologies—and Internet-based meetings form a part of the technology support for the business process layer.

Roles and Metrics Layer: Judging Performance Quality

As discussed in Chapter Three, the roles part of roles and metrics is concerned with understanding what organizations and people do, and the metrics part is concerned with measuring how well they do it. Externally, this domain is ruled by the marketplace, where a company's role is its place in the overall marketplace—as a services provider or a product provider, as a high-value player or a low-cost player, and so on—and where the company's performance is judged by the price that its shares bring on a stock exchange. Internally, this domain includes incentive plans, and employee goal setting and review, business planning and the business' performance against that plan. What are the drivers to walk up this part of the stack, and what role does technology play in walking across this layer?

The financial markets have a major codifying influence in this domain. Each company is perceived by the market as playing by a set of roles, and associated with those roles is a set of metrics by which the market judges the performance of the company, and by which the market either rewards or punishes the company through its price-setting mechanisms. For example, a professional services provider might be measured on performance metrics such as the percentage of time professional staff is working on billable client engagements or on how much business is carried into the financial reporting period due to long-term contracts. To the degree that a company is composed of multiple business units, the performance of each of those units rolls up to the overall performance of the company. Why are we discussing this in a chapter on technology in a book about collaboration?

Because a company that is being punished by the markets will find it difficult to collaborate with anyone—at least part of the perception of your potential collaborative partners will be based on its market perception of you (How many companies have lost business because a potential customer was uneasy about a sinking share price?), and if they have a bad impression, it will be difficult to create a favorable relationship. Technology offers help by influencing the processes by which the organization is structured, run, and measured—which affects the market's perception of the role of the company—by providing the infrastructure for the effective collection and reporting of appropriate metrics for the day-to-day management of the company, and for reporting to the people who are tracking the company's performance. Thus, the technology organization has some specific roles of its own to play in this layer of the stack:

- Providing the architectural thought leadership to apply to the overall structure of the organization. This requires the technology organization to understand the difference between a technology architecture and the concepts of architecture as applied to the business, as well as requiring the business to understand that the engineering disciplines have something to offer.

- Creating the environment for component organizations to effectively externalize things like workflow and business rules that are needed for the business processes of the architected organization.

- Leading the way to the common shared vocabulary for expressing, communicating, collecting, and reporting the associated metrics.

Figure 6.1 shows how these elements work together to provide the sort of visibility into the business operation that is needed for day-to-day management, accurate reporting, and (probably most important in the current business climate) no surprises. Note that the existence of well-defined architectural components and interactions as shown in Figure 6.1 also becomes an enabling factor for creating value ports.

Recall that another major codification that has happened in this domain has come from the increased use of managed services and outsourcing. Coupled with the codifications that we discussed in this chapter in the architecture and application layers, this identification and externalization of significant business components has driven the need to objectively specify roles and responsibilities across organizations, and to specify equally objectively the levels of service that are expected, and to monitor the service that is provided. A company entering an outsourcing relationship must externalize those parts of its organization that have to

FIGURE 6.1 ARCHITECT FOR ORGANIZATION AND BUSINESS REPORTING

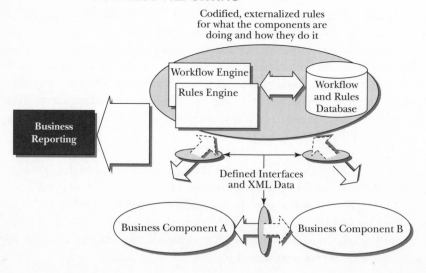

interact with the outsourcer. From the perspective of this chapter, this implies that some degree of architecturally oriented thought has been applied to the organization (to identify, partition, and encapsulate the business function that is to be outsourced, as well as the business function that has to interface with the part that is outsourced). The technology organization must also be in a position to provide thought leadership and guidance on the construction and monitoring of the agreements that govern the performance expectations of the service provider—so called service level agreements (SLAs).

Finally, in this domain, an architected organization with its well-defined business components provides the basis for a fluid, dynamic organization. For the organization to actually *act* dynamically, it is necessary for the people in the organization to have confidence that they will be properly cared for as their roles, and therefore the organization's expectations, change. For this, it is necessary to provide the organizational infrastructure that supports people changing jobs easily, easy and frequent updating of goals, tracking of those goals, changing of incentives and compensation, and so on. Technology again has a role to play in the architecture of the organization to create well-defined organizational components to service these needs, in rationalizing the organizational data involved in this infrastructure, and in putting much of the ability to create, track, and update that data in the hands of the employees through technologies that allow more responsibility to move to the edge of the organization—that is, into the hands of the people who are actually affected by the information.

Behaviors/Values Layer: Understanding Patterns of Group Behavior

Behaviors/values has to do with the organizational culture: How people act, how the organization acts, and how the people act on behalf of the organization. From the perspective of the semantic stack, this is the domain of assumptions—actual as opposed to espoused values.

As noted in Chapter Three, there has been very little activity that points toward what, if any, codification is likely to happen in this area, at least as regards external codification for the purposes of collaboration. There are no extant standards bodies codifying the behaviors/values domain—at least none with which we are familiar. That said, in Chapters Four and Five, we discussed the organizational and people aspects of collaboration, and discussed some of the imperatives to walk across this layer of the stack. We discussed an example of collaboration where there was a need, at the point where two groups of people from different organizations meet, to match titles and levels so that people on one team understand roughly the roles played by the people on the other team, and that imperfect communication in the matching process—due to the highly tacit nature—leads to miscommunication, misconception, and missed opportunities. In Chapter Three, we used this example in the roles/metrics domain, and here we draw on it one level up to note the relationship of roles/metrics to the behaviors/values that are the subject of this layer.

Much has been written over the past 10 years on organizational alignment, generally taken to be the degree to which the people of the organization all work toward the strategic goals of that organization.[10] Alignment begins with the statement of strategy, and finds its way through enterprise plans, into business unit plans, into group and individual performance goals, and finally into individual behaviors and values, generally tied to compensation, incentives, and career advancement. As we discussed in Chapter Four, organizations who are looking for collaborative partners will use, as at least a part of their selection criteria, the potential partner's corporate behaviors and values—a caring/nurturing organization, for example, might think twice before getting into a close relationship with a more driven, predatory organization (or might preferentially select such an organization as a complement for a particular venture). The selection for an initial collaborative venture might be made on the basis of market perceptions and top-level meetings. Whether the relationship then extends to other ventures will likely depend, at least partially, on the extent to which the participants in the collaboration actually reflect the corporate behaviors and values. Therefore, alignment is important to collaboration in the Jericho Zone, and technology has a role to play in alignment.

The technology responsibilities here, at least initially, focus on fostering communication and on creating a structured vocabulary for action on that communication. For communication, e-mail, Enterprise Information Portals,[11] and the Web-based collaboration tools and e-learning technologies that we discussed earlier all contribute to the communication of corporate goals and objectives. There is a key role for the technology that creates pervasive communications as part of the fabric of the everyday business process. The structured vocabulary requires some additional discussion.

We have been involved in several client projects aimed at using technology to help with capturing and mobilizing the tacit knowledge of the organization. Sometimes the projects are labeled as knowledge management projects, sometimes as collaboration projects, and sometimes—in the best cases—they are labeled as the implementation phase of an ongoing corporate culture of best practices and knowledge sharing. An excellent example of this is an initiative at ChevronTexaco,[12] where there is a deeply rooted culture of operational excellence, best practices, and mobilization of expertise, where the mantra of the project was "Quality Answers in Minutes, not Days." In the ChevronTexaco case, the goals of the project were to mobilize information to enable question-and-answer (Q&A) access for people with an immediate need, the collection of best practices to form the organizational benchmark for how to do things right the first time, and to push best practices into the planning process, so that business units will all, over time, converge on the best practices. In effect, the project used technology and leveraged ChevronTexaco's existing vocabulary for best practices and operational excellence, to create structured communication processes for propagating best practices, on demand in the case of Q&A, as a pervasive process in the case of business planning. This is the structured vocabulary that gives ChevronTexaco the ability to execute on the communication of best practices. Technology is not *the* answer here, but technology plays a crucial role in connecting the organization, culture, and business process to make the implementation practical.

Environment Layer: Recognition and Support of Tacit Understanding

From the perspective of the semantic stack, the environment layer is the domain of how the business relates to the marketplace and how the business relates to the economy. As with behaviors/values, there has been very little activity that points toward what, if any, codification is likely to happen in this area, at least as regards external codification for the purposes of innovation. That said, technology has a major role to play in this layer as, more and more, businesses connect to their revenue sources through technology. If those last two sentences appear contradictory, let's stop and be more explicit. Remember that codification for the purposes of collaboration refers to the framing that enables the people who actually innovate at the edges to get on with the innovation part of their work quickly and effectively. In the environment layer, that would imply codification of the highest level business consciousness so that something like, say, a merger, could be accomplished mechanically, and the people involved in the value that is supposed to result from the merger could concentrate all of their energies on driving the merged entity into its new markets. There is little cross-industry effort at codification at this layer; this layer continues to be so rich in tacit knowledge, hence high margin and highly differentiated value, that it remains a vibrant competitive battlefield of semantic differences.

However, this is the layer in which the business connects with customers to sell its goods, connects with the marketplace for market intelligence that drives strategy, and connects to the financial markets for capital. In these areas, there has been a great deal of codification. Thus, this is the layer where the role of technology is to enable the connection of the business to supply chains, such as the Covisint example that we discussed in Chapters Two and Four, and to online marketplaces such as Creditex for online trading of credit derivatives. We discuss the implications of such external connectivity later in this chapter.

Observation 2: Technology at the Edges—Innovate or Pay the Price

The codification in the lower layers of the semantic stack is far advanced compared to the higher levels of the stack. This codification is an inevitable result of the Red Queen acting in the market, as we discussed in Chapter Five. In these markets that were once a hot bed of widely dispersed innovation and centrifugal differentiation, knowledge, and business practices have become so highly executable that it is now a self-evident marketing advantage for a product in this space to adhere to a standard. Every institutional software salesman in the world must have a story as to how their product fits in seamlessly with their customer's current systems, usually indicating a strict adherence to some set of standards that are in use by the customer. Why? Because, as we saw in Chapters Four and Five, there is no longer any high margin here to exploit, so the ventures within the Collaborative Landscape have moved down and to the left.

But even within the lower levels of the stack, there is a great deal of tacit knowledge and innovation, as well as opportunity for profit. Recall the innovator's dilemma: In established markets, the innovation goes toward incremental improvement of the existing products. This means that the nature of competition and resulting economics that need to be supported in the lower layers is different from that of the upper layers. A low-margin game requires high-volume transactions; there is simply no room for operational error to meet quarterly and razor-thin margins; hence, the relentless focus on operational excellence and ever more aggressive attempts to streamline logistics and global supply chains to eliminate as much process inefficiency as possible. Thus, the focus of the technology organization in supporting innovation in collaborations that are targeted in the lower layers of the stack will be on the relentlessly critical, minute, and incremental improvements that create more productivity, scalability, or accessibility at lower cost or higher productivity.

It further means that the technology organization has two distinct focuses for innovation, related to the two uses of technology that we discussed in the first paragraphs of this section. For the operational use of technology in the core of the business, technology innovations focus on increased productivity and reduced cost. For the support of the innovation processes by which the company creates new value, technology focuses on the things that we discussed in our walk through the semantic stack: the things that support the architected organization, and the people that work at the edges within that organization.

Stated differently, innovation focuses on burrowing down or blowing up existing entities. Lowered margins bring in competition—the barriers to entry simply aren't there. Consequently, the competitive game has no choice but to shift in terms of being operationally excellent (competing in terms of who has the best codified set of practices) or resetting the competitive barrier and returning to a high-margin competitive game. It is exactly for this reason that as layers of the semantic stack become more codified and therefore more scalable and executable, leading vendors begin to blur their stack focus; as they move across the semantic stack, they begin, at the same time, to move up the stack as well—into areas of higher margin, more tacit-rich environments.

This dynamic remains the same, regardless of focus, regardless of what layer of the semantic stack is being attacked. This is, again, one of the key characteristics of the Red Queen: She runs, and she runs relentlessly. As layers of the stack become executable and the semantics become shared, the nature of competition shifts. What was once high margin becomes lower margin with significant competitive and strategic shifts. Using our model again, the lines between the layers become blurred and high-margin competition begins anew—but simply in a new competitive arena again with higher margins to realize. The semantic stack tends to have blurred horizontal boundaries as new technologies are introduced, get adopted, and mature into integrated product offerings by the vendor community.

On and on the Red Queen runs. Up and across the semantic stack, your technology organization supports your core business and your innovation process, and the technology vendors compete in creating their own view of the relationship of technology to business. Each of these observations reflects collaborative opportunities resulting from understanding the dynamics underlying the semantic stack. Each also has significant organizational implications to accelerate exploiting those opportunities.

Some Implications of What This Means to You

Implication 1: Staying Abreast of Technology
Trends—the Evangelist

As discussed in Chapter Five, staying ahead of the Red Queen requires celebrating the edges—the edge of technologies, the edge of business models, the edges of knowledge. By its very nature, the edge is unknown by most, and knowable by few. Yet, it is an area that must be explored and aggressively exploited. Given the role that technology plays in supporting the core business and supporting the innovation of the business, it becomes critical to figure out how to harvest the tacit knowledge from the leading edges of technology, and then manage and, as appropriate, institutionalize it.

One approach that we have used is to identify people to play the role of advanced technology scouts and market evangelists. The scout, first defined by John Mashey,[13] is a person whose job it is to find new technologies that might be interesting to an organization, how they might be used and what the impact might be to the organization's future direction. Most organizations have some form of the scout role, typically using the label *advanced technology*. The market evangelist has a related but different responsibility that includes staying abreast of industry and technology trends and working with key customers to determine how they might best take advantage of them. At Unisys, we established a Global Transformation Team to work with and stay abreast of business, technology, and client "edges." Cisco Systems had their Internet Services Business Group (ISBG) that are market evangelists with respect to emerging networking technologies and their range of possible impacts on yet-to-be determined business practices. Microsoft Corporation has defined a new evangelist role in their aggressive stance toward becoming more relevant to the larger enterprise marketplace. Their objective is to serve as dialogue partners discussing and clarifying business issues, then evangelizing the role Microsoft technologies could help address those issues. Many other companies have similar evangelist and scout roles (or an internal change agent role).

This role of staying abreast of the curve is not a simple one: It is not easily boxed within the traditional expense and revenue metrics used to run the organization, yet neither is it one that can be ignored. The evangelist's job, at its essence, involves figuring how to manage the creative tension between the operational realities of what and how you conduct business today and how you prepare for emerging competitive opportunities at the point in the future where the arrows in the three-arrow picture start to bend in noticeable ways. The evangelist's job, in short, is staying ahead of the Red Queen—exploring what is still new—and tacit—and figuring out how to make it operationally viable. And this leads us to the second implication.

Implication 2: The Movement toward Semantic Architecture

Architectural semantics is a focal point for guiding technology strategy, innovation, and implementation, leveraging organizational IT assets within the emerging models that use business collaboration to create business value. This is different from the viewpoint of system integration that we discussed in Chapter Three, where the focus is on technology architectures that help make it easier to make systems work together to create a specific business value. The systems integration point of view is of necessity a narrow one given the need to make things work together in the best possible way. The semantic architecture view is much more open, looking at the longer, deeper, wider strategic goals of enhancing the semantic positioning of an organization including:

- Deliberately working technology up the stack and also using technology as appropriate to codify the more human aspects of the stack
- Providing technology support for those human activities so critical to innovation
- Leveraging technology, standards, and architecture that are themselves highly codified so that connecting with another organization via a value port is as painless as possible

From this semantic architectural view, technology architecture has as a goal—not the *only* goal or even the most important goal, but *an* important goal—to support the domains of the semantic stack. This statement is obvious in light of the focus of this book. However, it represents a very large increase in scope compared to the traditional architectural focus of technology organizations. Think again from the viewpoint of the system integrator.

Internal IT efforts traditionally approach technology from the perspective of a business service (aligned with an organizational component in the core of the business), a support service (e.g., human resources), or a utility service (e.g., a business rules engine or a specialty calculator for the performance of a variable annuity). They add to or modify an existing set of functionality, or they substitute a current service through, for example, package replacement or outsourcing. This makes sense because the portfolio of applications in an enterprise comprises the functionality needed for the internal organization to create value for its customers. We call architecture with this focus *syntactic architecture.* We cannot emphasize enough that this is a descriptive term, not a pejorative term. As we discussed, technology innovation in the context of syntactic architecture is focused on productivity enhancement, either through increased scale or reduced cost, or for support of new products or product extensions. In this context, it is the system integrator's point of view that applies: Efficiently create business value by leveraging existing assets through reuse and re-engineering, and develop new software where necessary.

In the Jericho Zone, there is an additional architectural focus—not to replace syntactic architecture, but to augment it with an explicit charter to exploit technology to codify higher layers of (or walk across) the semantic stack to enhance the organization's ability to collaborate. This broader charter, with its focus on deeper transformational semantic enabling, implies designing architectures with an explicit goal of accommodating collaborative activities—particularly those that enable rapid and multiple collaborations and the management of intellectual property required to keep a lid on the leakage of increasingly valuable intellectual property.

At some level, syntactic and semantic architecture deal with the same sorts of stuff—business components, technology components, servers, applications, and so on. Critically, however, they take divergent views of this stuff, which creates a dynamic tension between the two viewpoints. We take an example from Enterprise Application Integration (EAI). From the viewpoint of syntactic architecture, applications are aligned with business functionality. A typical application implements a piece of business functionality and interacts with other applications and services—for example, a workflow engine, or a service that knows how to send messages between applications to productively function on the enterprise's production floor. Software tool vendors, understanding this need, have assembled product suites that provide access to needed services in a fully integrated, one-stop-shop package. These include product suites such as IBM's WebSphere, and the offerings from generally recognized EAI vendors such as SeeBeyond or Vitria. These products allow applications an easy integration point using standards-based technologies such as XML, however, they provide their various services using internal, sometimes proprietary, interfaces.

From the viewpoint of the application developer, this is convenient. From the viewpoint of the syntactic architect, it is troubling; the very bundling of functionality that makes the product suite attractive to the developer works against the architect's desire to identify, partition, and encapsulate. Since these product suites are generally fashioned from standard architectural elements, a syntactic architect can hold his or her nose and accept the bundling, understanding that the organization is accepting vendor dependence in exchange for the convenience of integrated functionality. However, from the viewpoint of the semantic architecture, the bundling is disastrous. The vendor bundling of application services cuts through the vertical layers of the stack—for example, through the network layer (messaging), the application layer, and the business process layer (workflow and rules). However, the semantic architect is focused also on connecting with other organizations in value ports that match up horizontally, at specific layers of the stack. A vertical bundling that is syntactically good is likely to be semantically bad, unless the various bundled components are accessible layer-by-layer through standards-based interfaces. For example, if the workflow engine in a vendor's EAI offering can be unbundled and accessed via Web services, then the semantic architect stands a chance of connecting to another organization's workflow at the business process layer. If not, the expenditure on the EAI package offers *syntactic value* but with no corresponding increase in codification that is necessary for it to offer *semantic value*. From this, we get to the aspect of semantic architecture that leads to the next implication.

Implication 3: Standards, Standards, Standards

Thinking about technology using the Collaborative Landscape as the model brings up the notion of semantic architecture, that is, architecture strategically associated with the semantic stack, and thus with the goals of the organization to innovate one step ahead of the Red Queen through frequent, efficient, and effective collaboration. The architectural implication, then, is to use collaboration as a key guiding principle when defining the necessary technology services and the interactions among them. Recognizing opportunities, potential collaborators, and the construction of more and more intellectual property occurring in the Jericho Zone among multiple interests will need to be conveyed, managed, and proliferated via technology. Organizing architecture from an intellectual property or semantic point of view better supports the handling of a huge increase in complexity with both better economic incentives and technical monitoring tools.

Semantic architecture is targeted to supporting higher and higher levels of (as well as walking across) the semantic stack, providing more and more codification. In supporting the domains of the semantic stack, even as the subject matter of the domain gets more and more tacit, it is important that the technology used to support it relies on highly codified technology standards and interfaces. In this way, technologists can satisfy in their own way the tenet so important to medical doctors: Do no harm. As we saw in Chapter Three, and have revisited in this chapter, technology has driven an enormous amount of codification, generally through the mechanism of the standards bodies.

The standards organizations are the embodiment of processes in which tacit understanding becomes increasingly codified. The notion of standards has become imbedded in our thinking as a fundamental quality for stable interactive products. Can it work with other products? This question cannot be considered absent standards. Eventually, as we have discussed numerous times in this book, the high-value interactions among participants in any subject domain become generally understandable through an incremental refinement process that creates shared semantics within a community of practitioners and across a population of casual users. This process of recognition and refined communication, which is at the heart of every standards body in the world, has accelerated, formalized, and proliferated the habit of standardization in most disciplines. It has become a basic part of the DNA of doing business.

As a kind of working model, we can think of standards bodies as expert facilitators of collaboration techniques across increasingly varied participants. That is, we have discussed the need to walk up and across the stack, and standards bodies have been doing this—usually working with a fairly unruly bunch of participants—for years. The business benefits that have accrued due to codification in the lower engineering layers of the semantic stack will be overshadowed by the business benefits yet to be realized in the codification of the higher layers as more and more semantic levels of the enterprise require collaboration.

The implication on technology is clear: Demand standards-based products and interfaces to products from your vendors. Demand standards-based development practices from your developers. Keep your scouts and evangelists on the alert for upcoming standards that you can influence or leverage, or that will cause you pain. By driving your supporting technology to a standards-basis, you will make sure that it stays in the supporting role that you want, rather than becoming the star of a debacle.

Implication 4: The Critical Role of the Collaborative Value Port

In Chapter Three, we introduced the concept of the value port as a conceptual way of exposing business process and knowledge at some layer of the semantic stack, thus enhancing the speed and efficiency of collaboration. If we look back at technologies like Web services, there is a definite trend toward greater end user control through self-configuration and empowerment at the edges. Combining Web services with the greater codification of business processes, and some of the technologies like Digital Rights Management that exist as initial approaches to maintaining control of intellectual property, we have a nascent workbench on which to build collaboration-oriented services that will let us walk up the semantic stack. With this nascent workbench, we can begin linking up the user-centric interactions at the edges with business process, adding technologies that support measurement of services, and a degree of control of content (which is a form of intellectual property) distribution and usage that will likely be available from core IT components. This gets us perilously close to the technology conditions needed for a value port.

The value port concept is focused on providing enterprise-level higher value collaboration and collaborative services, focused on externalizing the layers of the semantic stack in a reasonably codified way, and enabling innovation at the edges. Creation of value ports requires the semantic architecture that, as we have discussed, is designed specifically to support walking up and across the semantic stack placing the exploitation of intellectual property in the lead position.

The walk across the semantic stack from tacit understanding to execution has, to date, not been sufficiently recognized as an important goal, so the focus in technology implementation has been on the need for in-house transactional consistency. As a result, companies tend to have an inefficient internal process for recognizing their internal capabilities and an even less efficient process for finding much less-exploiting external capabilities beyond their traditional business. In the face of a potential opportunity, such a transactional—or what we characterized as a syntactic-oriented—emphasis constrains an organizational approach around particular internal capabilities. To enhance collaborative effectiveness, it is critical to provide views and capabilities that slice through the semantic stack and provide access to intellectual property (or other components of the value-bundle) that might belong to a customer, a competitor, or a current or potential partner, to apply and leverage in increasingly complex global ventures with an array of internal and external partners.

Thinking of an organization's capabilities in terms of Lego blocks, an organization that only looks internally for resources constrains itself to addressing opportunities with its own set of Legos. This is restrictive. It is important to realize that in-house operational constraints will inevitably occur no matter how extensive their collection of Legos. At some point, as we have said repeatedly, external resources must be mobilized to fulfill the needs of the opportunity. To apply a value port mind-set on this discussion, the collaborative architect really needs to look at the company's response to such opportunities in terms of the services—the Lego blocks—available in the company, identify the blocks that had to be melted or snapped in half or otherwise violated to creatively construct a response for the opportunity. These blocks represent the places where innovation occurred as well as the potential for codification about what was learned and how to use it the next time.

Implication 5: The Emergence of the Collaborative Architect

Enterprise technology architects have many issues to tackle: online business, production systems to run the core business (such as the clearing and settlement functions in a brokerage house), and new technologies to evaluate to name a few. Collaboration is one among many, and its architectural implications, though potentially profound, are just a part of the overall picture. For these reasons, we describe a role called the *collaborative architect* whose focus is to create the technological base for collaboration. Architecting for collaboration is the semantic architecture we discussed earlier, fundamentally different from traditional syntactic architecture.

The collaborative architect's scope is wide. With the increasing semantic definition and support for the full product and business life cycles, the new collaborative architect must design for a much larger canvas, must support a full business life cycle (from discovery, creation, deployment, differentiation, and renewal), and must chart the maturation of the business in terms of movement or drift on the collaborative grid with the different value ports (defined in Chapter Three) identified for building, buying, or subscribing to collaborations as they evolve over time. Next, we characterize some of the key characteristics of the technologies that lie within the purview of the collaborative architect.

Customization

The ability of end users to customize their interaction with technology is a basic need to support collaborative interactions. This may take the form of setting personal preferences for subscriptions, filters, and rules and may vary based on a particular collaborative context (e.g., a client, project, or location). One immediate architectural impact of the need to accommodate different contexts and versions is the multiplied increase in storage requirements per collaborator especially when the granularity of the collaborator is human-to-human and not enterprise-to-enterprise. Directory services, which we discussed in Chapter Three, and event services—services that allow for the enterprise wide definition and delivery of event information to and from applications—are key infrastructure capabilities that applications can leverage to achieve high degrees of customization.

Dynamic Transformation

Once again, based on customizable rules and dynamic circumstances, a collaborative environment can transform content as well as be deployed on various appropriate devices or communicate with various protocols, such as the ability to intelligently search the Internet for appropriate opportunities or additional resources and determine the relevance of collected information. One immediate operational impact of the need to accommodate different rule sets for presentation and deployment of content is the open-ended nature of maintaining potentially large numbers of distinct rule sets. Transformation services using eXtensible Markup Language (XML) and various emerging standard industry vocabularies, device standards, and emerging IT description standards in conjunction with event services are the key infrastructure capabilities that application services can use to deploy content appropriately.

Accessibility

Bandwidth, access rights, and adherence to emerging interface standards are necessary to allow high performance connectivity among collaborators. This poses an immediate operational risk as networks must be opened to external contributors, with consequent security and privacy impact. Key technologies to help mitigate the risk are quality of service (QOS) technologies that offer direct support for different levels of performance, accessibility, and various forms of network monitoring and problem detection. Additionally, content caching, which moves Web content physically closer to the edges of your organization to improve performance, will play a role in performance enhancement and facilitate delivery of content from trusted sources. Crucially, Web services, as the emerging Web standard for offering peer-to-peer computing capability, will be the preeminent influence on accessibility as the way services will be uniformly discovered, assessed, and procured.

Assurance

Collaborations create output, and in the Jericho Zone that output must be retained, measured, maintained, and monitored. For example, ongoing maintenance and monitoring for intellectual property created in a collaboration might include tracing portions of copyrighted material and or royalties as the intellectual property gets used and reused in various forms. Digital rights management—to protect the digital content forms of intellectual property that organizations contribute to, create, and harvest in the innovation process—business process monitoring to make sure that business processes are operating correctly, as well as Web services are the key technologies affecting assurance.

Where do we find these technologies and how are they currently used by the business? Many of the things outlined here can be found under different, though familiar, labels: personalization; content management; customer relationship management; EAI; digital rights management; and workforce optimization. These really are not technology terms. These are marketing bundles that combine sets of useful functions many of which can facilitate many forms of collaboration. As we've observed, most IT spending has focused on *syntactic* support where such vertical bundling of component functionality is welcome, and we have also observed that these vertical bundles often contain functional components that align nicely with the semantic stack. As a whole, architects have not focused on the upper right quadrant and Jericho Zone collaboration. We can be reasonably optimistic that as businesses more and more understand the need for collaboration, vendors will follow.

To be prudent, the collaborative architect needs to look at how to accommodate creative or consultative teams in any number of irregularly recurring business activities using the technology to support enterprise value ports that enable the teams. We have discussed the notion of value ports in some detail—technologically, enterprise value ports will be designed to allow the basic technologies we discuss in this chapter—such as directory services, quality of service, digital rights management, event services—to naturally support highly dynamic internal and external interactions. The way forward is tricky.

Key Requirements of the Collaborative Architect

The foremost implication of operating in the Jericho Zone is the requirement to put greater power in the hands of end users, both technically and organizationally through greater independence from their host enterprise. Simply put, the technique of well-designed encapsulation and simplifying layers of technical complexity gives end users more powerful levers to control. This greater independence is needed because the people working at the edge of the collaboration, by definition, are often doing things that are outside the envelope of the core company activities and thus need a malleable, dynamic toolset that they can shape to their unique needs.

As we've discussed, organizations possess at least some of the technology needed to support organizational collaboration, but we are still in the business environment of trying to realize efficiencies within the layers.

The possibility of a further distribution of power to end users places increased importance in understanding Jericho Zone activities where high-value individual collaborative capability may challenge institutional ownership and management of intellectual property. For the collaborative architect, this points to some specific requirements:

REQUIREMENT 1: ENABLE CROSS-BOUNDARY COMMUNICATION   Whether the boundary is internal business silos, technical silos, or different enterprises, the ability to communicate or transform communication to and from many sources is crucial, and XML plays a central role. If an enterprise is not already committed then it must extend investment into XML adoption or research and development. Aside from understanding the basic transactional semantics of the enterprise's internal systems in an XML syntax, determine the critical and secondary content/intellectual property produced by the organization.

REQUIREMENT 2: PARTITION YOUR BUSINESS SERVICES   Understanding your business functionality, organization/location, and processes in terms of the semantic stack becomes an important activity to support collaboration. It is important for the collaborative architect to understand the relationship between business processes at the transactional level and the role that those processes play within the semantic stack, and thus in collaboration.

REQUIREMENT 3: DETERMINE THE BUSINESS/COMMERCIAL MODEL   Which processes are at risk in terms of intellectual property ownership? How much is the purely transactional business worth in the market? What direction, what collaborations (contexts), and what investments are needed now and all along the business gestation process? Microsoft may have the lead in this understanding as they are committing to Microsoft.Net as a key distribution channel for their core products and extending MSN into a horizontal and targeted vertical distributed of business services. Valuable collaborative thinking should tend toward considering the degree of business change and ambition found in this example.

These requirements indicate only very rudimentary preparations that an architect needs to make to serve as a collaborative architect in an increasingly networked and collaborative business community. He or she will need to understand IT architecture in terms of business process, and in how the business processes feed the innovation process. The architect must ask questions, such as how will the business service or product mature? The architect must then design for platforms that can easily identify and use relevant Web services, expose internally developed Web services that clearly provide focused new value.

The architect needs to chart and design the technology gestation process that tracks the evolution of a collaborative venture described in Chapter Three, from the Jericho Zone out into lower margin, higher volume businesses. Should the venture progress through the upper left quadrant usage of full-functioned centrally supported applications? Or should the venture progress through the lower right quadrant of packaged solutions? The architect will need to understand to a greater level the life cycle and secondary markets for intellectual property in this gestation process as he or she supports keeping the lid on intellectual property.

To effectively design systems for the Jericho Zone, an architect cannot create a static vision of optimized functionality or a narrow technical view. The new collaborative architect must design for a much larger canvas—he must support the full business life cycle from discovery, creation, deployment, differentiation, through to renewal. Last, or maybe first, the collaboration architect *needs to understand who he works for.* Within the collaborative architect's domain, there are a few key business and technology areas that are particularly relevant. We discuss them in these next few sections.

Implication 5a: Business Processes in Collaborative Architecture

Business process is one of the current semantic battlegrounds we discussed earlier. Companies are beginning to recognize that codification of their business processes is key to understanding their business and to improving their process, and that using technology effectively in business process is key to running the business. For example, Gartner specifically recognizes the tacit knowledge and process that underlies much of business, and how technology can help: ". . . most enterprises are awash with information stored on databases and in the minds of its employees and managers, aggressive enterprises will be using business activity monitoring (BAM) to integrate and make intelligent real-time use of this information."[14]

Much of the pressure to achieve the evolutionary implementation of cross-institutional business process comes from the implementation of supply chain management technologies in many industries, and from inter-organizational utilities such as the Global Straight Through Processing Association (GSTPA) discussed in detail earlier in the book. These efforts have begun to impose a business imperative on companies to expose certain aspects of their business process to other companies. Just as software vendors have followed the business lead into software to improve business transactions, this trend toward codified and exposed business process will set a high-profile expectation on other industry software to be collaboration-ready. Already, the best practice in technology today is that serious software development must include coordinated business process understanding, requirements, and specification, and to determine and effect business value, the overall business performance requires tracking and measuring rather than discrete transactional system efficiency.

In today's environment, the collaborative architect can find many of the parts that can make up an initial workbench for collaborative architecture, for example:

- The Unified Modeling Language (UML), the common vocabulary used to express system design concepts, has found its way into the expression of business process through the Use Case, a UML construct that describes the interaction of an actor—typically a human, say, you—with a system.

- Product suites of standardized—or at least popular and familiar—architectural elements such as workflow engine, application server, transformation engine, and message queue that we see in the offerings of enterprise application integration (EAI) vendors such as Tibco, Vitria, and SeeBeyond have spurred the growth of third-party development, including a growing industry in developing connectors and adaptors between these and other commercial products.

- Vendor products and their packaging such as BEA's Weblogic and IBM's WebSphere, provide a practical environment for easily combining standardized architectural elements.

- Business process monitoring (BPM) tools that enable the measurement of process metrics and provide the ability to compare real time statistics against established business targets.

- Digital rights management (DRM) providing copyright protection from vendors such as Intertrust and Microsoft who have the ability to functionally prohibit or constrain the deployment of digital property based on rules established by the business—just as the BPM capability provides control over performance, DRM provides control on licensing.

Implication 5b: Web Services in Collaborative Architectures

Peer to peer (P2P) technology—made famous by the Napster file-sharing utility that shook the foundations of the music industry—is an approach to providing application functionality through resources that are at the edge of the Internet. It is not a coincidence that this at-the-edge computing is very important to the innovation at the edge that happens in the Jericho Zone. P2P has the power to put flexibility and governance in the hands of the people who need it. The increasing ability for creative, customer-facing people to configure-in-time products and services demonstrates that P2P architectures are defining and increasing the support for the full product and business life cycles—*not an evolutionary technical transition but a business process evolution.*

Web services is the codification of P2P principles into a standard for the Internet. What we have seen so far in terms of implementation of services has been quite conservative. IT departments are currently evaluating Web services mostly as a means to facilitate integration of existing, systems, and devices—a sort of EAI light. Business people, however, are thinking of Web services as a way to create new business opportunities by making previously internal assets available to the outside world. Somewhere in between theses two is the promise of Web services to facilitate interenterprise collaboration by leveraging the business process technology we just discussed to create ports—exposed via Web services—where external organizations can dock up and collaborate.

The promise could take the form of aggregating Web *and* human services, creating a process of perpetual custom assembly of services, for example, to implement a global complex time-critical event such as the Olympics or the World Cup. Enabling such collaborative tools and service discovery may prove to be the true disruptive value of Web services and P2P technologies—it is certainly the aspect of these technologies of most interest to the collaborative architect. In terms of the semantic stack, this would be a move into the environment layer, blurring the boundaries between it and the layers below it. While we don't yet have tools that are powerful enough to codify the environment layer, there are no real technical barriers to connect it with lower layers using Web services.

Implication 5c: Legacy Systems in Collaborative Architectures

Our focus is on the future and the edge of the organization. As a result, we tend not to immediately think of looking back to the legacy systems in the IT portfolio. The current state of the typical enterprise-installed base and legacy architectures creates a technical and cultural bias toward central governance and constrained user access. However, there are abundant technologies and functions that currently are fully focused on core business online transaction processing or online analytic processing that can have application to collaboration. Collaborative elements can be leveraged from institutional-centric packages that support cross-selling or self-service into more collaborative worker-centric objectives. Fitting inside a legacy of closed production technologies and attendant cultural and budgetary justifications may make it difficult to pursue new architectural paths to enable collaboration and will initially garner only conservative investments. The collaborative architect's strategy, therefore, needs to make the most of the conservative investments, to understand how to position collaboration in terms that are favorable with respect to legacy systems, and to understand how to gain collaborative leverage from legacy investments.

One opportunity exists because most institutions are engaged in a gradual effort to wrap (that is, put modern interfaces on), or re-factor (that is, separate out into separately usable services), or adapt complex and expensive infrastructure services to new business conditions. This has the affect of opening up functionality for use beyond the legacy application for which it was originally created, and also of opening up opportunities for vendors who can approximate the functionality of the newly available services. This in turn spells an opportunity for the collaborative architect in two ways: (1) in making some piece of the business process available in an open modern interface, and (2) through the potential for collaboration-friendly vendors to sneak into the computing environment if they can provide a good approximation of a newly exposed piece of legacy application functionality.

Another opportunity (or maybe coping strategy) is to have vendors do the work for you. Given that institutional IT will for some time remain institution-centric, real progress in collaboration, which is decidedly geared toward a user-centric advantage, may be more energetically and more effectively served by new players in the market. The new players will advocate for the user or team and offer a neutral workspace to solicit arrays of institution centric functions with the required cross-enterprise visibility standards. Forrester Research calls the software category involved in this intermediary domain extended resource management (XRM). Forrester suggests, for example, that a next generation supply chain management Web-based service would be the most ready to implement in this area.[15] It is still unclear whether large enterprises would sponsor XRM sites to draw transactional flow toward their matured infrastructure. Certainly one factor is the independence that an XRM effort would offer the end user or team from the sponsoring infrastructure. Regardless, the emergence of a new buzzword gives leverage in getting the attention of corporate IT departments.

As a final observation, collaboration, from the viewpoint of corporate IT departments, is a valid topic facilitating efficiencies along institution-centric lines. Thus, the most common collaboration strategies pursued by IT tend not to be for the benefit of the user or individual but for the benefit of the seller or institution. They tend to consider collaboration-friendly technologies from a seller's point of view and advocate user/customer or user-centric functionality as it suits them to lower costs or cheaply extend offerings through aggregation of Web-based products. While their motivation might not match the motivation of the collaborative architect, the fact that there are motivations in the legacy environment to examine collaboration tools and processes spells opportunity for the collaborative architect to make progress.

SUMMARY: TOWARD ARCHITECTURAL SEMANTICS AND ENABLING AGILE COLLABORATION

Architectural semantics is an unusual name for a pragmatic response to a critical imperative: namely, making collaborations more effective. Collaborations are innovation engines to take advantage of fast-moving business opportunities. From a technology perspective, this requires enabling your organization to adapt, exploit, and ensure an appropriate alignment between the value proposition, the appropriate value ports within the semantic stack, and the technical capabilities to make that alignment possible, quickly. Exploiting those opportunities quickly requires designing capabilities and building the capabilities to quickly walk up and across the semantic stack; it requires, as we've said many times in many different ways, understanding then exploiting the semantics of the processes involved—processes as a noun referring to the specific business activities underlying the collaborative venture and as a verb referring to the activities making the tacit knowledge more scalable, and hence more usable.

Tim Berners-Lee, the founder and proclaimed conscience of the World Wide Web, has called the next generation of the World Wide Web, the Semantic Web. There are three basic parts of speech, according to linguists: syntax, semantics, and pragmatics. Syntax refers to the placement of grammatical units—words—in some logical order. Semantics encompasses the understanding or meaning of those logically ordered units—they *mean* something. And pragmatics entails the use of those units for some purposes. This simple grammatical typology well distinguishes the rapid generation of the World Wide Web and, ultimately, our characterization of effective architectural trajectories. Berners-Lee's emphasis on the next generation Web as the Semantic Web is focused on how to transform the Web from a place of unstructured documents (syntax) with a set of search engines that can point someone to a set of organized materials (semantics) to an environment of useful personalized interactions determined and triggered by personal preferences *(Pragmatic Web)*. The Web can become the pragmatic action (a tautology if characterized by its linguistic usage) enabling only as its underlying technology and design supports semantic diversity and richness and if the underlying technology codifies the technical building blocks and engines necessary to support rapid selection and de-selection of shifting personal preferences and adaptations. Sound familiar? It should. The mutation of the World Web Wide can be explained as a process of walking up and across the semantic stack, and of attacking higher levels of the semantic stack as lower levels become commoditized and shared semantic building blocks for subsequent focus.

Returning to collaborations, fast-moving business opportunities require a rapidity of response—the enablers of which we characterized as value ports, and the effectiveness of which require capabilities to identify, exploit, select, and de-select functionality as needed quickly. While business opportunities are multiple and specific collaborative forms to address them equally numerous, there are a finite set of activities to design and build the adaptive capabilities needed—around the tacit knowledge and high margins inherent in all of these opportunities. The collaborative and competitive challenge then becomes how to exploit those high margin activities while building the capabilities to scale its underlying tacit knowledge as quickly as possible to—yes, yes, we'll say it again—walk up and across the semantic stack.

Conceptually, architectural semantics are an explanatory device for how and why particular technology trajectories are occurring. Operationally, they provide a powerful tool to make collaborations more effective. Their pragmatic import lies in how to help business partners align collaborative opportunities with technical capabilities. They become a focal point to creating business value from technology innovation and leveraging organizational IT assets within the emerging models of business collaboration. For this reason, we shied away from merely enumerating a variety of technologies and vendors in this chapter. What is more important than the shifting sands of competitive placement is exploring the underlying competitive bedrock of collaborative technology dynamics. Grounding this chapter around architectural semantics provides an initial simple, yet effective, means to cut through the tremendous amount of technology noise while focusing attention on the required energy for effecting effective collaborative opportunities.

CHAPTER HIGHLIGHTS

The Issue

What are technology implications of walking *up and across the stack?* What is the role of the technology organization and the technology implications of operating in the Jericho Zone of rapid, effective, and efficient collaboration?

The Insight

Technology has a key role to play in codifying large amounts of knowledge across large populations. In companies wishing to operate in the Jericho Zone, technology organizations must broaden their focus to create architectures that both serve the needs of the business in creating its products, and also help the business to walk up and across the semantic stack. Such semantic architecture focuses on enabling greater codification in higher layers of the semantic stack, helping to create the value ports that in turn enable collaboration.

The Phrases

Architectural semantics, value ports, collaborative architect.

The Implications

The implications of technology as an enabler up and across the stack include exploiting semantic architecture as a focal point for guiding technology strategy, innovation, and implementation. In turn, a new role, one of the *collaborative architect* becomes an important complementary role and supporting skill-set to drive and codify the semantics of business processes and collaborative activities.

   If you can easily plug into and out of collaborations via a value-port, you have significantly lowered your cost of doing so, broadened your competitive arsenal, and increased your competitive agility.

CHAPTER SEVEN

Collaborations as Emergent Behaviors

In the summer of 2002, an extraordinary book, *A New Kind of Science,* was published challenging much of how we understand and have explained the physical laws of our world.[1] Its premise is that our current scientific explanations attempt to capture the richness of our universe with complicated mathematical equations. Most of these explanations rest on the assumptions that what we characterize as *time* and *space* can be broken down into smaller and smaller discrete units and thereby described with unlimited, infinitesimal precision—requiring only the advancement of mathematical and engineering tools to do so. "Bunk," cries Stephen Wolfram, author of this brilliant book, computer scientist, and recipient of a MacArthur Genius Grant. At the heart of his book is the notion of modeling physical phenomena in terms of simple rules in simple computer programs—cellular automata—rather than complicated mathematical equations. Complex systems in nature—whether they are weather systems, fluid dynamics, biological adaptations, or brain synaptic structures—are governed, argues Wolfram, by small and simple sets of rules that interact to create complex emergent behavior. It is the simplicity of these rules that engenders—and enables us to explain—the apparent complexity of resultant forms. Throughout the book, Wolfram shows with countless examples how apparently simple systems can give rise to extraordinarily complex behavior.

Wolfram's insights result from providing a novel way of *making sense* of the bewildering complexity and range of natural phenomena. Rather than appending extensions onto preexisting theories thereby creating more and more complicated explanations understandable by fewer and fewer people, Wolfram steps back and suggests a new language or vocabulary to make sense of the same focus. Simplicity is gained. More can be explained by less. Equally importantly, scenarios can be built—or simulations run—to anticipate what types of behaviors will emerge over time. Thus, *making sense,* for Wolfram, results from discerning the underlying patterns and resulting dynamics, of physical behaviors.

Our focus is not nearly so broad, nor our claims nearly as grand as Wolfram's. Yet, our message is similar in spirit and rests on similarly founded assumptions. There are multiple forms of collaborations; there always have been and always will be. Yet, what is important to discern, from a pragmatic perspective, is less their differences than their similarities. Knowing that differences exist is important. Knowing which forms align with your business objective is, obviously, critical. However, enumerating multiple collaborative options or attempting to follow the fractal-like trail of describing the multiple collaborative forms that exist today, much less those likely to mutate into different forms tomorrow, is tiresome, and ultimately not instructive. What *is* important to understand are the underlying dynamics and mechanisms to make each of these forms more effective, and thereby knowing what collaborative forms most effectively suit your specific business objectives.

Therefore, knowing the underlying dynamics—the simple rules or what we have been calling the *collaborative DNA*—is more than an exercise; it is a competitive requirement. Making collaborations more effective involves manipulating these underlying DNA strands more so than their surface or symptomatic behaviors. From our perspective, making sense of collaboration requires understanding these underlying dynamics. Why? Because collaborations change over time. Organizations must build with sensors and capabilities to know *when* and *how* to adapt or end collaborations and prepare themselves for subsequent ones. This temporal aspect of collaborations is critical. Understanding how to identify and exploit it and its underlying dynamics becomes important. This is the similarity that underlies collaborative differences that needs to be identified, understood, and effectively exploited. We hope that we have provided a start on a set of relatively simple models that together make sense of collaborations' complex external behaviors.

Collaborations are ubiquitous. They take multiple forms that continue to multiply as they mutate and respond to changing technology and business opportunities. Yet, there are several constants within this collaborative variety. Our final chapter summarizes these constants. We also build on them to suggest some different directions collaborative forms may take over the next several years. There is no doubt that the roles and structures of organizations have changed. There is equally no doubt that we are merely at the edge of an enormous playing field of collaborative venturing. We're just beginning—in recognizing, in understanding, and in executing powerfully dynamic collaborations. We have attempted to paint a collaborative landscape, to identify some patterns of different types of collaborations, and to suggest some of their underlying dynamics. In this final chapter, we step back and summarize what we see as those collaborative dynamics, what's driving them, and the emerging patterns of effective collaborative behaviors.

WHAT IS DRIVING THE COLLABORATIVE IMPERATIVE?

What is driving the focus and increased attention around collaborative forms? We have all observed and many of us experienced islands of collaboration around shared value propositions. As many of us are experiencing, more and more of the islands are rising into connected continents, driven by fundamental changes in technologies and business models that, in turn, are driving fundamental changes in interactions. We've explored these changes from different perspectives in each of our chapters. Tying together these different perspectives has been a set of transformational activities that we used as starting points or coordinates to guide our discussion. Restated briefly, these coordinates are:

- *The broadening of the network metaphor.* Often, this metaphor is tied to the Internet and its enabling protocols to physically connect people, processes, and supporting organizations. However, as we saw, this connectivity has implications as much on people and processes as on enabling technologies. Collaborative forms differ in structure, process, and certainly competitive pressures depending on what part of the semantic stack becomes the organizing collaborative principle. Connectivity, then, has very different meanings and implications depending on what part of the stack is being addressed. The network metaphor needs to be broadened to discern what these different implications are and how to exploit them, in a focused and effective manner.

- *The Red Queen runs, and she runs relentlessly.* Collaborations are inherently risky. Making them effective requires being clear regarding the specific value proposition, ensuring the creation of mutual value, and managing distributed risk, over time. It requires knowing where and how to walk up and across the semantic stack—as the margins inherent in the initial phases of the collaboration become squeezed and the tacit knowledge on which they are built become codified. This is a characteristic as much of general competitive life as of collaborations. However, the distributed and risky nature of collaborations is what makes the clarity of the propositions and their underlying knowledge assets so critical. Fundamentally, the Red Queen issue, while an inexorable competitive dynamic, is a story of thorough leadership and knowledge management—the process of walking up and across the semantic stack. Stated even more strongly, the Red Queen story *is the story of the underlying collaborative dynamic.*

- *Metcalfe meets Coase.* Metcalfe's Law states that the value of a network goes up with the square of the number of users. This means that more and more value will be harnessed into our applications, our processes, and our intellectual property as they become available through the growing network reducing the marginal costs of communication and coordination and thereby lowering the organizational barriers of communication. Coase's Law states that organizational structures can be explained as a simple balance between the value derived and the costs incurred of internalizing transaction and communication activities. As communication and coordination costs come down, inexorable pressures to collaborate go up. It's that simple.

Each of our chapters explored these dynamics from different perspectives. Each identified specific implications of these dynamics—from organizational, process, people, leadership, and technical perspectives on collaborative behaviors. Through these explorations, we discovered that all roads lead to a simple observation: Organizational walls are coming down, and they are coming down quickly. *The Jericho Principle* excavates this simple but profound observation. Each of the perspectives explored are horn blasts from Joshua's trumpet putting pressure on organizational walls. We described the pressures and resulting implications on both the need for and tangible steps to make collaborations more effective.

We've summarized part of the answer to the question: Why now? We've summarized the pressures on organizational walls that open up opportunities for collaborative behavior. But we haven't answered the question: Why collaboration? What is it about collaboration that makes it a strategic requirement? Our answer so far has answered the operational question: Why collaboration? The operational answer is one of expediency or pragmatism. But what is the strategic need driving collaboration? *What transforms collaboration from merely an operational option to a strategic imperative?*

The answer is as simple to state as it is difficult to implement.

We exist in an uncertain environment—competitive, political, economic, and technological. In an uncertain environment, the best we can do, and what is incumbent upon us to do, is to acknowledge, embrace, then attack the uncertainty (yes, embrace, then attack—modifying Sun-Tzu's admonition to "Keep your friends close, and your *competitors* even closer."). Planning from presumptions of certainty in today's marketplace is unwarranted. Thus, one of the most important strategic and leadership challenges—and talents—is precisely how to make the most out of uncertainty, rather than the chimera of certainty. This remains a key challenge. The processes, the products and services, and the leadership that have so far made us successful are very often the obstacles to harnessing the potential of marketplace uncertainty. There is no guarantee that what has made us successful in the past will make us successful in the future. By definition, an uncertain future cannot be known. Therefore, attempts to predict it or to control it are, at best, limited in impact and, at worst, a waste of resources.

By no means have we tried to say that attempting to create degrees of certainty through structured and standardized means is either inappropriate or futile. But we *do* say that a disproportionate amount of attention, from a leadership perspective, needs to focus on how to harness the process and underlying potential power of uncertainty. Building constant management philosophies, standardized procedures, control processes, and other managerial tools based on the premises of continuity and consistency only deadens the organization to the creative impulse and need to embrace the market forces of creative destruction. Companies get locked into their success and the underlying processes, incentives, and structures that made them successful make it difficult for them to adapt to new opportunities.[2] What worked for them once no longer does and what, in retrospect appeared certain, no longer is. This leads us back to how we started this chapter: The seductive and ultimately futile pursuit of certainty in an ever-uncertain competitive world. Leadership needs to recognize the sirens of certainty, of predictability, of assumptions of linear growth and internal rates of return, for what they are—seductive, but impossible to trust. Leadership needs to use the dynamics that coexist with uncertainty to drive their company forward. Uncertainty can be nerve-wracking, but it's a lot of fun.

Recognizing that uncertainty infuses the competitive environment in which we live requires that we acknowledge that no simple or single answer exists to navigate through that uncertainty. That is the lesson of the simple three-arrow picture presented in Chapter Two. That is the reality we face. Yet, how can we embrace this uncertainty with respect to emerging collaborative business opportunities and thereby begin to manage that uncertainty as we acknowledge its ubiquity?

What we can do and what we need to do are to build capabilities that allow us to identify opportunities, place bets, and move quickly to take advantage of them. What we can do is build an agility to innovate and to participate in fast-moving opportunities and, upon seeing where the opportunities lie and the benefits that result, reposition ourselves to continuously exploit such opportunities. What we need are capabilities and mechanisms to minimize risk, increase our agility, and enhance our strategic arsenal to attack fast-moving market opportunities. To do what? To not merely keep pace, but to pull ahead of the Red Queen.

This is precisely the role of collaboration. Strategically, collaborations, at their essence, are innovation engines, designed to exploit fast-moving business opportunities. They are a means to create new genes in your organizational DNA to enhance organizational capabilities and thereby more effectively harness the power of competitive uncertainty. This is not as far-fetched as it may sound.

We defined a collaboration as a set of business activities that created shared value while managing distributed risk. This is a fine, but ultimately static definition. Digging deeper, we characterized the strategic "whys" of collaborations as means to manage uncertainty and exploit fast-moving business opportunities. Digging even deeper, the fundamental "hows" of effective collaborations result from managing distributed risk and walking up and across the semantic stack. This archeological dig hit bedrock regarding how to characterize different collaborative forms, drive their execution, and anticipate their competitive relevance and evolution over time. Walking up and across the semantic stack makes us take stock of the business rationale for the collaboration, the tacit knowledge underlying its execution and the dynamic involved in harnessing and exploiting the resulting margins and competitive pressures in codifying and exploiting that tacit knowledge over time. Herein lies the dynamic rub: What is high-margin, tacit knowledge today, becomes lower margin, codified sets of executable—and therefore scalable—processes, standards, and technical enablers tomorrow. Thus, what is today's competitive advantage becomes tomorrow's table stakes to play the competitive game, which raises some challenges:

- The *strategic* challenge becomes one of viewing, positioning, and driving collaborations as *innovation engines* to continually exploit fast-moving business and high-margin arbitrage opportunities.

- The *operational* challenge becomes one of building the value ports—or capabilities to plug-and-play—into the relevant part of the semantic stack to differentiate yourself as well as to quickly either disengage or evolve the collaborative form as competitive conditions warrant.

- The *leadership* challenge becomes one of building collaborative skills as core competencies throughout the organization able to respond quickly to the opportunities.

- The *competitive* challenge becomes one of anticipating how the collaborative relevance shifts depending on the speed and impact of competition as the collaboration and competitive playing field impacts the process of walking up and across the semantic stack.

The Red Queen runs and she runs relentlessly. Understanding the answers to the questions of strategically "why," and operationally "how" to make collaborations more effective becomes critical to outrun the Red Queen.

WHAT'S NEXT? HOW WILL THE COLLABORATIVE IMPERATIVE PLAY OUT OVER THE NEXT 18 TO 36 MONTHS?

Is there an inevitability about collaborations? Does it make sense to talk about how collaborations will evolve over time? If so, should we talk about particular collaborative trajectories based on what we see occurring today? If the answer is yes to any of these questions, how can we get ready today for what may happen tomorrow, from a collaborative perspective?

The answer to all three questions is a definite maybe. We've spent much time discussing the inherent competitive uncertainty. If there is one thing that we can forecast with certainty, it is that the future will turn out in unexpected ways. If there is another forecast, it is that our competitive environment will continue to shift, again in unexpected ways. Consequently, as we stated before, one of our strategic imperatives is to learn how to harness the power and potential of uncertainty as both strategic and operational assets. We can never know, with clarity, what will happen or what we should do. But there are certainly mechanisms and guiding lights to help us peer into the haze of tomorrow's uncertain competitive environment. These guiding lights are the principles we've explored throughout the book, and the mechanisms are the use of collaborations as innovation engines. This immediately takes us back to the starting questions of this section and demands a clearer answer to them.

Charles Darwin, without doubt one of the greatest biologists and scientific minds of all time, figured out a mechanism to explain how animal species adapted to climatic, or environmental, changes. The explanation was elegantly simple: just spawn a lot of variations in each generation and, given the high mortality rate, only those variants better adapted to the current environment will survive long enough to reach reproductive age. Those lucky variants will spawn further variations to more effectively fit to the environment's opportunities and perils. Those variants better suited to some other climate do not grow up and reproduce; they simply die out.

There is nothing inherently automatic—or directional—about this evolutionary change. Adaptive fits do not necessarily mean sustainable change. A climatic change back to the original state can result in species adaptations tracking back to their previous traits. The important point is that many adaptations and innovations don't have necessary or clearly defined growth curves. As Oliver Sacks, a neurologist and wide-ranging author describes this point, using a different example, "if you invent a digging stick to expand the range of gathering possibilities, there isn't too much you can do to improve it into a shovel until a lot of ancillary improvements occur in the creation of sharp tools of the sort needed to make other tools. To redouble your payoff in terms of calories gathered via the digging stick takes a lot of further invention. If you invent soaking to help remove the bitter taste from plant toxins, it is again hard to double and redouble your payoff until you invent boiling. Efficiency improvements are often difficult."[3] Thus, adaptive fits result from a whole range of additional changes; it is the set or suite of complementary changes that make any evolutionary shift sustainable.

Taking us back to answering the collaborative evolutionary questions, there is no doubt that there is an inevitability about collaborations and the increasing use and critical role of them as both strategic options and operational extensions. *The Jericho Principle* encapsulates what we are all experiencing: Organizational walls are coming down requiring adaptive shifts in strategy and execution to aggressively exploit fast-moving business opportunities with our customers, clients, and business partners. The collaborative imperative is as strategic as it is operational. Collaborative skills will become a core competency critical to support the ubiquity of the ventures they need to engender. Of this there is little doubt. What is in doubt are the specific forms collaborative ventures will take. Collaboration can play a role regardless of which of the three arrows—scenarios we discussed in Chapter Two—play out over time; that role becomes more crucial as the arrow we are on turns more sharply.

The Collaborative Landscape provides a framework to characterize different types of collaborations. The semantic stack provides a means to explain the underlying business logic, competitive pressures, and likely competitive trajectory the collaborations will take. Different competitive dynamics exist depending on the part of the semantic stack that serves as the organizing focus for the collaboration as well as the degree to which the collaboration supports the range from tacit to codified knowledge. A key strategic challenge is to clearly identify which part of the Collaborative Landscape as well as which part of the semantic stack needs to become the foundation for any collaborative venture; and the corollary operational challenge is how to align the process, the people, and the technology both to exploit and to hasten the movement up and across the semantic stack. We've provided frameworks, examples, observations, and implications to build the language to help us make sense as well as take effective action to make collaborations more effectively. *Walking up and across the semantic stack and understanding how collaborations in the different parts of the Collaborative Landscape evolve, get sustained, or die across time are key strategic requirements and challenges, to instilling collaborative capabilities as core competencies.*

Yet, even doing so, it remains apparent that we haven't yet answered the question: Can we predict the specific path a collaboration will take? The simple answer is, no. Knowing that collaborations are inevitable and will become ever more so is not the same as being able to predict which collaborations will be sustainable and which ones will not, over time. But we can predict the *type* of evolutionary path a collaboration will take and suggest how to make them more effective and thereby create some of the ancillary improvements necessary to increase their adaptive fit to our changing competitive environment. That is what we have attempted to do in this book—namely, *discern collaborative patterns, identify their dynamics, and recommend specific actions to make your collaborative options clearer and operationally more effective.*

Any collaboration will be as effective as strategically, it is clear, and operationally, it is enabled. We identified a broad range of ancillary implications and improvements to enhance your collaborative fit. Each of these is complementary with the others. All of them are small, but powerful pressures on organizational walls. As such, all of them both engender the business need for collaborations and are determinants of their effectiveness.

Let's go back to the beginning of this section. Are collaborations inevitable? Absolutely. Will they become strategically more critical over the next 18 to 36 months? Without a doubt. *The Jericho Principle* well exemplifies what many of us are experiencing. Our organizational walls are coming down. The role of the Internet and other communications, connectivity and coordination technologies broaden our potential range of cross-organizational collaborations; the ever-increasing process perspective demands that we do so; and the Red Queen relentlessly pushes us to build adaptive and agile capabilities to exploit the fast-moving, short-term high-margin opportunities that can only be capitalized through collaborations. Creating value ports to rapidly plug in and out of different collaborative ventures requires an architectural trajectory, process sensitivity, knowledge sensitivity, and leadership skills that recognize the semantics underlying, and the processes critical to exploit, the tacit knowledge and practices necessary to scale the codified knowledge underlying collaborative ventures. Collaboration is simply a means of creating new genes to create new organizational capacities. Each chapter has attempted to identify particular strands of collaborative DNA necessary to support these enhancements.

What is key is to make sense of our current collaborative marketplace noise and take action that exploits the emerging business opportunities. We have endeavored to *make sense* and *take action* to identify, to exploit, to accommodate, and to guide the collaborative trajectories that can be, need to be, and will be as critical strategically tomorrow as they are operationally relevant today. We have endeavored to start building a road on which we can all travel.

CHAPTER HIGHLIGHTS

The Issue

Are collaborations inevitable over the next 18 to 36 months? Why do we care now?

The Insight

There are multiple forms of collaborations; there always have been and always will be. Yet, what is important to discern, from a pragmatic perspective, is less their differences than their similarities. Knowing that differences exist is important. Knowing which forms align with your business objective is critical. However, enumerating multiple collaborative options or attempting to follow the fractal-like trail of describing the multiple collaborative forms that exist today, much less those likely to mutate into different forms tomorrow, is tiresome and ultimately not instructive. What *is* important to understand are the underlying dynamics and mechanisms to make each of these forms more effective, and thereby knowing what collaborative forms most effectively suit *your* specific business objectives. This understanding is based on identifying, knowing, and exploiting collaborative DNA (shared value, managing distributed risk, and walking up and across the semantic stack) and its underlying dynamics. The inevitabilities of increased, more focused, and dynamic collaborations are not in doubt. The challenge is to build organizational core competencies now and to begin exploiting their inherent dynamics later.

The Phrases

The collaborative imperative; collaborative ubiquity.

The Implications

The *strategic* challenge becomes one of viewing, positioning, and driving collaborations as *innovation engines* to continually exploit fast-moving business and high-margin arbitrage opportunities.

The *operational* challenge becomes one of building the value ports—or capabilities to plug-and-play—into the relevant part of the semantic stack to differentiate yourself as well as to quickly either disengage or evolve the collaborative form as competitive conditions warrant.

(continued)

The *leadership* challenge becomes one of building collaborative skills as core competencies throughout the organization able to respond quickly to the opportunities.

The *competitive* challenge becomes one of anticipating how the collaborative relevance shifts depending on the speed and impact of competition as the collaboration and competitive playing field impacts the process of walking up and across the semantic stack.

Bottom line: Walking up and across the semantic stack and understanding how collaborations in different parts of the Collaborative Landscape evolve, get sustained, or die across time are key strategic requirements and opportunities to instilling collaborative capabilities as core competencies.

NOTES

CHAPTER ONE

1. William James, *Some Problems of Philosophy* (New York: Longman's Green, 1911), p. 47.

2. Manuel Castells, *The Internet Galaxy: Reflections on the Internet, Business, and Society* (New York: Oxford University Press, 2001).

3. Matt Ridley, *The Red Queen: Sex and the Evolution of Human Nature* (New York: Macmillan, 1993).

4. James C. Collins, *Good to Great: Why Some Companies Make the Leap . . . and Others Don't* (New York: HarperCollins, 2001).

5. Antonio Machado, Proverbios y Cantares from "Campos de Castilla" (1907–1917), from *Machado: Campos de Castilla* by R. Havard (ed.), September 1997. The full quote is "traveler there is no road/we build the road as we travel" (caminante no hay camino/se hace camino al andar).

CHAPTER TWO

1. Michael E. Gazala, "Making Open Finance Pay," *Forrester Research* (April 1999).

2. eBondTrade is at http://www.ebondtrade.com; Creditex is at http://www.creditex.com.

3. Clayton M. Christensen, *The Innovator's Dilemma: When New Technologies Cause Great Firms to Fail* (New York: HarperBusiness, 1997).

4. Hugh Courtney, *20/20 Foresight: Crafting Strategy in an Uncertain World* (Boston: Harvard Business School Press, 2001).

5. Michael Treacy and Fred Wiersema, *The Discipline of Market Leaders* (Reading, MA: Addison-Wesley, 1995).

6. Available http://www.wallstreetandtech.com/story/supp /WST20010406S0001 and http://www.wallstreetandtech.com/story /stp/WST20020304S0001.

7. For detailed descriptions of these processes, see, for example, Marcia Stigum, *After the Trade: Dealer and Clearing Bank Operations in Money Market and Government Securities* (Homewood, IL: Dow Jones-Irwin, 1988).

8. Available http://www.wallstreetandtech.com/story/supp/WST20010406S0001.

9. See note 8.

10. Available http://www.axion4.com/cm/index/maintree/gstp-index/gstp-background.htm.

11. See note 10.

12. Discussion with Steve Crosby, June 2002.

13. Metal Bulletin PLC, *Interoperability High Noon*, Global Investment Services, May 2002, http://www.globalinvestmentservices.co.uk/pdfs/Coverstory_May2002web.pdf.

14. Available http://www.gs.com/news/2000/bondbook_06132000.html.

15. Peter L. Levin and Reinhold Ludwig, "Crossroads for Mixed-Signal Chips: Cutting and Pasting Intellectual Property Speeds the Design of a System on Chip by Fabless Semiconductor Companies," *IEEE Spectrum* (March 2002).

16. Ronald H. Coase, *The Firm, The Market, and The Law* (Chicago: University of Chicago Press, 1990).

17. See, for example, Oliver Williamson, *The Economic Institutions of Capitalism* (New York: Free Press, 1985); and Oliver Williamson, "Vertical Integration and Related Variations on a Transaction—Cost Economics Theme," *New Developments in the Analysis of Market Structure*, eds. Joseph Stiglitz and G. Frank Mathewson (Cambridge, MA: MIT Press, 1986).

CHAPTER THREE

1. Sandra Rogers, Carl W. Olofson, and Dirk Coburn, *IDC Application Development and Deployment Enterprise Integration Software Program* (IDC IT Professional Web Conference Series, April 30, 2002). See also the author's note on "Business Blueprints" on p. 265.

2. For an excellent introduction to Web Services and related technologies, see Nicholas D. Evans, *Business Innovation and Disruptive Technology* (Financial Times Prentice Hall, 2002).

3. See note 2.

4. See note 2.

5. See note 2.

6. Available http://www.ietf.org, quote from http://www.ietf.org/overview.html.

7. The classic text in the field for at least the past 15 years is Andrew Tannenbaum, *Computer Networks,* 3rd ed. (Englewood Cliffs, NJ: Prentice Hall, 1996).

8. See note 7.

9. See, for example, Charles C. Mann, "Why Software Is So Bad," *MIT Technology Review* (August, 2002).

10. Steven Pinker, *How the Mind Works*(New York: Norton, 1997).

11. Geoffrey Moore, *Crossing the Chasm* (New York: HarperBusiness, 1982); and Geoffrey Moore, *Living on the Fault Line: Managing for Shareholder Value in the Age of the Internet* (New York: HarperBusiness, 2000).

12. It is never possible to have a "fully set of executable" practices—at any level. However, our intention and our depiction are simply to indicate the relative amount of codification that exists for the core set of activities that the layer depicts. A needed activity to actually explore the dynamics of this codification is to delve into each cell of the semantic stack to understand the specific pressures and codification activities. See also the author's note on "Business Blueprints" on p. 265.

13. Available http://www.opengroup.org, quote from http://www .opengroup.org/togaf.

14. See http://www.systar.com.

15. See http://www.kintana.com.

16. For much more on the underlying organizational and behavioral patterns, see Ralph Welborn, "Invisible Actions, Visible Impacts," draft manuscript.

17. Michael Treacy and Fred Wiersema, *The Discipline of Market Leaders: Choose Your Customers, Narrow Your Focus, Dominate Your Market* (Cambridge, MA: Perseus Publishing, 1997).

CHAPTER FOUR

1. John H. Holland, *Hidden Order: How Adaptation Builds Complexity* (Reading, MA: Helix Books, 1995); Steven Johnson, *Emergence: The Connected Lives of Ants, Brains, Cities, and Software* (New York: Scribner, 2001); Stuart Kauffman, *At Home in the Universe: The Search for the Laws of Self-Organization and Complexity* (New York: Oxford University Press, 1995). There exists a fair number of business books that have attempted to draw lessons from the fields of "chaos and complexity" for our management practices. See, for example, an early one by Ralph Stacey, *Managing the Unknowable: Strategic Boundaries between Order and Chaos in Organizations* (San Francisco: Jossey-Bass, 1992).

2. Hugh Courtney, "Making the Most of Uncertainty," *McKinsey Quarterly*, no. 4 (2001), pp. 1–3. Michael Lewis, *The New New Thing: A Silicon Valley Story* (New York: Penguin, 2001).

3. Robert Foster and Sarah Kaplan, *Creative Destruction: Why Companies That Are Built to Last Underperform the Market* (New York: Currency Books, 2001).

4. James Collins, *Good to Great: Why Some Companies Make the Leap . . . and Others Don't* (New York: HarperCollins, 2001).

5. Clayton M. Christensen, *The Innovator's Dilemma: When New Technologies Cause Great Firms to Fail* (New York: HarperBusiness, 1997).

6. Peter Drucker, "The Near Future," *The Economist* (November 1, 2001).

7. Ronald Coase, an economist, developed this "transactional model" theory to explain the dynamics of organizational forms, for which he received the 1991 Nobel Prize in economics. See Coase, *The Firm, The Market, and The Law* (Chicago: University of Chicago Press, 1990).

8. For example, see George Gilder, *Telocosm: How Infinite Bandwidth Will Revolutionize Our World* (New York: Free Press, 2000).

9. See note 6.

10. The Internet was developed not as a network to leverage or drive down transaction costs. That came later; 30 years later. The Internet originated as a research and communications tool among scientists to share their research results quickly, irrespective of their geographical boundaries and organizational affiliations.

11. *Harvard Business Review* (Summer 2002); Survey on Leadership, Howard Gardner, *Leading Minds: An Anatomy of Leadership* (New York: Basic Books, 1996); Warren Bennis, *On Becoming a Leader* (Cambridge, MA: Perseus Books, 1994); and Shoshana Zuboff, *In the Age of the Smart Machine: The Future of Work and Power* (New York: Basic Books, 1988).

12. Daniel H. Pink, *Free Agent Nation: How America's New Independent Workers Are Transforming the Way We Live* (New York: Warner Books, 2001). This book also provides the title to Observation #1.

13. See note 12, pp. 45–55.

14. See note 12, p. 53.

15. Donald D. Davis, PhD and Karen A. Polonko, PhD, "Telework in the United States: Telework America Survey 2001," *International Telework Association and Council* (October, 2001).

16. In India, the largest IT outsourcing companies grow in revenue and influence, seemingly independent of the strength of the global economy. See "Survival of the Biggest," *Dataquest*. Available http://www.dataquest.com, quote from http://www.dqindia.com/content/dq_top20/2002/102081201.asp.

17. See note 6.

18. See note 12, p. 84.

19. Ken Berryman and Stefan Heck, "Is the Third Time the Charm for B2B?" *McKinsey Quarterly*, No. 2 (2001), pp. 19–20. This particular version of *McKinsey Quarterly* is solely dedicated to B2B lessons.

20. See note 19, p. 20.

21. Steve Bodow, "The Care and Feeding of a Killer App," *Business 2.0* (August 2002), p. 77.

22. See note 21

23. Remo Hacki and Julian Lighton, "The Future of the Networked Company," *McKinsey Quarterly*, no. 3 (2001), pp. 26–39.

24. Michael Hammer, *The Agenda: What Every Business Must Do to Dominate the Decade* (New York: Random House, 2001), p. 53. See also the author's note on "Business Blueprints" on p. 265.

25. Paul Greenberg, *CRM at the Speed of Light: Capturing and Keeping Customers in Internet Real Time* (New York: McGraw-Hill, 2001).

26. See Chapter 4, also Kevin Rivette and David Kline, *Rembrandts in the Attic: Unlocking the Hidden Value of Patents* (Boston: Harvard Business School, 2000).

27. See note 24, p. 69.

28. See note 24, p. 132.

29. The title of this section is drawn from Geoffrey Moore's work. Geoffrey Moore, *Crossing the Chasm* (New York: HarperBusiness, 1982); and Geoffrey Moore, *Living on the Fault Line: Managing for Shareholder Value in the Age of the Internet* (New York: HarperBusiness, 2000).

30. Goldman Sachs Global Equity Research, *IT Services Weekly* (2002).

31. For our purposes, what differs between them is less important than their similarities.

32. Thomas Malone and Robert Laubacher, "The Dawn of the eLance Economy," *Harvard Business Review* (September 1, 1998). Available http://harvardbusinessonline.hbsp.harvard.edu/b02/en/common/item_detail.jhtml?id=98508.

33. See note 12, p. 303.

34. David Campbell and Ron Hulme, "The Winner-Takes-All Economy," *McKinsey Quarterly*, no. 3 (2001), pp. 82–91.

35. "What Should B2B Sell-Side Apps Do?" *Forrester Research* (December 2001), p. 16.

36. Ted Schadler, "The Truth about Web Services," *Forrester Research* (May 2002).

37. See note 36, p. 4. Figure 4.1 is taken from this report.

38. See note 36, p. 5.

39. See note 36, pp. 6–7.

40. See note 12.

41. See Albert-Laszlo Barabasi, *Linked: The New Science of Networks* (Cambridge, MA: Perseus Publishing, 2002); Nitan Nohria and Robert Eccles, Eds., *Networks and Organizations: Structure, Form, and Action* (Boston: Harvard Business School Press, 1992); and for a set of social network tools, see John Scott, *Social Network Analysis: A Handbook* (London: Sage Publications, 1991). See also the author's note on "Business Blueprints" on p. 265.

42. Interview in London, June 18, 2002.

43. Carol Rozwell, "Sourcing: How to Evaluate Your Readiness to Make a Commitment," *The Gartner Group* (2002).

CHAPTER FIVE

1. Robert Foster and Sarah Kaplan, *Creative Destruction: Why Companies That Are Built to Last Underperform the Market* (New York: Currency Books, 2001).

2. Clayton M. Christensen, *The Innovator's Dilemma: When New Technologies Cause Great Firms to Fail* (New York: HarperBusiness, 1997).

3. Michael Treacy and Fred Wiersema, *The Discipline of Market Leaders* (Reading, MA: Addison-Wesley, 1995).

4. Larry Bossidy and Ram Charan, *Execution: The Discipline of Getting Things Done* (New York: Crown Business, 2002). In their book, Bossidy, a former vice chairman and a chairman of Honeywell International, and Ram Charan, a consultant, provide lessons from their careers and experience at General Electric and Honeywell of why big ideas often fall flat, exploring the "externalities"—both benign and harmful—of who knows what and uses it where . . . and why.

5. Many books can be cited here, starting with many of Peter Drucker's works, including his *Post-Capitalist Society* (New York: HarperBusiness, 1993). Other books include Kenneth Arrow's seminal work on the role of knowledge and resource allocation, *Studies in Resource Allocation Processes* (Cambridge, MA: Cambridge University Press, 1977); Shoshana Zuboff, *In the Age of the Smart Machine* (New York: Basic Books, 1988); Kenichi Ohmae, *The Invisible Continent: Four Stratetic Imperatives of the New Economy* (New York: HarperBusiness, 2000); and Thomas A. Stewart, *The Wealth of Knowledge: Intellectual Capital and the Twenty-First Century Organization* (New York: Currency, 2001).

6. See notes 1 and 2.

7. In the 1980s and early 1990s, many heralded artificial intelligence as being able to mimic how people think; consequently, it was an era of extreme optimism about being able to create automated business processes. Since then we have learned that we can increasingly model how people make decisions but not supplant those processes. Tacit knowledge remains tacit. As we have seen, it is tacit knowledge that is the basis for identifying, creating, and initially operating collaborative ventures. It is tacit knowledge that is the basis of the IP "leakage" that results from such collaborations as well.

8. For an entertaining and informative discussion of both Nike and Starbucks branding strategy and aggressive continual moves to transform their market positions, see former head of marketing for both Nike and Starbucks; Scott Bedbury, *A New Brand World: 8 Principles for Achieving Brand Leadership in the Twenty-First Century* (New York: Viking, 2002).

9. Geoffrey Moore, *Crossing the Chasm* (New York: HarperBusiness, 1982). Geoffrey Moore's technology adoption curve has become a mainstay of technology, and increasingly other production-based companies in terms of the criticality, yet challenge, of "crossing the chasm" from early adopter to mass market capabilities. In it, he well explores the challenges and differing operating models and cost challenges crossing the chasms.

10. Lock-in happens in many contexts. For a good discussion of the various forms of customer lock-in, see Carl Shapiro and Hal R. Varian, *Information Rules: A Strategic Guide to the Network Economy* (Cambridge, MA: Harvard Business School Press, 1988). Much of the emphasis on Customer Relationship Management has been to generate customer lock-in. For a discussion of CRM and customer lock-in strategies, see Jim Highsmith et. al, "CRM: Implementing Customer-Centric Strategies," *Cutter Consortium* (2000).

11. This merger was scrutinized closely by the Federal Communications Commission (FCC) and the Department of Justice, as well as by the media and industry pundits. TimeWarner's Gerald Levine described the benefits of this merger, saying, "The public will benefit from the new company's ability to offer diversity in interactive television content, offer multiple ISP access over our Road Runner service, forcing other cable operators to follow suit, and deliver broadband services that will break down the digital divide. The Internet is the technology of human freedom." At the same time, Esther Dyson, chairperson of EDventure Holdings, Inc. and the Internet Corporation for Assigned Names and Numbers (ICANN, the nonprofit corporation that administers IP address assignments and the Intenet's domain name space) recognized the potential benefits of the

merger, but also recognized the lock-in (and lock-out) potential of the merger, cautioning about the potential of AOL to preferentially steer consumers toward the links and products of favored advertisers, noting that "consumers can only exercise choice and force rivals to compete when they are informed of their options." Patricia Fusco, "AOL, TimeWarner Stump for Merger" (The Internet News, July 27, 2000), available http://www.internetnews.com/xSP/article.php/8_424741.

12.   Available http://www.axion4.com/cm/index/maintree/gstp-index /gstp-background.htm.

13.   Frances Cairncross, *The Company of the Future: How the Communications Revolution Is Changing Management* (Boston: Harvest Business School Press, 2002).

14.   See note 13, pp. 5–6.

15.   For a discussion of how Procter & Gamble has teamed with Los Alamos National Laboratory, see Matthew Boyle, "Using Rocket Science to Make Sugar Drinks," *Fortune Magazine* (November 26, 2001).

16.   This collaborative venture, CoKinetic Systems Corporation, released its first commercial product to a major company in August 2001. For information about CoKinetic, see http://www.cokinetic.com.

17.   Private conversation. John McKinley, Global CTO of Merrill Lynch (June 2001).

18.   See, for example, Rebecca Scholl, Ted Kempf, and Debashish Sinha, "Cross-Border Collaboration: A Service Aggregator Model for Offshore IT Services," *The Gartner Group* (October 5, 2001).

19.   See note 18.

20.   The Collaborative Delivery Framework, which we examine in the next section, handles the methods and process side of effectively executing projects using a team comprising people from different organizations using different methods. To maximize the impact and leverage of such projects, it is crucial that the overall portfolio of projects be aligned, coordinated, and focused on creating business value. We have identified a new business function—the Strategic Implementation Office—to drive implementation activities and coordinate the moving parts across the organization, working toward the shared goals of advancing the corporate strategic vision, satisfying the business and time-to-market needs of the business units, and maximizing the impact of the resulting investment outlay. The Strategic Implementation Office has wide responsibility, including: creating the agenda for strategic implementation efforts across and within the various business units of an organization; defining requirements and business architecture for strategic implementations;

interfacing with the CIO and IT organizations to coordinate strategic technology implementation and strategy efforts with the overall IT strategy (this is the essential bridge function that aligns the business needs with the IT agenda; setting a common vocabulary; rationalizing and coordinating activities across projects to minimize conflict and duplication of effort); and articulating business-aware criteria for vendor selection and interfacing with the CIO and IT organizations to establish a business-friendly vendor selection process. The Strategic Implementation Office would be a compact, efficient organization, comprising a senior management lead, a senior technology architect to serve as liaison to IT and business unit architects, a senior strategist to serve as liaison with the business units and the corporate strategy organization, driving strategic alignment, and business unit CTOs. The Strategic Implementation Office is complementary to the typical corporate CIO and CTO positions, acting as the "strike team" for the CIO, and the source of initiative and funding for the CTO. See also the author's note on "Business Blueprints" on p. 265.

21. Eric S. Raymond, *The Cathedral and the Bazaar: Musings on Linux and Open Source by an Accidental Revolutionary* (Cambridge, MA: O'Reilly, 2001).

CHAPTER SIX

1. http://www.webex.com.
2. http://www.netmeeting.com.
3. SharePoint is a trademark of Microsoft, Inc.
4. PeopleSoft is a registered trademark of PeopleSoft, Inc.
5. The Unified Modeling Language and UML are trademarks of the Object Management Group (OMG), http://www.omg.org/. UML documentation is available at the OMG website and also on the website of Rational Software Corporation—the current home of Grady Booch, Ivar Jacobson, and James Rumbaugh whose research and thought leadership over the years led to the creation of the Unified Modeling Language in 1997—at http://www.rational.com/uml/resources/documentation/index .jsp. See also the author's note on "Business Blueprints" on p. 265.
6. http://www.tibco.com.
7. http://www.vitria.com.
8. http://www.neon.com.
9. Increased focus on business process leads to increased codification of business processes and regularity in the approach that businesses

take to the processes they share. In turn, opportunities arise for outsourcing of business process. This is discussed in Rebecca Scholl, *Business Process Outsourcing at the Crossroads,* (The Gartner Group, January 31, 2002).

10. For a discussion of organizational alignment and the role of program management tools in helping to drive alignment, see Lee E. Heindel and Vincent A. Kasten, "P++: A Prototype PC-Based Enterprise Management System," *The International Journal of Project Management* (December 1996); see also, Lee E. Heindel and Vincent A. Kasten, "Next Generation PC-Based Project Management Systems: Implementation Considerations," *The International Journal of Project Management* (October 1996). See also the author's note on "Business Blueprints" on p. 265.

11. For a general discussion of Internet-based enterprise portals and enterprise information portals specifically, see Susan Landry and Kimberly Harris, *Financial Services Enterprise Portal: A Cog in the Wheel,* (The Gartner Group, January 14, 2002).

12. Personal communication with Stephen Woodruff, ChevronTexaco (September 2002).

13. The role of the scout was defined in a classic early talk on software engineering given by John Mashey, then at Bell Laboratories. The original reference is John Mashey, "The Software Army on the March," *Proceedings of UNICOM 1983* (1983). The notes for the talk, as well as some background, are available at http://www.usenix.org/events/bsdcon02/mashey_army.

14. Milind Govekar and Roy Schulte, *BAM Architecture: More Building Blocks Than You Think* (The Gartner Group, April 1, 2002).

15. Navi Radjou with Laurie M. Orlov and Meredith Child, *The X Internet Powers Collaborative XRM Apps,* The Forrester Brief, Forrester Research, November 19, 2001.

CHAPTER SEVEN

1. Stephen Wolfram, *A New Kind of Science* (Boston: Wolfram Media, 2002).

2. Clayton M. Christensen, *The Innovator's Dilemma: When New Technologies Cause Great Firms to Fail* (New York: HarperBusiness, 1997).

3. William H. Calvin, *A Brain for All Seasons: Human Evolution and Abrupt Climate Change* (Chicago: University of Chicago Press, 2002), p. 106.

AUTHOR'S NOTE: PATTERNS, PATTERNS EVERYWHERE: UNISYS CORPORATION'S BUSINESS BLUEPRINTS

Effective collaboration rests on exploiting the rich semantics of different types of activities. The semantic stack presented in this book depicts a layered set of domains, each of which benefits from semantic agreement that codifies them into something increasingly executable. We explored how one of the key challenges for effective collaborations is the construction and use of a shared vocabulary or semantic base that reconciles different understandings, expectations, and processes. Given the vital role of technology to enable effective collaborations, aggressively exploiting *semantic architecture* becomes critical to support the agility and scale needed across multiple collaborative ventures. This is where Unisys Corporation's Business Blueprints come in.

Business Blueprints are a set of tools, methods, and repositories of organizational patterns, business processes, and technology implemention options that provide a connected, consistent model for your business from strategic initiatives through to technology implementations. They form a practical, actionable approach and toolset for driving an organization in its walk up and across the semantic stack to meet the collaborative requirements and design principles of the Jericho Principle.

The term *blueprint* refers to an abstraction of functionality, performance, and structure using standard forms of description. Blueprints serve as communication tools, highlighting relevant patterns of what something is and thereby guiding how to use it more quickly, more easily, more flexibly. Unisys Corporation's Business Blueprints serve precisely this function within and across the layers of a company, with the commensurate business benefits of enabling organizations and businesses to identify their tangible and intangible IP assets and reuse, reconfigure, or renew them as necessary to take advantage of fast-moving business opportunities. Unisys—building on its rich heritage of designing, building, deploying and managing large-scale and mission-critical systems to support the core asset base, focus, and strategy of companies globally—has created repositories of industry-specific (and, working with its clients, *client-specific*), mission-critical, organizational patterns, business processes, and technology options independent of any particular technology implementation. Clients can exploit this intellectual property quickly, either themselves and/or with business partners, collaboratively, enabling them to execute on the imperative we articulate throughout the book regarding competition and collaboration.

Competitive uncertainty is real and will remain so. Within such uncertainty lies the potential of significant marketplace power—a power to *embrace* the uncertainty, *understand* the patterns, *explore* the options, and *exploit* the opportunities with speed, agility, and purpose. This rests, in turn, on a commitment to and passion for standards-based agility and the infrastructure to enable continual innovation, reuse, reconfiguration, and renewal in exploiting the tacit knowledge, the intellectual property, and the high-margin or high-revenue potential of fast-moving business opportunities again and again. It requires the capabilities to leverage the organizational patterns, the business processes, and technology implementation options quickly, effectively, and predictably. These are the requirements for many businesses today as they recognize the potential power of embracing and exploiting competitive uncertainty. And these are some of the key design principles of Unisys' Business Blueprints and the reality of the value they offer their clients. These are the makings of a collaborative powerhouse; they are the makings of a marketplace leader; and they are the makings of marketplace opportunities that Unisys has, is, and will continue to create with their clients. We joined Unisys to be part of this marketplace potential, of navigating the shoals of uncertainty with the sails of grounded and groundable blueprints.

The Red Queen will continue to run. Outrunning her requires the ability to recognize how to leverage the semantic richness of your intellectual property and do so collaboratively. Unisys Corporation's Business Blueprints are designed to extract, codify, and exploit the semantic richness for the agility needed, the visiblity required, and the scalability critical to embrace the uncertainty we all face, and exploit its rich opportunity.

INDEX

ABB, 127
Abstractions, 75–76, 87, 146
Accessibility, 231–232
Access protocols, 66
Action taking *vs.* sense making, 55, 100, 244
Activities, 143
Adaptive fit, 250
Adaptive mechanism as core asset, 54
Aero Exchange International, 123
Aggregation, business (collaborative form), 45
Aggregator, solutions, 192–194
Agreement:
  codification and, 75, 76, 146
  semantic (degrees of), 82–83, 90, 108
AIG Avantrust, 152
Amazon.com, 29
AOL/Time Warner merger, 182
Application(s):
  EAI (Enterprise Application Integration), 145, 146, 148, 149, 226, 227,
  integrator (role), 194
  interaction, 62
  N-tier architecture, 215
  vs. process, 121–131
  semantic stack layer (patterns and best practices), 80, 84, 89–91, 213–215
Application Integration Software (AIS), 60
Application service providers (ASPs), 135
Architect, collaborative, 207, 230–234
  accessibility, 231–232
  assurance, 232
  customization, 231
  determining business/commercial model, 233–234

dynamic transformation, 231
enabling cross-boundary communication, 233
partitioning your business services, 233
requirements of, 233–234
Architectural semantics, 12–13, 88, 206, 207, 238–240
Architecture:
  codification and, 71–73
  semantic (*see* Semantic architecture)
  syntactic (*see* Syntactic architect/ architecture)
  technology/business and, 87
Architecture and platform layer, in semantic stack, 80, 84, 86–89, 210–213
ARPANet, 68, 76
ASCII (American Standard Code for Information Interchange), 70, 75, 76, 78
Assurance, 232
Atriax, 123
AT&T, 188
Avanade, 169–170, 187
B2B (business to business), 122, 123–127, 152

Back-to-the-basics as "return-to-the-future," 4–5, 106–109
Bandwidth/accessibility, 231–232
BankOne, 170
Barlow, John, 122
Barnes & Noble, 29
"Bars" zone (quadrant in Collaborative Landscape), 41, 42
BEA's Weblogic, 236
Behavior(s):
  complex emergent, 243
  observations from the field, 117–140